YOUR
FIRST
SAILBOAT

YOUR FIRST SAILBOAT

How to Find and Sail the Right Boat for You

DANIEL SPURR

International Marine / McGraw-Hill

Camden, Maine ▪ New York ▪ Chicago ▪ San Francisco
Lisbon ▪ London ▪ Madrid ▪ Mexico City ▪ Milan
New Delhi ▪ San Juan ▪ Seoul ▪ Singapore ▪ Sydney ▪ Toronto

For Gene Correll and Robert Lindy,
who taught me a lot of what's in this book.

The **McGraw·Hill** Companies

2 3 4 5 6 7 8 9 DOC DOC 0 9 8 7 6 5

Library of Congress Cataloging-in-Publication Data
Spurr, Daniel, 1947–
  Your first sailboat : how to find and sail the right boat for you / Daniel Spurr.
      p.   cm.
Includes bibliographical references and index.
  ISBN 0-07-142216-1 (pbk. : alk. paper)
 1. Sailboats. 2. Sailing. I. Title.
  VM351.S64 2004
  623.822'3—dc22   2004006425

Questions regarding the content of this book
should be addressed to
International Marine
P.O. Box 220
Camden, ME 04843
www.internationalmarine.com

Questions regarding the ordering of this book
should be addressed to
The McGraw-Hill Companies
Customer Service Department
P.O. Box 547
Blacklick, OH 43004
Retail customers: 1-800-262-4729
Bookstores: 1-800-722-4726

Illustration credits may be found on pages 269–71.

Contents

Part Three **Maintaining Your First Sailboat**

Part Four **Navigation**

So You Want to Buy a Sailboat?

O K, your wife or your husband says you're nuts but you're going ahead anyway. You've told your friends the plan and they don't have a clue.

"You're giving up the golf league?"

"You're not quitting the Elks, are you?"

"What does Fred say about this?"

You might even have discussed the matter with your therapist, and all she can say is that you have some unresolved issues surrounding your birth (the water thing, you know) and had better start coming in twice a week.

Undaunted, unswayed, and unmoved, you're sticking to your guns. You don't care what anyone says: You are about to buy your first sailboat.

No one understands why you want to do such a fool thing.

Well, they raise good points: a boat is not exactly the best investment in the world (though occasionally you might sell it at a profit), other pastimes tend to fade in favor of weekends afloat, and you begin to speak a language that to most of your friends might as well be Swahili.

When I was in my early twenties, I talked my best friend into going partners on a new Catalina 22 swing-keel trailer sailer. We applied for a loan from my friend's brother, a bank manager. After I told Bill that his brother Jim and I wanted to borrow $4,000 for a sailboat, there was a long silence. He leaned back in his leather chair with his hands cupping the back of his head, staring at me, trying to . . . I'm not sure . . . either figure me out or give me a "correction," like I was a puppy being trained not to pee on the carpet. At long last, he said, "Why do you want to buy a boat?"

I wasn't prepared for such an odd question.

After an awkward moment, I replied, "Why? Well, I don't know. Do I have to have a reason?"

"Well, $4,000 is a lot of money," he said. "I'd be happy to loan you the money for something sensible, like, well, why not put an addition on your house? It'll increase your equity."

That made way too much sense.

Improving my net worth was the farthest thing from my mind. (Fortunately, or unfortunately, that does change with age.) Like the Frenchman Bernard Moitessier, who in 1968 kept sailing around the world instead of claiming the prize for the first person to circumnavigate nonstop alone, I was more concerned with saving my soul.

Well, that may be an overly dramatic description of what I was about back then, but it does accurately reflect the difference between those who keep their feet in the sidewalk squares and those who step on the cracks.

Jim and I emptied our savings accounts and bought the Catalina 22 anyway. This was my first boat with a cabin and sleeping accommodations, and what a thrill it was to sit below in its self-contained world, complete with berths, toilet, and galley. Why ever leave?

It also was my first boat with a ballast keel. Under way, one could walk around the deck without making the boat tip over. This felt like the real thing, an oceangoing boat that could take us someplace far away. Warm breezes. Palm trees. Coral reefs. White sand beaches. Bougainvillea. Beautiful people. You have the picture. You've seen it. You've dreamed it.

My friend, you are not crazy, irresponsible, or stupid . . . well, at least not for wanting a boat!

You might be having a midlife crisis. You might be ridden with angst. You might be thinking that a sailboat is a vote against mediocrity, a stand against boredom, a kick in the butt of the 9-to-5 establishment, a voice in the existential dark screaming, "Yes, I want more out of life. I want to LIVE!"

Or maybe the idea of sailing has simply and suddenly attracted your interest, like when you were young and first noticed an attractive member of the opposite sex—ping!

Where did it come from?

Perhaps you were turned on by a television commercial. A photo in a magazine. The account of a friend who went sailing. Or maybe you got out on the water with a friend and she put your hand on the helm. There you were, holding the wind in one hand and the sea in the other, balancing the two in such a perfectly harmonious way that the boat mysteriously moved

forward, responding to your every adjustment of the sails and tiller.

How did it do that?

And so quietly?

No fumes. No roar of engines.

Consumer surveys of recreational interests usually rank sailing as a sport a lot of people would like to try, but one for which few are willing to take the first step. And what is that first step, anyway?

"I wouldn't know where to start."

"Where would I even find a boat to try it out?"

"It seems so complicated!"

"Rich man's sport."

"I get seasick."

"What do you do with all those ropes, anyway?"

Well, I'm here to tell you that all of the above are true. And none of them.

Don't know where to start? You bought this book, didn't you? You're on your way. Next question.

Boats are available for rent in many communities. Along the coasts and on major lakes there are community sailing clubs for the express purpose of making sailing available and affordable to anyone interested. Look in your phone book. No luck? Call a sailboat dealer and ask him.

Too difficult? Ever try hitting a golf ball 250 yards? Straight? I guarantee this book will get you sailing in a straight line faster than you can get that hook out of your drive.

Expensive? You can get into sailing for as little or as much money as you want. What does a good set of skis and boots cost? Five hundred bucks? A thousand? Check the classifieds of your local paper for older sailboats, and you'll find something in your price range. Maybe a one-man Laser. Maybe a two-woman Snipe. Perhaps even a small cruiser with a cabin. It might need some work, but hey, learning how to care for your boat is part of the deal and part of the appeal. And marina fees are likely to be less than greens fees—especially if your marina is the boat trailer in your driveway.

Seasick? Just about anyone can get seasick. And just about anyone can learn to deal with *mal de mer*. Overcoming any preexisting fears you may have is a start. And you do that by doing. If seasickness persists, there are numerous medical remedies—ranging from over-the-counter tablets such as Bonine and Dramamine, to acupuncture wrist bands, to prescription medicines such as scopolamine—that work like a charm on the vast majority of afflicted persons. And even if you do get seasick, you'll be over it as soon as the rolling stops, whereas tennis elbow can last a long, long time.

Some mariners, even famous ones, get sick every time they go out. But after a period of adjustment, they're fine, and the adventures they experience make the temporary discomfort a worthwhile trade-off.

Complicated? Too many ropes? Sailing is not as mystifying as it may look. Give this book a night. All you really need to know to become a competent sailor and boatowner will be revealed. Everything else is optional.

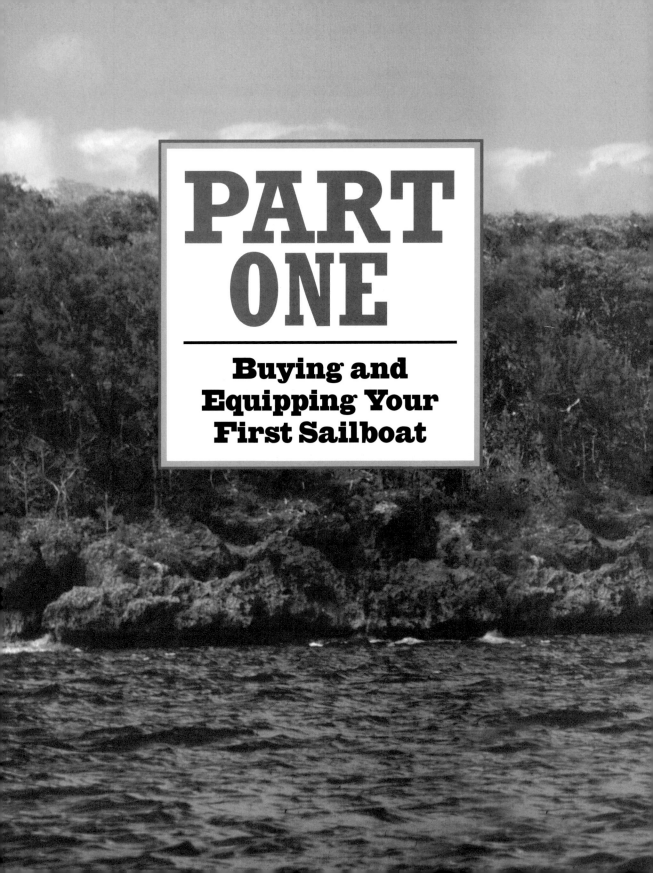

PART ONE

Buying and Equipping Your First Sailboat

What Kind of Boat Should I Buy?

At the heart of the mysterious allure of sailing lies the boat, what philosophers call "the thing in itself." To build a boat and sail out of sight across unknown waters to strange lands is one of man's most primal and mythic adventures. In the twelfth century BC, Odysseus sailed across the Mediterranean to wage war against Troy and then sailed 10 years home to Ithaca. St. Brendan purportedly sailed a goatskin boat across the North Atlantic from Ireland to Iceland in the thirteenth century AD. Polynesians navigated giant proas hundreds of miles between island groups of the Pacific. And in the early 1960s, a 14-year-old boy from Ann Arbor, Michigan, threw a sleeping bag and a can of Spam into a wooden Rhodes Bantam, sailed out into the vast waters of Barton Pond, beached the boat on the island at its center, and *almost* spent the night. Though that was 40 years ago, I still savor the memory. On any scale, the lure today remains unchanged from what it was 3,000 years ago.

There are at least three components to this fascination: the call of an exotic destination (the other side of the lake counts, as any reader of Arthur Ransome's "Swallows and Amazons" series knows well); the thrill of steering and handling the boat, even in circles; and the boat as an object of adoration.

Just as a carpenter has affection for a favorite saw or chisel, the golfer his favorite wood, and the hunter a handsome rifle, the sailor admires his boat for its many attributes—graceful lines, stout structure, and the fact that it is his (or hers). Ownership breeds pride.

OK. That all sounds good, but you ask, "What boat should I buy?"

The answer depends on what you plan to do with it. You could, of course, build your own boat, but most people will find it simpler to buy one new or used. Answer the following questions and we'll begin to work through the choices.

Where will you sail?

a. Small lake or bay, or close to harbor and home? Call these *protected waters*.
b. Big bays and sounds (San Francisco Bay, the Chesapeake Bay, Albemarle Sound, Puget Sound)? These are known as *semi-protected waters*.
c. The Great Lakes (Michigan, Superior, Huron, Ontario, Erie) or near-coastal

ocean waters? We'll call these *inshore waters.*

d. On the open ocean more than 20 miles from shore (Atlantic, Pacific, Indian, Caribbean, Mediterranean)? These are *unprotected waters,* mate.

Will you

a. Daysail only?
b. Sleep on the boat overnight?
c. Take weeklong cruises?
d. Voyage across large bodies of water?
e. Groove on going as fast as you can?
f. Take large groups sailing?

Do you

a. Want to keep your sailing simple?
b. Want to avoid yard fees?
c. Want this to be a family affair?
d. Have visions of tropical islands?
e. Have a strong competitive streak?
f. Have a pathological fear of tipping over?

How long can you tread water? (Just kidding. That's an old Bill Cosby line from his comedy piece, "Noah's Ark.")

If you answered one or more a's to the earlier questions, see the following Daysailers section. If you answered one or more b's or c's, jump to Trailer Sailers and General-Purpose Boats. If you answered one or more d's, scroll down to Cruisers. If your answers included e's, check out the Racers category. The smaller keel racers are typically campaigned on bays and inshore; the larger ones, such as the Farr 40 and Santa Cruz 52, sail offshore. Answers that included f's direct you to the Multihulls section, which includes daysailers for both pleasure and racing (Hobie 16 and Tornado), coastal cruisers (F-27 and Gemini 105), and offshore cruisers (PDQ 36).

Choosing a Sailboat. Below is a flowchart to help you organize your thoughts about sailboat choices. Use it in conjunction with this chapter

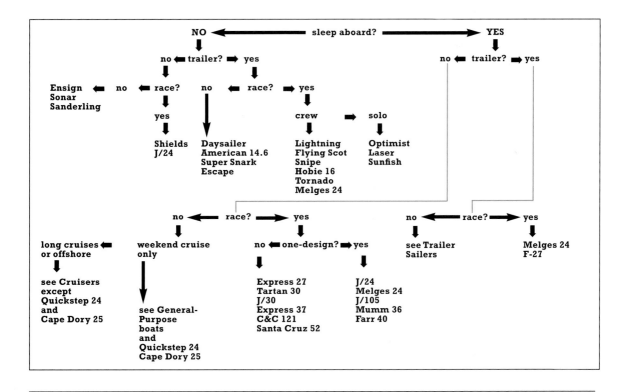

and the Sailboat Guide at the back of the book, but bear in mind that any such overview of categories has to make an arbitrary judgment here and there. For example, while it's true that Ensigns are less often raced than other daysailers, in some places they are. And so on.

Daysailers

If what you want to do is spend a Saturday sailing around a small lake, maybe picnicking and then going home, you don't need a big boat with a cabin and complicated electrical and plumbing systems. There are few pleasures in life more satisfying than sitting on the deep seat of a well-behaved family boat such as the O'Day Day Sailer, your back rested against the curved coaming, skimming across a lake.

Some daysailers are intended purely for relaxed sailing; others for spirited racing. Most small racing sailboats are called *one-designs*, which simply means that they are essentially identical, and compete without handicap—the first to finish wins.

If you want more thrills than the rather staid O'Day Day Sailer, try leaning out horizontally over the water, feet planted on the side of a 420 racing dinghy, your body held up by a trapeze wired between a chest harness and the masthead; or hiking out while flying a hull on a Hobie 16 catamaran. These are international designs: the International Sailing Federation (ISAF) has accepted them for event sponsorship. Some such classes are used in Olympic competition. (See the ISAF Classes sidebar for a complete list.)

Daysailers generally don't have cabins, though some have a partial shelter forward called a *cuddy cabin*. Sometimes these cabins have enough room for a portable toilet, which is much appreciated if you'll be away from shore for a few hours or longer. Otherwise, you have to lean over the side to relieve yourself, which is potentially dangerous and most times embarrassing; or use a bucket; or jump over the side.

Small boats are the best way to learn to sail. Unlike a big boat, your mistakes provide instant feedback. Everything happens faster on a lightweight daysailer than on a heavy keelboat, which seems sluggish by comparison, its tendencies camouflaged by its weight.

People who learn to sail on large boats miss many fundamental experiences like, well, capsizing. It's no big deal on a small centerboard boat. You stand on the centerboard, grab a halyard (the line that hoists the sail), lean back and pull the boat upright, climb in, bail, and get going again. No fears, right? R-i-i-i-i-i-ght! OK, I know the thought of being dumped into the water with all your clothes on might be intimidating, but just think of it as taking a swim without your suit. So you got wet? Live a little!

Daysailers can have nonballasted centerboards that pivot, or daggerboards that lift straight up, or fixed keels with ballast inside— like the Ensign and Sonar. Fixed keels are not practical to launch at a ramp; boats with keels usually are put in the water at the beginning of the season and left at a dock or mooring until fall. This way, you help support the marina owner, who is trying hard not to have to sell his valuable waterfront property to condominium developers. So, although it may seem like the money you're handing him is a lot for just being able to tie up your boat to a bunch of old boards, it's nothing compared to what Donald Developer is waggling in front of his tired old eyes.

Fixed-keel daysailers are probably best owned where there are active fleets for club racing, or perhaps by people with homes on the water who desire a "gentleman's" boat and have no real desire to sleep aboard. Their lack of portability and accommodations, and the absence of self-bailing cockpits, restrict their utility.

Centerboard and daggerboard boats can be *dry sailed*; that is, stored on a trailer in a driveway or backyard and launched every time you go

INTERNATIONAL SAILING FEDERATION (ISAF) CLASSES

Olympic Classes

How better to give you a sense of the fun to be had sailing one-design racers than in these photos of the nine Olympic sailing classes? These boats are fast, wet, and exciting. This is athletic sailing! (Photos by Daniel Forster.)

470: two-person dinghy

49er: two-person dinghy

Europe: one-person dinghy

Finn: one-person dinghy

Laser: one-person dinghy

Mistral: sailboard

(continued next page)

ISAF CLASSES (CONTINUED)

Star: two-person keelboat

Tornado: catamaran

Yngling: three-person keelboat

International Centerboard Boat Class Associations

14-foot dinghy	Laser
29er	Laser 4.7
420	Laser II
470	Laser Radial
49er	Lightning
505	Mirror
Cadet	Moth
Contender	OK Dinghy
Enterprise	Optimist
Europe	Snipe
Finn	Sunfish
Fireball	Topper
Flying Dutchman	Vaurien
Flying Junior	

International Keelboat Class Associations

11 meter	H-boat
12 meter	J/22
2.4 meter	J/24
5.5 meter	Melges 24
6 meter	Open 60 monohull
8 meter	Soling
Dragon	Star
Etchells	Tempest
Flying Fifteen	Yngling

International Multihull Class Associations

A-catamaran	Hobie 17
Dart 18	Hobie 18
Formula 18	Hobie Tiger
Hobie 14	Tornado
Hobie 16	

International Windsurfing Class Associations

Formula Windsufing	Mistral Junior
Funboard	Raceboard
Mistral	

Recognized Class Associations

Open 60 multihull	Mumm 30
Aloha	Open 50 monohull

ISAF CLASSES (CONTINUED)

B14	Sonar	**Classic Yacht Classes**	
Byte	Splash	GP14	Shark
Farr 40	Tasar	IOD	
J/80	X99		
Maxi One Design	Zoom 8		
Micro			

sailing. The shallower the draft with the board up, the easier the boat is to launch and haul out. The resulting cost savings and the flexibility of sailing on a lake one day and on a bay the next are somewhat offset by the hassle of rigging and unrigging the boat each time you go out.

Among monohulls, check out the 11-foot Escape, 14-foot Laser, 15-foot Snipe, 17-foot O'Day Day Sailer, 19-foot Lightning, 19-foot Flying Scot, and Rhodes 19. There is more information on each of these boats in the Sailboat Guide appendix. Of course, there are a lot of other designs to choose from, but this selection includes tried-and-true boats that also are affordable and widely available used.

The overriding advantages of daysailers are simplicity and economy. You'll have less hassle getting under way, spend less time on maintenance, and save money over larger boats. On the other hand, your destinations are more limited, as is the weather the boat can handle.

Daysailers

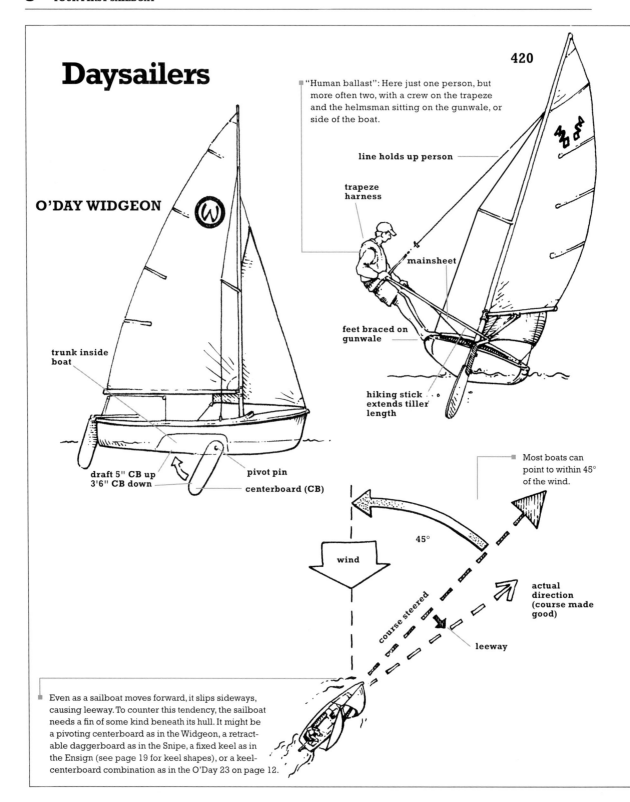

420

"Human ballast": Here just one person, but more often two, with a crew on the trapeze and the helmsman sitting on the gunwale, or side of the boat.

O'DAY WIDGEON

line holds up person

trapeze harness

mainsheet

feet braced on gunwale

trunk inside boat

hiking stick extends tiller length

draft 5" CB up
3'6" CB down

pivot pin

centerboard (CB)

Most boats can point to within 45° of the wind.

45°

wind

course steered

actual direction (course made good)

leeway

Even as a sailboat moves forward, it slips sideways, causing leeway. To counter this tendency, the sailboat needs a fin of some kind beneath its hull. It might be a pivoting centerboard as in the Widgeon, a retractable daggerboard as in the Snipe, a fixed keel as in the Ensign (see page 19 for keel shapes), or a keel-centerboard combination as in the O'Day 23 on page 12.

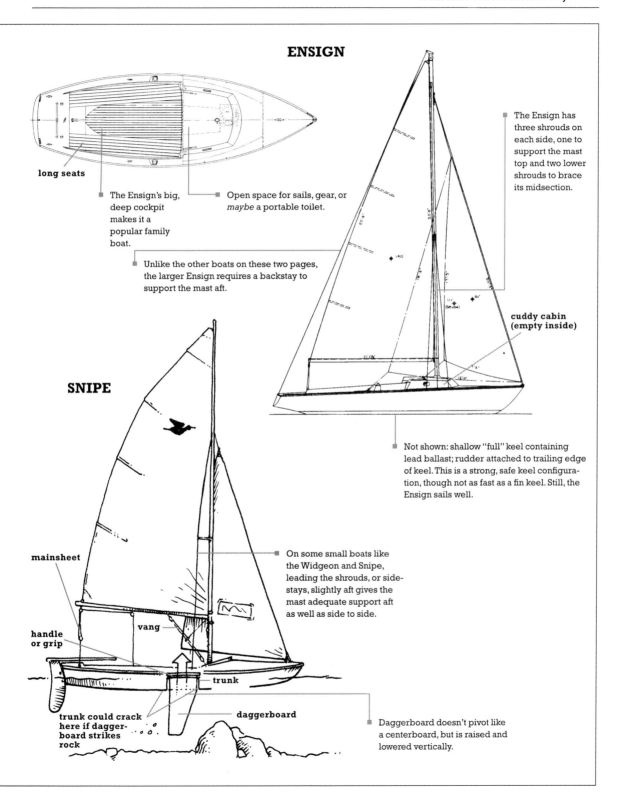

ENSIGN

long seats

The Ensign's big, deep cockpit makes it a popular family boat.

Open space for sails, gear, or *maybe* a portable toilet.

Unlike the other boats on these two pages, the larger Ensign requires a backstay to support the mast aft.

The Ensign has three shrouds on each side, one to support the mast top and two lower shrouds to brace its midsection.

cuddy cabin (empty inside)

Not shown: shallow "full" keel containing lead ballast; rudder attached to trailing edge of keel. This is a strong, safe keel configuration, though not as fast as a fin keel. Still, the Ensign sails well.

SNIPE

mainsheet

handle or grip

vang

trunk

trunk could crack here if daggerboard strikes rock

daggerboard

On some small boats like the Widgeon and Snipe, leading the shrouds, or sidestays, slightly aft gives the mast adequate support aft as well as side to side.

Daggerboard doesn't pivot like a centerboard, but is raised and lowered vertically.

Trailer Sailers

Bigger, heavier boats, usually with cabins, require more sail area to make them move. The more sail area, the stronger the need to counterbalance the tendency to tip or heel. Multihulls counter the force of the wind with very wide beams that resist heeling. Monohulls counter wind forces by adding ballasted keels below the hull. The deeper the ballast, the greater the righting force to resist heeling. But there's a trade-off because boats with deep keels are more limited as to where they can go without running aground.

Designers have developed several compromise solutions. One is the *swing keel*, which is basically a weighted centerboard that pivots up into a trunk when in shallow water or hauling out at a ramp. Because all its weight is placed on a single pivot pin, the pin must be very strong, and a winch might be necessary to lift and lower the swing keel. Several popular models of the past 25 years, now out of production, include the Chrysler 22, Venture 22, and Southcoast 22. The best-selling Catalina 22 continues in production as an updated MKII version of the original. The motivation behind all these models is not only stability, but trailerability as well.

The so-called "trailer sailer movement" originated in the late 1960s. An early proponent was Roger MacGregor, who designed and built the line of Venture swing-keel sloops. As of this writing, he is building the water-ballasted MacGregor 26, equipped with a 50 hp outboard motor that provides double-digit speeds under power. *Water ballast*, which is a fairly recent development, involves having a sealed tank in the bottom of the boat that is allowed to fill with water. As the boat is hauled onto a trailer, a plug is removed, and the water is drained. The advantage of this arrangement is that you don't have to lug all that weight down the highway. The disadvantage is that water is not nearly as dense as lead (the usual ballast material) and its location inside the hull doesn't provide much righting arm (leverage).

Keel-centerboard boats are part keelboat and part centerboarder. Generally, a shallow stub keel contains the majority of the ballast; a slot in its bottom allows a centerboard to be fitted that drops down in deep water to improve windward performance (as we'll see later, sailboats can indeed sail into the wind, not directly, but usually to within 40 to 45 degrees). The centerboard also reduces leeway, which is the tendency of a boat to be shoved sideways by the wind.

The trailerable O'Day 23, PY 23, and PY 26, also no longer made, are small keel-centerboarders still found on the used-boat market.

Very small cruising sailboats are called "pocket cruisers," and one of the most popular is the 15-foot West Wight Potter.

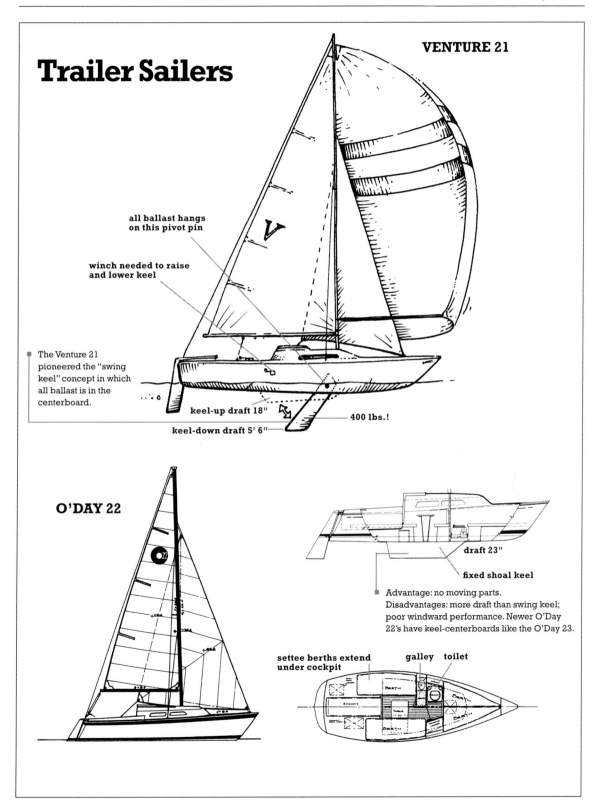

Trailer Sailers

VENTURE 21

all ballast hangs on this pivot pin

winch needed to raise and lower keel

The Venture 21 pioneered the "swing keel" concept in which all ballast is in the centerboard.

keel-up draft 18"

400 lbs.!

keel-down draft 5' 6"

O'DAY 22

draft 23"

fixed shoal keel

Advantage: no moving parts. Disadvantages: more draft than swing keel; poor windward performance. Newer O'Day 22's have keel-centerboards like the O'Day 23.

settee berths extend under cockpit

galley   toilet

TRAILER SAILERS (cont.)

O'DAY 23

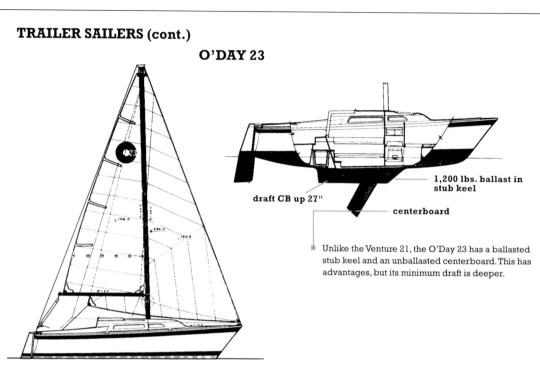

1,200 lbs. ballast in stub keel

draft CB up 27"

centerboard

Unlike the Venture 21, the O'Day 23 has a ballasted stub keel and an unballasted centerboard. This has advantages, but its minimum draft is deeper.

MacGREGOR 26

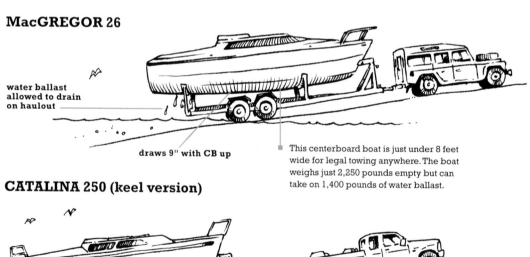

water ballast allowed to drain on haulout

draws 9" with CB up

This centerboard boat is just under 8 feet wide for legal towing anywhere. The boat weighs just 2,250 pounds empty but can take on 1,400 pounds of water ballast.

CATALINA 250 (keel version)

draft 3' 5"

The Catalina 250 is available in a keel or centerboard version. The keel version with its lead ballast weighs a thousand pounds more and is harder to launch, but it's also more stable and, without a centerboard trunk beneath the cabin floor, has 5 inches more headroom.

Sometimes a trailer tongue extension is needed to back a boat into deeper water without submerging the tow vehicle.

General-Purpose Boats

By far, the largest category of keelboats between 25 and 45 feet are so-called cruiser/racers. These are purported to be dual-purpose boats that can be competitive in club races and equally adept at a summer's cruise with the entire family aboard.

Designed and built for average weather conditions and use, general-purpose boats have moderate displacement, a decent turn of speed, and comfortable interiors. They are neither light enough nor powerful enough to be grand prix racers, nor are they built strong enough to cross an ocean. But because most boats are used only on summer weekends and are never taken too far from home port, the cruiser/racer can be built for a more affordable price than either the full-on racer or the offshore cruiser. You'll find descriptions of some of my favorites in the Sailboat Guide appendix.

Most general-purpose boats have a *fixed keel*, and these days that means a fin keel, although lengths (from front to back) and depths vary.

Large keel-centerboard boats, which were once popular for shallow-water cruising, have lost favor to the simpler wing keel in recent years. There are several reasons: First, at anchor, centerboards tend to "slat" inside their trunks, making an annoying noise; second, there is always the risk of the pivot pin failing or the board jamming; and third, a keel-centerboard configuration does not get the ballast as low as with a fixed keel, thereby reducing stability unless more weight is added to compensate for the shallow draft. Wing keels, though not as deep as ordinary fin keels, often have bulbs at the bottom to concentrate additional weight, and their horizontal "winglet" appendages provide some lift, like an airplane wing, to help the boat point closer to the wind ("higher") than it otherwise would.

Shoal keels like the keel-centerboard arrangement allow sailing in shallow water, as in the Florida Keys and the Bahamas, but offshore in deep water, a deep keel with the ballast low provides greater stability and safety.

General-purpose boats also have moderate amounts of sail area. This means they won't be the fastest boats around in light air, but they also won't have to be reefed as soon as a raceboat with a tall mast and acres of expensive Spectra and Kevlar threads.

The *sail area/displacement* (SA/D) ratio is a convenient way to compare the relative amounts of sail area on different boats. This number, coupled with the *displacement/length* (D/L) ratio, gives a fairly accurate picture of a boat's performance. A general-purpose boat will have a D/L ratio between about 200 and 300 and a SA/D ratio between about 15 and 17. See the illustrations on page 15 for the actual formulas.

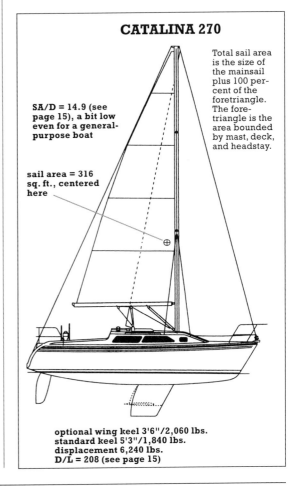

CATALINA 270

Total sail area is the size of the mainsail plus 100 percent of the foretriangle. The foretriangle is the area bounded by mast, deck, and headstay.

SA/D = 14.9 (see page 15), a bit low even for a general-purpose boat

sail area = 316 sq. ft., centered here

optional wing keel 3'6"/2,060 lbs.
standard keel 5'3"/1,840 lbs.
displacement 6,240 lbs.
D/L = 208 (see page 15)

General-Purpose Boats

PEARSON 30

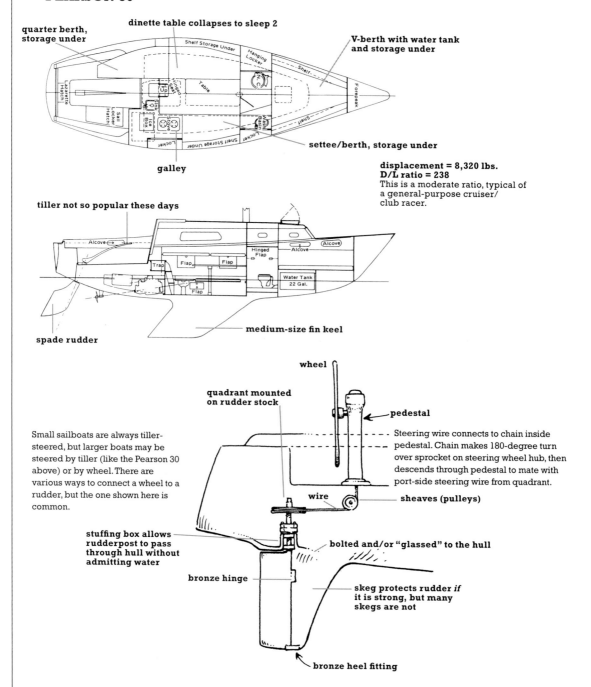

quarter berth, storage under

dinette table collapses to sleep 2

V-berth with water tank and storage under

Shelf Storage Under

Hanging Locker

Shelf

Lazarette Hatch

Sail Locker Hatch

Hinged Seat

Table

Up

Sink

Ice Box

Stove

Locker

Shelf Storage Under

Locker

Water Basin

Forepeak

Shelf

galley

settee/berth, storage under

displacement = 8,320 lbs.
D/L ratio = 238
This is a moderate ratio, typical of a general-purpose cruiser/club racer.

tiller not so popular these days

Alcove

Alcove

Alcove

Hinged Flap

Trap

Flap

Flap

Flap

Water Tank 22 Gal.

spade rudder

medium-size fin keel

wheel

quadrant mounted on rudder stock

pedestal

Small sailboats are always tiller-steered, but larger boats may be steered by tiller (like the Pearson 30 above) or by wheel. There are various ways to connect a wheel to a rudder, but the one shown here is common.

Steering wire connects to chain inside pedestal. Chain makes 180-degree turn over sprocket on steering wheel hub, then descends through pedestal to mate with port-side steering wire from quadrant.

wire

sheaves (pulleys)

stuffing box allows rudderpost to pass through hull without admitting water

bolted and/or "glassed" to the hull

bronze hinge

skeg protects rudder *if* it is strong, but many skegs are not

bronze heel fitting

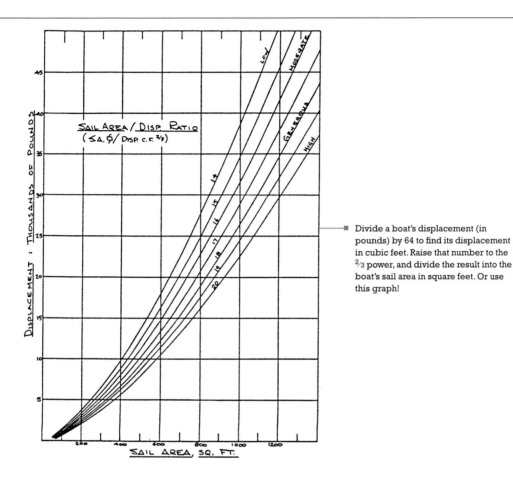

Divide a boat's displacement (in pounds) by 64 to find its displacement in cubic feet. Raise that number to the $\frac{2}{3}$ power, and divide the result into the boat's sail area in square feet. Or use this graph!

To get the D/L ratio, multiply the water-line length in feet by 0.01, raise the result to the third power, and divide that number into the displacement in long tons (2,240 lbs.).

$$D/L = \frac{\text{Displacement (long tons)}}{(\text{Length (ft) x } 0.01)^3}$$

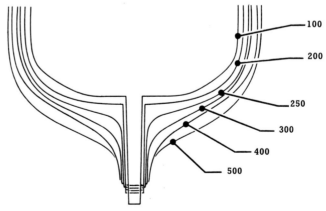

100: Strictly racing, thrill sailing, and overnighting.
200: Racing, weekending, and light cruising.
250: All-around good sailing, motoring, long and short cruising with moderate liveability.
300: Fair sailing for long cruises but excellent motoring with good liveability.
400: Poor sailing but excellent motoring, seakindliness, and liveability.
500: Terrible sailing, but superb liveabilty. Motoring is good with lots of power.

Cruisers

As noted previously, fixed keels provide superior stability and are favored for use in open water. The keel may extend from near the bow all the way to the stern, in which case it is called a *full keel*. More modern are *fin keels*, which are shorter from front to back, but deeper. Some have bulbs on the bottom to locate the ballast as low as possible. There are pros and cons to each (see the sidebars). Traditional cruising boats have full keels, but in the past 25 years, they have given way to fin keels, albeit longer than those found on modern raceboats.

But there's more to designing and building a safe offshore boat than just its keel. The windows and portlights must be strong and not too large. The cockpit must not hold too much water if flooded by a breaking wave. Hatches must be strong and not leak. The rig must be well

stayed and offer convenient ways to reduce sail in a storm. All hardware must be of good quality and well-fastened. The rudder must be well made, and an emergency steering system should be provided as backup.

The sloop rig is the most common, mainly because it is the simplest and least expensive. The cutter rig has two headsails, so reducing sail is easy. Ketches and yawls have mizzenmasts, which add complexity and cost; their mizzensails add nothing in terms of speed upwind, but they balance the boat better when sailing on a reach.

The suitability of a given boat for deepwater cruising—or offshore racing, for that matter—depends on its design, the quality of its construction, and the crew's experience and skill. The cruisers in the Sailboat Guide appendix are as good a starting place as any.

FULL KEEL

Advantages
- Easier to steer straight ("tracks" well)
- Sits level (fore and aft) when aground
- Inside ballast can't fall off
- Protects rudder from collision
- Propeller in aperture is somewhat protected from being fouled by lines in the water, such as those (called *warps*) used to tether lobster pots

- Hull usually has more volume, so stowage is increased

Disadvantages
- More wetted-surface area means more friction and makes the boat slower
- Wider turning radius
- Increased volume makes the boat more expensive to build

FIN KEEL

Advantages
- Less wetted-surface area makes the boat faster
- Shorter turning radius
- Lower ballast makes the boat "stiffer" (doesn't heel as much)
- Points higher (sails closer to the wind)
- Spade rudders often provide better steering control

Disadvantages
- High loads are placed on the bolts that hold the keel to the hull

- More easily damaged in a grounding
- Less stowage
- Some have such shallow bilges that even a little water collected there can pour out on the *sole* (the floor) when the boat is heeled—a real drag if it also contains engine oil drippings
- May not track as well; if the helm is left untended even for an instant, the boat may start to turn

Cruisers

Not all cruising is offshore; this innovative boat is especially designed for cruising very shallow water, like Florida Bay.

SHANNON SHOALSAILER

LOA	32'
LWL	30'
beam	12'9"
draft	30"
displacement	9,500 lb.
sail area	450 sq. ft.

SLOOP

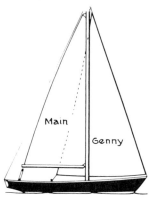

CUTTER

YAWL

KETCH

CRUISERS (cont.)

VALIANT 50

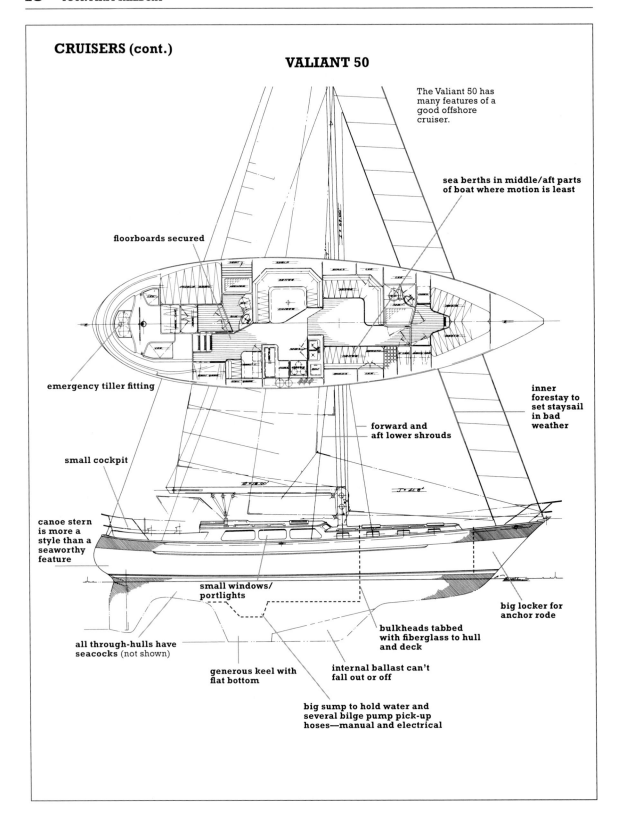

The Valiant 50 has many features of a good offshore cruiser.

floorboards secured

sea berths in middle/aft parts of boat where motion is least

emergency tiller fitting

inner forestay to set staysail in bad weather

forward and aft lower shrouds

small cockpit

canoe stern is more a style than a seaworthy feature

small windows/ portlights

big locker for anchor rode

bulkheads tabbed with fiberglass to hull and deck

all through-hulls have seacocks (not shown)

generous keel with flat bottom

internal ballast can't fall out or off

big sump to hold water and several bilge pump pick-up hoses—manual and electrical

Keel Configurations

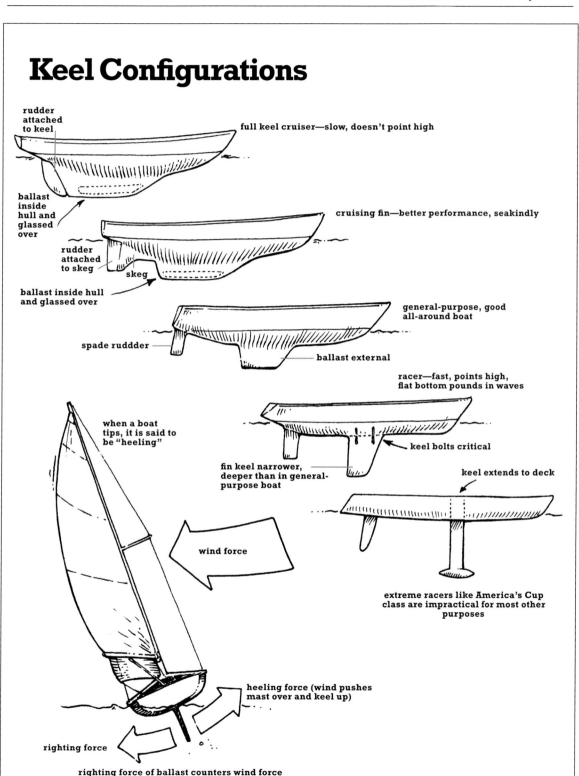

rudder attached to keel

full keel cruiser—slow, doesn't point high

ballast inside hull and glassed over

cruising fin—better performance, seakindly

rudder attached to skeg

skeg

ballast inside hull and glassed over

general-purpose, good all-around boat

spade ruddder

ballast external

racer—fast, points high, flat bottom pounds in waves

keel bolts critical

when a boat tips, it is said to be "heeling"

fin keel narrower, deeper than in general-purpose boat

keel extends to deck

wind force

extreme racers like America's Cup class are impractical for most other purposes

heeling force (wind pushes mast over and keel up)

righting force

righting force of ballast counters wind force

Racers

By nature, racing sailboats are lighter than cruising sailboats, usually with deeper fixed keels and taller masts for carrying more sail area. They may be one-designs, like the J/24 and Melges 24, or designed for favorable ratings under one of the various handicap rules, such as the International Measurement System (IMS).

Racers usually have fairly spartan interiors and, despite frequent claims to the contrary, they are less-than-ideal as off-duty cruisers.

Modern racers have become so light that they depend on human ballast (so-called "rail meat," which are crew sitting on the "high side"—feet overboard) to prevent excessive heel.

Nevertheless, campaigning a boat can be wonderfully rewarding. You quickly learn how to trim sails for maximum speed, how to determine and plot the fastest course between two points, and how to steer effectively. Equally important, you learn teamwork and the pleasures of camaraderie. And some sailors are simply more temperamentally inclined to the competitive excitement and goal attainment of racing than the Zen of leisurely sailing.

The cost of equipping and maintaining a raceboat can be considerable, so it's best to consult with other owners. To be competitive, new sails usually have to be purchased every year or two or three. The bottom must be sanded and polished smooth—sometimes more than once a season. Worn lines must be replaced. Boats campaigned on a national circuit must be trucked from one event to the next. It's the cost of racing that no doubt has led many young sailors to cry out the acronym "OPB!" when asked how they manage. (*OPB* means "other people's boats.")

The J/24 is one of the most popular one-design keelboats in the world, with more than 11,000 sold since its inception in 1977. Notice the "rail meat"!

Racers

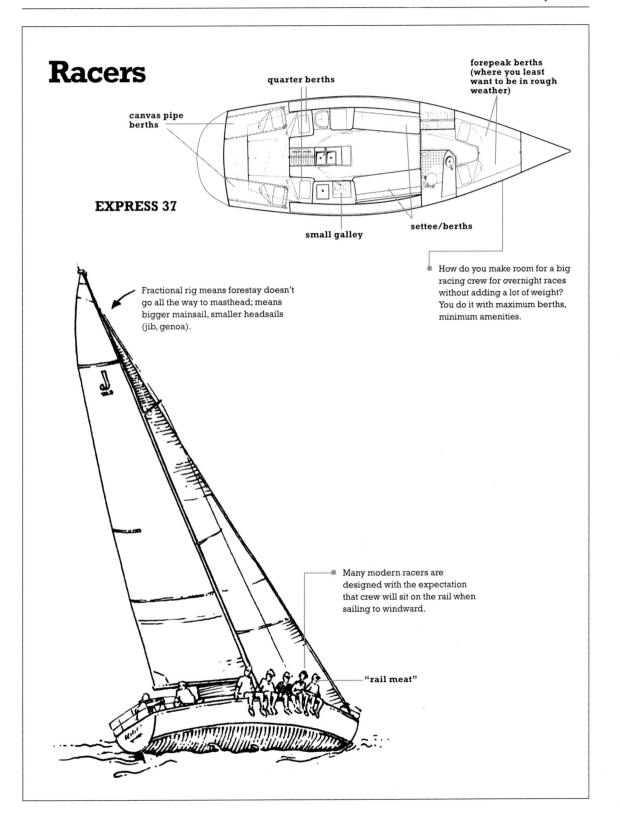

EXPRESS 37

quarter berths

canvas pipe berths

forepeak berths (where you least want to be in rough weather)

small galley

settee/berths

How do you make room for a big racing crew for overnight races without adding a lot of weight? You do it with maximum berths, minimum amenities.

Fractional rig means forestay doesn't go all the way to masthead; means bigger mainsail, smaller headsails (jib, genoa).

Many modern racers are designed with the expectation that crew will sit on the rail when sailing to windward.

"rail meat"

Multihulls

The earliest multihulls were probably dugout canoes lashed together for increased stability. At some point, the crossbeams connecting them were lengthened. The greater the distance between the two hulls, the harder they are to capsize. And because they don't need ballast for stability, they are lighter than monohulls and therefore much faster. The only problem with multihulls is that if they capsize and turn turtle, they are stable upside down and are often impossible to right. On the plus side, they won't sink, and a well-designed cruising catamaran or trimaran is very stable and will flip only in the most extreme circumstances.

Popular daysailing multihulls, all catamarans because most small trimarans are impractical, include the 12-foot Aqua Cat, the Hobie 14 and 16, the 20-foot Nacra, and the 20-foot Tornado. The Hobie 16 and Tornado are international classes. Most are trailerable despite their wide beams. Some larger multihull daysailers can be canted on the trailer to reduce beam and thereby meet state highway requirements.

Larger mutihulls, such as the folding F-27 trimaran and Gemini catamaran, generally cost considerably more than monohulls of the same length because there are many more parts. Again due to their great beam, there is much more deck space. Although a trimaran's interior is often smaller than a monohull of equivalent length, the cruising catamaran offers living space in both hulls and on the connecting bridge deck.

Racing multihulls are very fast, with speeds in the teens and higher. Cruising multihulls have shorter masts to reduce the odds of capsizing. A 30-footer might typically cruise at 8 to 9 knots (1 knot = 1.15 miles per hour), which may not seem very fast until you realize that this is 60 percent faster than the 5 to 6 knots made by most 30-foot monohulls!

Due to their lightness, multihulls have a much faster motion in waves than monohulls do. Though they stay mostly level, the movement of their hulls up and down is accurately described as "snappy." These boats are an absolute delight to sail in calm conditions, but potential buyers are strongly advised to test-sail a multihull in choppy water before making a final decision.

■ ■ ■

Most people are introduced to sailing by a friend who already owns a boat. Your first impulse may be to buy the same one, and that may work out fine. Or it may not. Try to sail as many kinds of boats as you can before putting down your cash. The more experience you have, the wiser your choice. Then again, at some point you just have to jump in. Remember that you are likely to outgrow your first boat within a few years, so resale value is an important consideration in protecting your investment . . . and your marriage, should you be fortunate enough to be so engaged.

The F-27 trimaran folds up to a road-ready 8' 5" beam. Speeds of 20 knots under sail are possible.

Multihulls

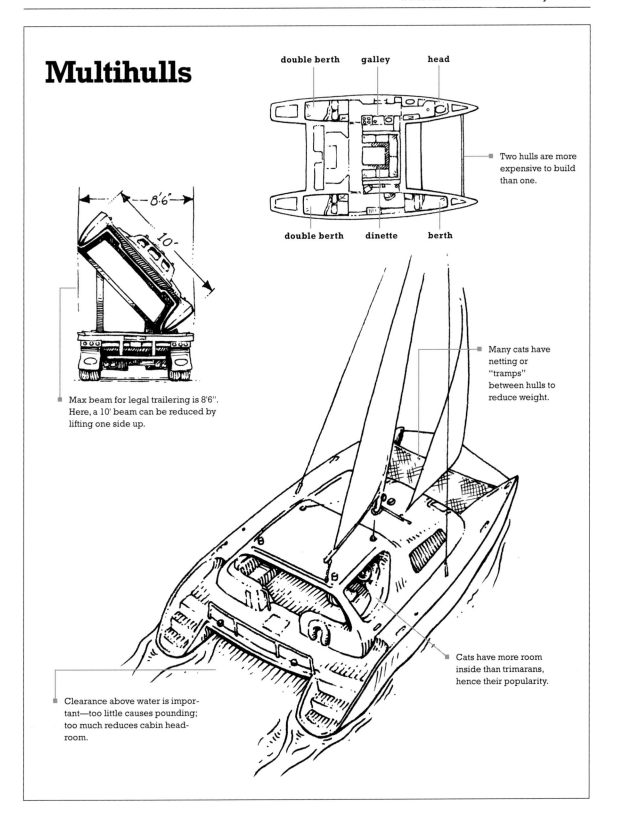

double berth   galley   head

Two hulls are more expensive to build than one.

double berth   dinette   berth

Max beam for legal trailering is 8'6". Here, a 10' beam can be reduced by lifting one side up.

Many cats have netting or "tramps" between hulls to reduce weight.

Cats have more room inside than trimarans, hence their popularity.

Clearance above water is important—too little causes pounding; too much reduces cabin headroom.

MULTIHULLS (cont.)

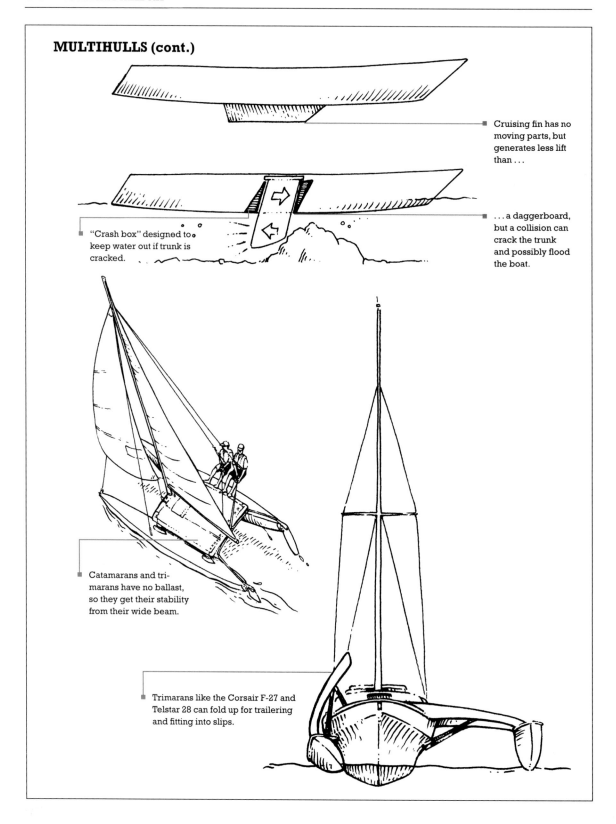

Cruising fin has no moving parts, but generates less lift than . . .

. . . a daggerboard, but a collision can crack the trunk and possibly flood the boat.

"Crash box" designed to keep water out if trunk is cracked.

Catamarans and trimarans have no ballast, so they get their stability from their wide beam.

Trimarans like the Corsair F-27 and Telstar 28 can fold up for trailering and fitting into slips.

First-Time Sailor's Survival Guide

The last chapter urged you to sail as many boats as possible before deciding what to buy, and one excellent way to do that is to sail on other people's boats. So OK, you've been invited to go sailing with a friend. Maybe it'll be your first time on a sailboat. You're excited, but also a little nervous. Will you bring the right stuff? Embarrass yourself because the only knot you know is a granny? Fall off the boat when it heels?

Here's all you need to know:

- Ask what to wear. Soft, white-soled shoes are best; black-soled shoes, unless you know for certain they will not leave scuff marks on a deck, are a bad idea. It might be cooler on the water than ashore, so take layers of clothing—pants for when your shorts don't keep you warm, a polar fleece to wear over your T-shirt, and a windbreaker to wear over that. Take a small canvas bag for these items plus a hat, sunscreen, and any personal items you require. And take sunglasses—sunlight reflected from water is hard on unprotected eyes.

- Ask if you'll be eating on board. If the answer is no, minimize the chances of seasickness by eating at least an hour beforehand. Nothing greasy. Bring some dry crackers and cola drinks in case you do get woozy. If you do eat aboard, don't overdo it.

- Seasickness strikes more often on bigger boats with slower roll periods. It's less likely to grip you on a daysailer.

- If you are prone to seasickness, take a medication BEFORE getting on board, usually an hour or more in advance. Dramamine and Bonine motion-sickness pills help many people, but not all. Probably the most effective preventive is scopalomine, sold under the name Transderm Scop. Ask your doctor for a prescription for this patch that is applied behind the ear. If you do have to throw up (toss your cookies, feed the fish), lean far enough overboard so you won't take the varnish off your host's *brightwork* (that means all that painstakingly varnished wood).

- Drug-free remedies for seasickness: Steer the boat yourself. Lie down and stare at the sails and sky. Eat ginger and sip cola. Some people wear elastic pressure bands on their wrists and swear these help.

- Ask what you can do to help. If the owner asks you to get aboard while he pushes off, look around to see whether you're going to hit anything when leaving the dock. Be prepared to push off a piling or neighboring boat, but be careful not to get any part of your body between the hull and the stationary object—big boats won't even know you're there. Crunch! Bring lines and fenders to the cockpit and ask where to stow them. Coil the lines and secure them in some manner so they don't come undone when retrieved later. If the owner asks you to stay on the dock and push off while he steers, walk the boat forward, a foot off the dock. Keep one hand on some part of the boat to help you get aboard. Ask when to step aboard. Don't wait too long! (See chapter 16 for more on leaving the dock.)

- The owner may ask you to raise the sails while he or she steers. Don't be afraid to ask for instructions. Haul on the halyard until the sail's *luff* (the vertical part next to the mast) is taut; then ask if it should be taken up more. See chapter 12 for an illustration of how to belay a line—in this case the halyard—on a cleat.

- If you have to use the toilet, ask if there's anything you need to know first. Most marine "heads" require several steps to flush: After use, open the water inlet valve, pump continuously until the contents are gone, and then pump another five or so times to make sure the contents make it through the hose all the way to the holding tank or overboard, as the case may be; then close the inlet valve. Never put any-

thing else into the toilet except toilet paper. Clearing a clogged hose is a nasty, nasty job!

- Can the boat capsize? Ask the owner. If it's a small daysailer, the answer may be yes. Ask what to do in that event. Whatever he tells you, don't leave the boat. Most capsizable daysailers have flotation and will not sink, so hang on and be ready to help right it (see chapter 21.) Your chances of encountering conditions extreme enough on an afternoon sail to capsize a keelboat—which could sink—are roughly equivalent to being struck by a meteor. Simply put, this is not something to worry about. Even in a small centerboard boat, your skipper should have enough warning of a freshening breeze to get home or get the sails down well before you capsize.

- All sailboats heel, so don't be alarmed. Catamarans heel very little, and trimarans heel only about 15 degrees under most conditions. Sit on the "high" or windward side. This helps keep the boat level and the fear lobes in your brain from panicking. Don't worry until water enters the cockpit. You'll feel better if you're wearing a life jacket, and so will your skipper.

- Relax and enjoy the experience. Observe how the boat is tacked and jibed, with sails going over to the other side as the boat turns and then trimmed to the new course. The more you know, the less anxious you'll feel. And maybe you won't feel anxious anyway; not everyone does.

- The best way to get invited back is to be helpful and to have fun. Back at the dock, help put away the sails, cushions, and lines. Rinse the deck. Offer to bring beer, or soda, or sandwiches for the next outing.

How Big Should My First Boat Be and What Should It Be Built of?

How Big?

Like cars and houses, most people want the biggest boat they can, er . . . talk someone else into. (I was going to say "afford," but lack of money doesn't stop people nowadays.) Even in Texas, however, bigger isn't always better, especially when it comes to your first boat. The cost of ownership always exceeds the purchase price. And then there are the intangibles, such as how much bottom sanding your triceps can tolerate before wilting. Or for the status-conscious, how small a "yacht" your psyche can stand before it's just totally embarrassing.

Further, it is likely you'll keep your first boat just two or three years, after which time you'll have acquired sufficient experience and skill to justify spending trainloads of money on something larger. Being on the shoal end of the learning curve now, however, is a good reason for choosing a smaller and less-expensive boat. What you think you will want in two years and what in two years you actually want may be very different. You may think now that you want a world cruiser, but in two years you might want a round-the-buoys racer or maybe even (gasp!) an RV.

But for now, you're going to buy a boat. Good. And size is a relevant avenue of study. Emerson said there is no virtue in size, yet there is an undeniable attraction: When it comes to boats, longer is faster. Bigger is roomier. Heavier is more seaworthy. All at a price, naturally. A price many of us are more than willing to pay.

If you're the suspicious sort, however, you might have guessed there are other important factors involved in sizing a boat besides the thickness of your wallet. Consider:

- *The number of people aboard at any one time.* For planning purposes, four is a good number. I'm always surprised that even on a 40-footer, more than four people seems like a crowd. (If you are a family of seven, you need either a very large boat or another sport.)
- *Where you sail.* Small boats are safest in protected waters, such as small lakes. In big waves, longer, heavier boats are safer and more comfortable.
- *The amount of maintenance you're willing to do.* Of course, bigger boats require more upkeep: sanding and painting the bottom

DAYSAIL
RACE
CRUISE

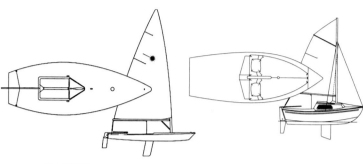

DAY SAILER
16'9"   575 lbs.
$2,000   crew 1–4

LASER
13'10"   130 lbs.
$1,200   crew 1–2

WEST WIGHT POTTER
15'0"   495 lbs.
$3,000   crew 1–3   sleeps 2

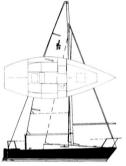

ENSIGN
22'6"   3,000 lbs.
$5,500   crew 1–4

J/24
24'0"   3,100 lbs.
$19,000   crew 4–5

SABRE 28
28'0"   7,900 lbs.
$25,000   crew 1–4   sleeps 4

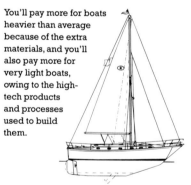

You'll pay more for boats heavier than average because of the extra materials, and you'll also pay more for very light boats, owing to the high-tech products and processes used to build them.

SHIELDS 30
30'0"   4,600 lbs.
$20,000   crew 1–5

FARR 40
40'9"   10,917 lbs.
$150,000 crew 8–11
(when not racing, fewer crew can sail the boat leisurely)

ISLAND PACKET 38
38'   21,500 lbs.
$150,000 crew 2–5   sleeps 6

Whether for daysailing, racing, or cruising, a bigger boat is a heavier boat, more expensive to buy and to own. These are representative used-boat prices.

Increasing Size and Cost

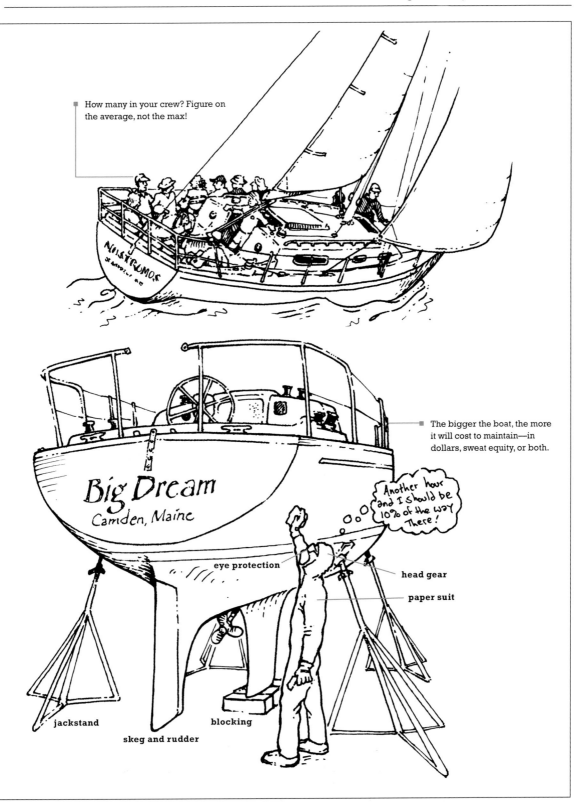

with antifouling paint each season; waxing the topsides to protect the gelcoat; replacing equipment that wears out, such as lines, fenders, lights, hoses, and electronics. If you don't do the work, you'll have to pay someone else to do it for you. Many marinas require that you commission them and pay their hourly rates for sanding the bottom—even when performed by an adenoidal 18-year-old—maybe $50 per hour or more. Unless you're Joe Millionaire, it makes a lot of sense to do as much of your own maintenance as possible on your first boat. If nothing else, it will give you the experience to supervise the work of others on later boats.

- *That boat size increases exponentially with length.* This means that a 10 percent increase in length might increase weight and volume (called *displacement*) by 25 percent or more. The cost of practically every associated expense increases as well: slip space; insurance; the cost of a sail, rope, or anchor; bottom job; wax job, and so on.
- *That the larger the boat, the less sense it makes for impromptu sailing.* A J/24 can be handled easily by one or two people, and you can get under way in less than 10 minutes and put the boat to bed just as quickly at the end of an afternoon. A bigger boat, with bigger sails and bigger gear, takes more hands and more time to sail comfortably. A 35-footer makes no sense for daysailing, but if that's what you want, there are no rules that say you can't have it!

What Material?

Boats are made of wood (planks or plywood), steel, aluminum, various plastics, and fiberglass. There also are a few old boats still around made of something called ferro-cement, which is basically plaster and cement on chicken wire and is to be avoided.

Metal is too heavy for dinghies and daysailers, and should be considered only for cruising boats about 35 feet and longer. During the 1970s and 1980s, aluminum was a reasonable choice for a raceboat of about 45 feet and longer, but today's raceboats are almost entirely made of *composites*, which means making the hull laminate of several materials—such as fiberglass or carbon fibers—sandwiched on both sides of a lightweight balsa, foam, or plastic core.

Until the late 1940s, nearly all boats were made of wood. As wonderful as it is to work with, as amazing as its properties are, and as beautiful as its grain may be, wood has one major weakness: it rots. Oh, it can last 100 years . . . if you devote your life or your income to its preservation. And unless the boat is a valuable antique, resale value is dubious.

A process called *cold molding*, in which thin veneers of wood are bent over frames and then set in epoxy resin, makes for a strong, stiff, lightweight hull. Nearly all boats built with this method are custom, however, so this is not the best choice for your first boat.

The development of fiberglass during World War II revolutionized the boating industry—making tough, long-lasting, economical boats available for the first time to the middle class. Since then, the vast majority of boats have been molded in fiberglass.

In the past decade, certain plastics have become so sufficiently strong and durable that small boats, such as the popular Escape and Pico dinghies and some Hobie catamarans, can successfully and economically be made using such techniques as rotomolding polyethylene and thermoforming ABS (acrylonitrile-butadiene-styrene). But these plastics still lack the strength to support large structures subject to the dynamic loads of wind and wave, and they're heavy.

Unless you choose one of the small boats mentioned above, your first boat should be fiberglass. Later, after you learn more about boat ownership, you can consider wood and metal.

From Whom Should I Buy?

Well, the choices are about the same as for an automobile:
- Dealer
- Private individual

And you find them the same way: Yellow Pages, newspaper ads, and now the Internet. Because big expensive boats take longer to sell than most cars, and the audience is necessarily smaller, some boats are advertised only in magazines and through brokerage firms. That's when a boat becomes less like a car and more like a real estate property, making you think you need an agent to locate a buyer and negotiate the transaction. You don't.

Here's what I do when I'm looking to buy a boat:
- I subscribe to *Soundings* boating newspaper because it has thousands of classified ads for all types of boats.
- I check Internet sites such as www.boat traderonline.com, which also lists thousands of boats.
- I verify price ranges by checking the BUC *Used Boat Price Guide*. These books are ex-

pensive to purchase, but you can request a report on a single boat for a more reasonable price (online at www.bucnet.com). Alternatively, your library might have copies, but you're more likely to find the three-volume set in the office of a yacht broker. BUC's guides are published several times a year, but any volume less than a year old will do. There are other price guides for boats, such as NADA (National Automobile Dealers Association). None is perfect; there are frequent accusations that individual boat prices don't always reflect actual sale prices, but are merely statistical adjustments based on what the publishers believe to be happening to the economy in general and to segments of the boating market in particular. Competition and faults aside, I've found BUC the most comprehensive and reliable. Nevertheless, temper even BUC's figures with your own market research.
- I look at as many examples of a target boat as I can possibly find. This usually requires some driving time, even overnight trips when I get serious or when I can work in the visit with some other purpose.

For most of the boat models I've desired over the years (ah, and there have been many!), I've usually managed to see just two or three before making a choice. More often than not, my choice has been to buy something else entirely. Why? The closer you look, the more a boat reveals about itself.

I was once enamored with a Dufour 35, a popular French-built sloop of the 1970s. I was fortunate enough to have cruised aboard one for two weeks along the coast of Turkey and came to admire many of its attributes. It was a decent sailer, well-mannered, and reasonably fast. The galley was workable, and I liked the offset double berth forward (not found on all Dufour 35s). When one became available in my hometown, I got excited, visiting the boat with the seller's broker several times. But then I started seeing things I didn't like, such as the small European-size Eno stove; a U.S. stove was too wide to fit the small swing space, so there wasn't much opportunity to upgrade when the Eno failed (and everything on a boat eventually does). And the fiberglass-pan interior stretched all the way from the sole up the sides of the hull and to the deck. Such large interior moldings have several drawbacks when compared with wood interiors: more condensation, louder noise, and greater difficulty in accessing all parts of the hull. On this boat, there was no access to areas behind the settee backrests. What happens if there's a collision and you need to stuff a towel in the crack, but the crack is in the hull, inches away on the other side of the strong fiberglass liner? While you're staring at the shiny gelcoat surface, water pours in between the hull and pan, filling the bilge. Uh-oh.

Whether you work through a broker on any transaction is purely personal. There are advantages (you don't have to deal directly with the other party) and disadvantages (the seller pays a commission).

I've never bought a boat from a broker, but that is merely coincidental. Although I've never used an agent to sell anything, especially houses where the commissions are large, I have nothing against buying from one. Indeed, brokers can make the whole process of negotiation much simpler and less stressful, mainly because you don't have to deal with an emotional seller who takes any offer under the asking price as a personal insult. Avoid, if you can, dealing with such persons: first, because unless you're hard-nosed they'll probably get their way, which means you'll pay more than you should; and second, what should be a good experience becomes less than pleasant, sometimes even coyote ugly. Who needs it?

Opposite: An assortment of for-sale ads for J/24's and Sabre 28's, to show how prices vary with age, condition, and equipment. (Sellers' names and phone numbers removed for privacy.)

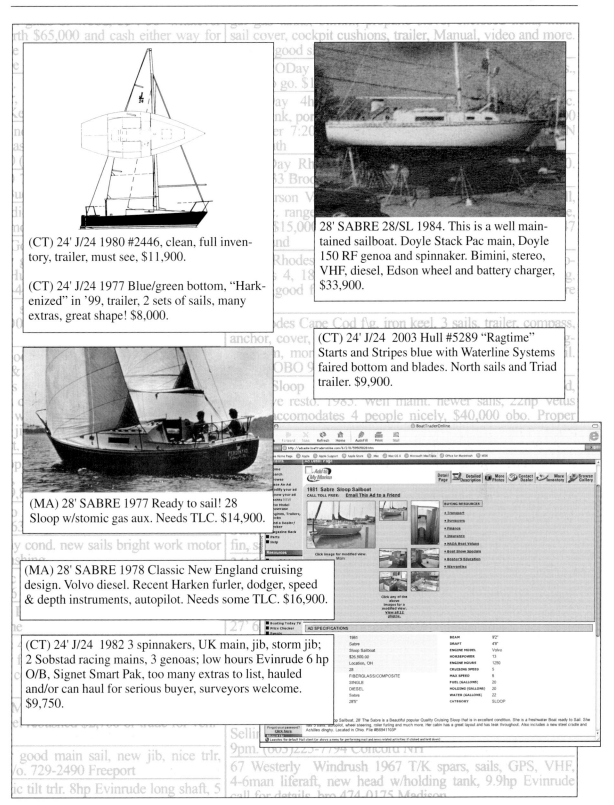

(CT) 24' J/24 1980 #2446, clean, full inventory, trailer, must see, $11,900.

(CT) 24' J/24 1977 Blue/green bottom, "Harkenized" in '99, trailer, 2 sets of sails, many extras, great shape! $8,000.

28' SABRE 28/SL 1984. This is a well maintained sailboat. Doyle Stack Pac main, Doyle 150 RF genoa and spinnaker. Bimini, stereo, VHF, diesel, Edson wheel and battery charger, $33,900.

(CT) 24' J/24 2003 Hull #5289 "Ragtime" Starts and Stripes blue with Waterline Systems faired bottom and blades. North sails and Triad trailer. $9,900.

(MA) 28' SABRE 1977 Ready to sail! 28 Sloop w/stomic gas aux. Needs TLC. $14,900.

(MA) 28' SABRE 1978 Classic New England cruising design. Volvo diesel. Recent Harken furler, dodger, speed & depth instruments, autopilot. Needs some TLC. $16,900.

(CT) 24' J/24 1982 3 spinnakers, UK main, jib, storm jib; 2 Sobstad racing mains, 3 genoas; low hours Evinrude 6 hp O/B, Signet Smart Pak, too many extras to list, hauled and/or can haul for serious buyer, surveyors welcome. $9,750.

New or Used?

As we learned in the previous chapter, fiberglass boatbuilding started to replace wooden boats beginning in the late 1940s. Say what you will about plastic, it made boating affordable for the middle class. Boats became faster and cheaper to build. But there was another factor no one anticipated: fiberglass boats last a long time! So long that some builders have jokingly talked of inventing fiberglass-eating bugs called "polyestermites" to eat them away like teredo worms eat wood.

Although the life span of a fiberglass boat depends on many factors—quality of construction, frequency and quality of maintenance, how hard it is used, and how much time it spends in the water and is subjected to intense ultraviolet rays—40 to 50 years isn't a bad estimate. That's a lot longer than an automobile. The engine, sails and rigging, and electrical gear will need to be replaced at some interval or intervals during those years, but buying used still can produce spectacular savings.

Here's another thing boats and cars don't have in common: depreciation. Although an automobile begins to lose value the moment it is driven off the lot, sailboats often increase in value the first few years. The reasons are several:

- Gear added after purchase—such as extra sails, anchors, docklines, life jackets, and radios—increases the value of the boat.
- During the first few years, the price of a used boat tracks new boat prices. For example, suppose that the price of a 2003 Sun Sloop 20 is $10,000. You buy one. Two years later, the price of a 2005 Sun Sloop 20 has increased to $12,000 (inflation, energy costs, and so on.). How much can you get for your 2003 model? Unlike a car, there is no odometer on a sailboat to betray how many miles it has traveled. If it has been well cared for and gear has been added, it might well be worth it to some bloke to pay you, say, $11,000 or even $12,500 for your used 2003 model, rather than $12,000 for a new 2005 model that still needs an anchor, docklines, life jackets, and a VHF radio. So it's two years old? You sailed it only during the summer and then just on weekends and a one-week family cruise. The engine was run barely

15 hours each summer. Why, it's hardly broken in, for cryin' out loud!

- Eventually, new and used prices begin to diverge. The reasons are at least twofold: sails, engines, and other gear begin to wear out, necessitating costly replacement; and newer models appear with desirable features that are lacking on older boats. When buying used, the trick is to find a boat well depreciated for its age, but not requiring more work and cost than you can handle.
- A builder's capacity to produce new boats may be limited, and when a backlog of orders piles up, anxious customers may be more than happy to pay like-new prices for a good used boat.
- Popular models no longer in production also may bring higher-than-expected prices simply because consumer demand is greater than the supply. Examples include the Westsail 32, Hood 38, and Cape Dory 300MS. Such demand may last for years, but not forever.

Eventually, of course, age catches up with everything, including a sailboat, and its resale value diminishes. As its value falls, the work required to maintain it in top condition increases. When the sails lose shape after 5 or 10 years, they should be replaced. When rigging wires begin to part or corrode, they, too, need replacement. So the decision whether to purchase a new or used boat should weigh the savings of buying old versus the cost of upgrades and maintenance. A surveyor can help you measure these variables. Like a home appraiser, a marine surveyor inspects boats in detail and gives the buyer a report itemizing necessary repairs as well as an overall value based on his knowledge of the boat, the builder's reputation, and the used boat market. Employ a surveyor on any purchase that costs more than you can afford to lose. You wouldn't normally pay a surveyor to look at a 10-year-old Sunfish, but you certainly would on a $300,000 Swan 44. Call in the surveyor only after making your own preliminary inspection, but never be fooled into thinking you've uncovered all its flaws; a professional will find problems you've never even heard of.

Here's another potential blunder: I once bought a 1967 Pearson Vanguard that had been extensively cruised by a previous owner and seemed ready to go again. It had been repowered with a Westerbeke diesel, was equipped with a windlass on the foredeck, and had a unique downwind rig that was touted as being much easier to handle than a spinnaker. I paid top dollah! During the next two years, as I prepared the boat and my life for cruising, the boat started to fall apart. The engine, it turned out, was quite old and leaked oil badly. The Simpson-Lawrence windlass, a vinyl-covered aluminum casting, was corroding to powder underneath. And the two-pole downwind butterfly rig required three people to set up reliably—hardly a shorthanded arrangement. The moral is twofold: even "new" gear starts aging from the moment it is installed and soon becomes old gear; and retaining a surveyor is always a good idea, no matter how much you know and how much you trust the seller.

So Why Buy New?

Good question. The reasons are several:

- Yacht design is a rapidly changing field, and if you race and want to stay competitive, you may have to buy a new boat every few years.
- The same holds true for boatbuilding technology: materials and processes continue to improve, making new boats stronger, lighter, and faster than their predecessors. One example is the increasing use of car-

bon fiber in strategic areas in which its super strength and light weight make it far superior to glass fibers.

■ Like anything else, new products generally have fewer problems than worn ones . . . except for lemons, of course, but losers right out of the box are becoming rarer in all fields of manufacturing.

■ A new boat is yours and yours alone. You don't have to live with the previous owner's choice of cushion fabric or shag carpeting; you can fill in the holes he drilled in a bulkhead to hang (and later remove) his favorite painting of a clipper ship; you can get rid of the smells of his cooking, and the oil he left dripping in the bilge.

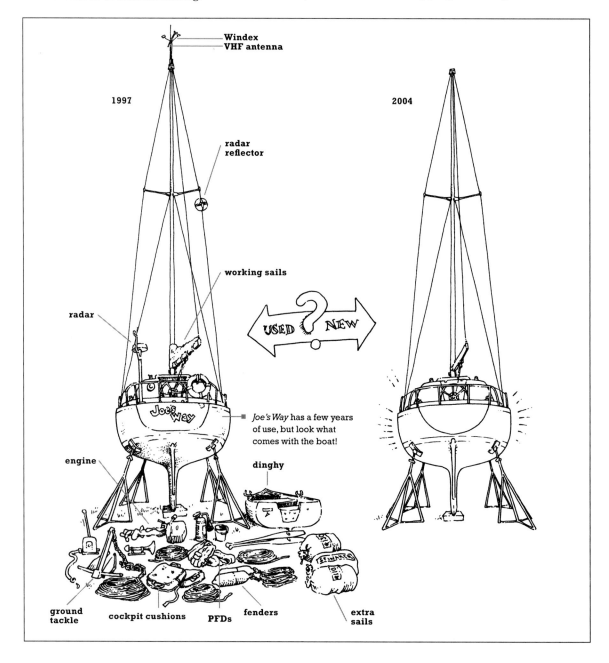

Joe's Way has a few years of use, but look what comes with the boat!

So How Do I Sort This Out?

- First, determine how much money you have to spend.
- Second, see what sizes and types of boats fit your budget. You may discover that you can afford a new 25-footer or a 5-year-old 28-footer. But the new boat is very cool and the used boat a little frumpy . . . what to do? It's your call, pal, and yours alone. Just remember, there's no wrong choice. (The only wrong choice is buying a bad boat—an unpopular design that will be hard to resell, or one with hidden defects that either impair its performance or will cost you dearly to fix.)
- Add to the purchase price of a used boat any necessary repairs and upgrades, and add to the new boat's price the cost of gear to outfit it properly. Ask yourself whether you can do any of the work yourself or if you'll have to job it out to qualified mechanics and riggers.
- It seldom pays to buy the biggest boat. Instead, buy the boat that represents the best combination of size, style, quality, and reputation. New or used matters little then.

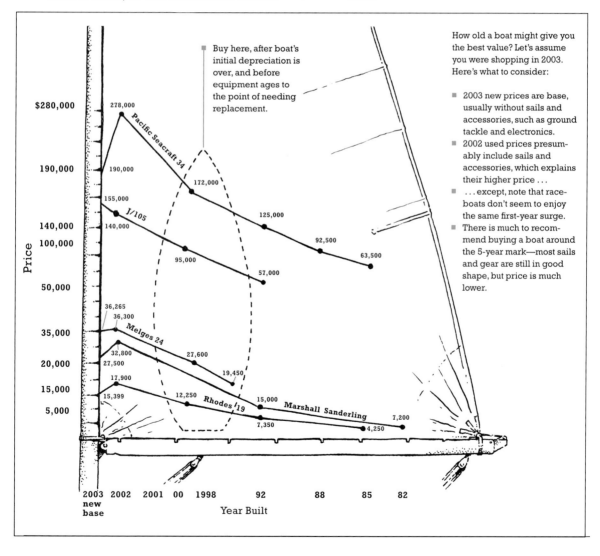

Buy here, after boat's initial depreciation is over, and before equipment ages to the point of needing replacement.

How old a boat might give you the best value? Let's assume you were shopping in 2003. Here's what to consider:

- 2003 new prices are base, usually without sails and accessories, such as ground tackle and electronics.
- 2002 used prices presumably include sails and accessories, which explains their higher price . . .
- . . . except, note that raceboats don't seem to enjoy the same first-year surge.
- There is much to recommend buying a boat around the 5-year mark—most sails and gear are still in good shape, but price is much lower.

How Do I Know If a Used Boat Is Used Up?

Awell-built, well-maintained fiberglass sailboat will last for decades—
50 years and longer. A 1947 Beetle
Cat, one of the first fiberglass sailboats ever built, is still sailed every
summer by staff at the Museum of Yachting in
Newport, Rhode Island. Is it as good as new?
Probably not. But if its hull laminate is, say, 80
percent as strong as it was originally, it is still
plenty strong enough to sail the wide and
choppy waters of Narragansett Bay. The sails
and ropes have been replaced, of course, probably several times. And the centerboard trunk
may have developed a crack at one time, but
fiberglass repairs are relatively simple to make,
so a structural fracture is not fatal.

Still, there comes a time in the life of every
boat when it is time for the owner to throw
down his scraper and say, "This doesn't make
sense!" Recognizing the moment of your
epiphany is sometimes difficult; other times, it's
so doggone obvious you'd have to be blind not
to see it.

Generally speaking, a boat is no longer worth
fixing up when the cost to do so exceeds its resale value. This rule of thumb doesn't consider

sentimental value; there's no accounting for the
affection you may feel toward your first boat or
your dearly departed father's last boat. I felt
that way about a red '57 Chevy convertible
once, but I got over it.

Here are additional tips:

- Remember that a boat is an investment,
  just like a house, an RV, or an automobile.
  You won't own it forever, and when the
  day comes to sell, you'll thank yourself
  that you chose a decent boat with a decent reputation and decent resale value.
- For the preceding reason and many more,
  avoid old wood, steel, and ferro-cement
  boats. You may see Tahiti through the
  open seams and behind the scales of rust,
  but what you think are moonbeams are really just the glitter from the last coins in
  your bank account being emptied into
  Davy Jones's locker.

An old fiberglass boat is ready for the landfill
when:

- Large areas of the deck core are wet and
  delaminated, and they feel spongy when

walked on. Yes, the deck can be repaired, but the expense is usually too great because it involves peeling off either the top or bottom skin, drying the core, and then replacing the skin.

- So many of the following conditions are found that you don't know where to start:
    massive gelcoat cracking
    green (corroded) electrical wiring
        throughout
    rust bleeding from an iron keel
    rust bleeding through the fiberglass
        rudder skin
    major leaking through the hull-to-deck
        joint
    meat hooks in the rigging wires
    baggy, dirty, stained sails
    crazed portlight lenses
    inboard engine is a hunk of rust and
        won't run
    plumbing that looks brown and smells
        worse
    flaking interior paint and peeling vinyl
        liners

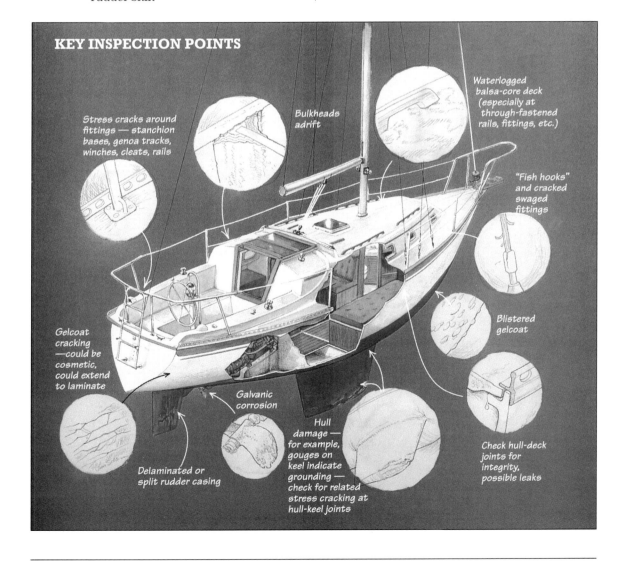

KEY INSPECTION POINTS

Stress cracks around fittings — stanchion bases, genoa tracks, winches, cleats, rails

Bulkheads adrift

Waterlogged balsa-core deck (especially at through-fastened rails, fittings, etc.)

"Fish hooks" and cracked swaged fittings

Blistered gelcoat

Gelcoat cracking —could be cosmetic, could extend to laminate

Galvanic corrosion

Hull damage — for example, gouges on keel indicate grounding — check for related stress cracking at hull-keel joints

Check hull-deck joints for integrity, possible leaks

Delaminated or split rudder casing

THE 10-MINUTE SURVEY

One of the best of boating times is looking at boats, hunting down specific ones for sale, or simply wandering through a yard full of hulls on the hard. Although I highly recommend retaining the services of a professional marine surveyor before finalizing the sale of expensive boats, you can quickly determine whether a given boat is worth looking into further by conducting your own 10-minute survey.

Here are the key things to look for:

- Check the hull for signs of damage: cracks; deformities (sight down the hull from each end) such as hollow areas or hard spots where interior bulkheads or furniture are pushing through; and asymmetrical sections (may have been built that way or may have been poorly repaired).

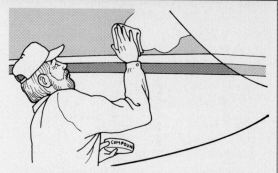

Is the gelcoat dull or chalky? If it is, and you can't restore it with a rubbing compound, you'll have to paint the boat.

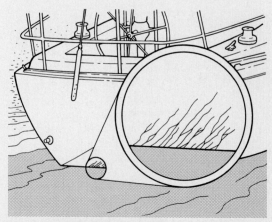

Stress cracks usually have an ongoing cause—in this case, excessive backstay tension.

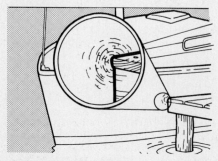

Do you see any signs of hull damage like the impact damage here from the corner of a dock?

- Stress cracks in the gelcoat. Random cracks may be just cosmetic surface crazing, but if there is a pattern or obvious cause, such as around stanchions, they may run deeper into the laminate, thereby allowing water to enter and causing weakness in the structure.

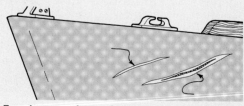

Even deep scratches can be repaired. (See chapter 23.)

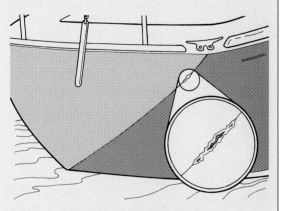

Do you see any places where the gelcoat has chipped away because there was a void underneath (usually at sharp turns where the fiberglass pulled away from the corner during lay-up)? These can be repaired with gelcoat putty.

THE 10-MINUTE SURVEY (CONTINUED)

Gelcoat Blisters

Blisters occur because free water-soluble chemicals inside the laminate exert an osmotic pull on water outside, and some water molecules find a way through the slightly permeable gelcoat. As more water is attracted into the enclosed space, internal pressure builds. The water molecules aren't squirted back out the way they came in because they combine with the attracting chemicals into a solution with a larger molecular structure. Instead, the pressure pushes the covering gelcoat into a dome—a blister.

Examine the hull bottom, below the waterline. Do you see any blisters, or domes in the gelcoat? If so, break a sample blister to assess the condition. Wear goggles because pressures can exceed 150 psi and the liquid that comes spraying out is acid. Scrub out the blister with water and a brush and examine the underlying laminate. If the laminate is perfect—the usual finding—the blister is primarily a cosmetic flaw, although taking steps to prevent water from reaching the laminate may be prudent.

If the underlying laminate is damaged, repairs will be more extensive, but this is still not a dangerous condition as long as the number of blisters is small. Use a knife point to find the depth of the damage. Laminate blisters most often occur between the initial layer(s) of mat and the first layer of woven roving.

- Rusty water weeping from the keel may indicate an iron keel that is corroding underneath the paint, or water on the inside leaking through the hull-to-keel joint. Rusty water weeping through the sides of the rudder indicates corrosion of the metal framework inside.

- Walk around the deck—and don't tread lightly. Soft or bouncy spots suggest delamination of the fiberglass skins from the core (almost all fiberglass boat decks are cored, usually with end-grain balsa, but sometimes with other materials such as foam).

Tap the deck with the handle of a screwdriver. If the sharp tapping moise turns into a full thud, you might have found an area where the fiberglass has delaminated, or separated, from its balsa core. If there is a hump there or alligatoring in the gelcoat, count on it.

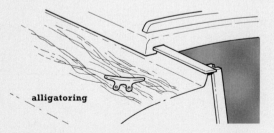

alligatoring

- Check the mast for dings and kinks and the standing wire rigging for meat hooks. Look at the sails because they're expensive to replace. Are they clean or stained, thin or thick? New sails are stiff; worn ones are pliable.

(continued next page)

THE 10-MINUTE SURVEY (CONTINUED)

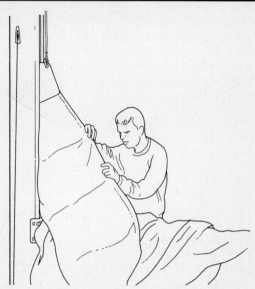

Check the sails. Are they thin, worn, frayed, stained? Is the stitching intact? Do you see pinholes or minor tears? If yes, you'll need new sails soon.

■ Inside the cabin (if there is one), check for moisture. Although water at one time or another generally gets everywhere in a boat, a dry boat is a better boat than a wet one. Water corrodes wiring and metal, rots wood, and ruins fabrics. Look for telltale signs such as watermarks on bulkheads. Especially important is the integrity of the wood where the chainplates fasten. If you can get away with it, poke the wood around the chainplate with a semisharp object.

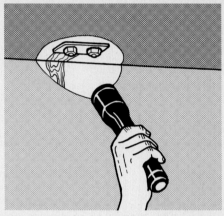

Look for signs of leaks under hardware, hull-to-deck joints, etc.

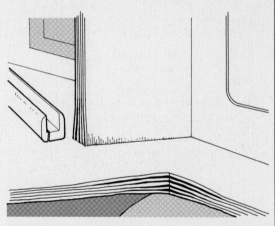

Plywood soles and bulkheads will delaminate if habitually wet.

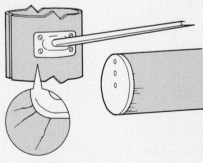

Look for cracks in an aluminum spar—for example, where the spreaders land on the mast.

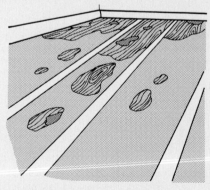

Black stains under varnish indicate water damage.

THE 10-MINUTE SURVEY (CONTINUED)

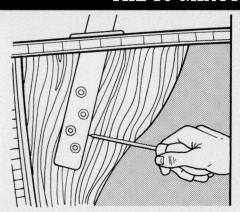

Check for wood rot on knees, bulkheads around chainplate attachments, etc. Rot in these places results from leakage.

■ Has the owner customized the boat in ways that deviate significantly from the original, such as installing an easy chair for a settee? Are there a lot of covered up or poorly filled holes in the deck and cockpit, indicating the removel of old gear?

■ It's easy to tell a boat that's well cared for from one that's been poorly loved. As Gil Scott-Heron once sang, the truth is deeper still. Rein in your desires and keep looking, because what you see is probably just the edge of the big black hole that's about to suck in all your money.

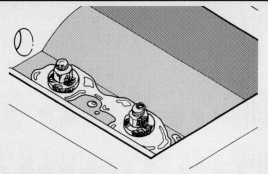

If the keel bolts fail, you lose the keel—and that's not something you want to do. Failure of good bronze or stainless steel keel bolts on an otherwise sound fiberglass boat is highly unlikely, but to be certain you can have the keel X-rayed. If the bolts are exposed, visually check them for corrosion and signs of leakage. They should have a generous shoulder washer under the nut.

When a keel is bolted directly to the hull, the bolts should pass through floor "frames" or a reinforcing grid. Check the floors for any signs of stress cracking.

Many of these conditions indicate that the boat is wetter inside than out. There's a saying that eventually water gets everywhere. How did it get in? The ways are many: drippy-lippy hatches, weepy-leaky portlights, sneaky-leaky hull-to-deck joints, dried bedding around deck hardware, loosey-goosey keel bolts, and trickle-down trickles on the inside of a keel-stepped mast.

Like a punky deck, each of these conditions can be repaired, but if the basic value of the boat isn't there, forget it. There are thousands of boats for sale, so try to resist the incredible $500 bargain sitting in the weeds at the back of the boatyard, or the sweetheart of a deal your neighbor is offering.

Many of the boats I've bought have required major work. Each spring, I tackle one or two big jobs and many smaller ones. Some years I'm lucky to launch by the Fourth of July. I momentarily pause from my boatyard labors to watch the boats sailing on the bay, some of which have been in since early spring. Inevitably, I then spot the bumper sticker that says, "I'd rather be sailing."

Amen.

How Do I Recognize Quality?

Distinguishing among varying levels of workmanship isn't easy. Often, we confuse style for quality. For example, if you were shown the radio knobs of a KIA and a Cadillac, could you identify the type of plastic used to make each one? Could you honestly say one was more durable, or superior in some way to the other? If you looked under the hood of each car, the Cadillac would have a much bigger engine and more stuff—wires and hoses. More chrome perhaps. But beyond that, could you really say one was better made than the other? The truth is that most of us don't even know what we're looking at. Perhaps one car has an iron engine block and the other an aluminum alloy block. Not many of us know the comparative physical properties of each or the pros and cons of the respective materials.

Recognizing differences in quality takes a trained eye. When it comes to boats, much is hidden. Take lifeline stanchions, for instance. They all look pretty much the same. But if you walk down the dock at a boat show and begin pulling stanchions out of their bases and measuring wall thickness with a micrometer, you'll find differ-ences. Thick-wall pipe is much stronger and more expensive than thin-wall pipe, which might dimple too easily and bend over like a tulip when someone falls against it. But from the outside, hey, both look shiny and fine!

There are reasons for price differences between boats. Why does a 40-foot Beneteau cost $160,000 and a comparably sized Hinckley cost three times as much? Beyond the fact that the former is built in days on an assembly line and the latter is hand-built over many months, there are some things you can look for.

Signs of Good Quality

- Smooth and fair hull
- Lead keel rather than iron
- Wood furniture tabbed (fiberglassed) to the hull
- All areas of hull accessible from inside, so cracks can be temporarily filled in an emergency and later repaired
- Hull and deck feel solid and don't *oilcan*, or flex
- Rubrail covering hull-to-deck joint is straight and neatly fitted

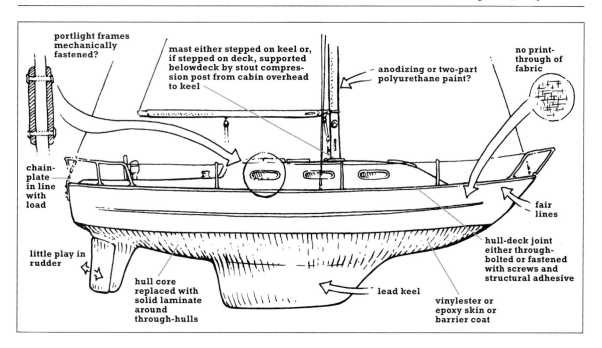

portlight frames mechanically fastened?

mast either stepped on keel or, if stepped on deck, supported belowdeck by stout compression post from cabin overhead to keel

anodizing or two-part polyurethane paint?

no print-through of fabric

chain-plate in line with load

fair lines

little play in rudder

hull core replaced with solid laminate around through-hulls

lead keel

hull-deck joint either through-bolted or fastened with screws and structural adhesive

vinylester or epoxy skin or barrier coat

- Bulkheads are tabbed (fiberglassed) to the hull AND deck
- Large backing plates on undersides of all deck hardware through which the bolts pass; this distributes loads and helps prevent deck cracks
- Through-bolts with washers and nuts at the hull-to-deck joint (a modern trend is the use of structural adhesives with bolts only at certain locations, and this is acceptable)

A smooth, fair hull.

All areas of the hull are accessible from the inside.

Rubrail covering hull-to-deck joint straight and neatly fitted.

Large backing plates for hardware fasteners.

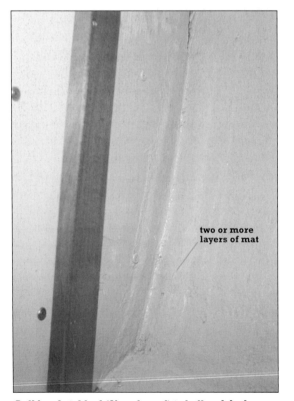

two or more layers of mat

Bulkheads tabbed (fiberglassed) to hull and deck.

Through-bolts with washers and nuts along the hull-deck joint.

Window and portlight frames mechanically fastened.

Chainplates lead fair.

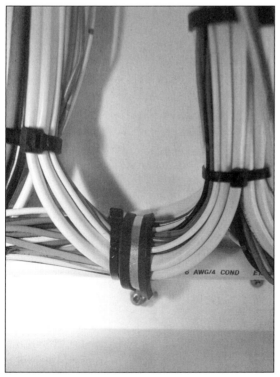

Wiring and plumbing runs are neat, well supported, and clearly labeled.

Chainplate anchor is strong and waterproof.

- Window and portlight frames mechanically fastened
- Deck core removed and filled where hardware will be bolted
- Interior plywood end grain sealed
- Adequate number of drawers for stowage
- Solid woods and thick veneers used for furniture and cabinetry
- Plumbing and wiring runs are neat, follow surfaces, are supported at short intervals, and are identified
- Deck-stepped mast well supported underneath
- Chainplates lead fair to shrouds and stays
- Chainplate anchors are strong and waterproof

Here's a couple you can't see but should ask about:

- Vinylester or epoxy resin used in the skin coat of the hull to prevent blisters
- Kerfs in the core material filled with resin

Signs of Lesser Quality

- Bulges and depressions, however faint, in the hull
- Print-through pattern of underlying fiberglass can be seen on gelcoat
- Iron keel
- Large fiberglass-pan interior
- Some areas of hull not accessible
- Pushing or jumping on areas of hull and deck results in flex, or oilcanning
- Rubrail covering hull-to-deck joint wavy
- Bulkheads simply fitted into molded slots in the overhead
- Washers only (no backing plates) on undersides of deck hardware bolts
- Screws or pop rivets fastening the hull-to-deck joint
- Window and portlight lenses held in only by rubber gasket
- Hardware installed through deck core, risking water entry to core
- Interior plywood end grain left unsealed, risking water absorption

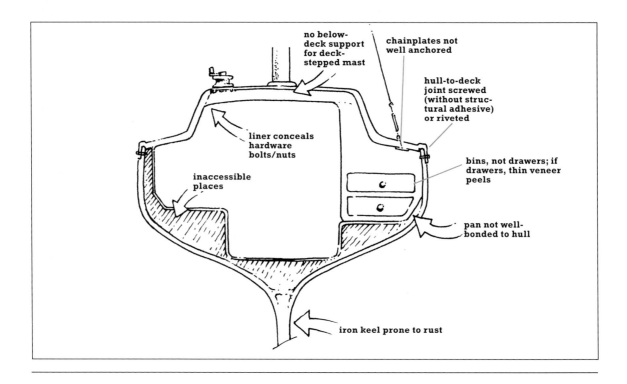

- More bins and few drawers for stowage
- Thin veneers used for furniture and cabinetry
- Plumbing and wiring runs cut across areas, droop, and are not identified
- Deck-stepped mast poorly supported underneath, resulting in deck compression
- Angle rather than fair lead between chainplates and shrouds or stays (most often seen on transom-mounted chainplates)
- Chainplates bolted through unreinforced or unwaterproofed plywood bulkheads

Another indicator is price. I suppose you could say that in most cases you get what you pay for—the more you pay, the more quality you get. But that is not always true, especially

Bulges or depressions visible in topsides.

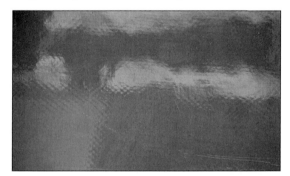

Print-through of fabric.

Sooner or later, an iron keel may look like this.

Fiberglass pan interior restricts access to inside of hull and deck.

Waviness in rubrail.

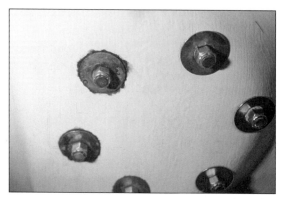

Hardware fasteners backed up with washers rather than sturdy backing plates.

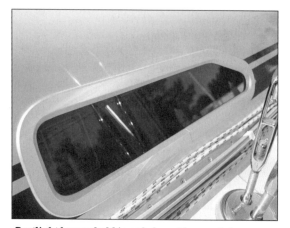

Portlight lenses held in only by rubber gaskets.

Plumbing and wiring runs sloppy, unsupported, and not identified.

Chainplate out of line with shroud or stay.

This aluminum mast step for a deck-stepped mast is corroded, probably due to an airtight mast boot and lack of adequate drain holes.

SIGNS OF A GOOD ENGINE INSTALLATION

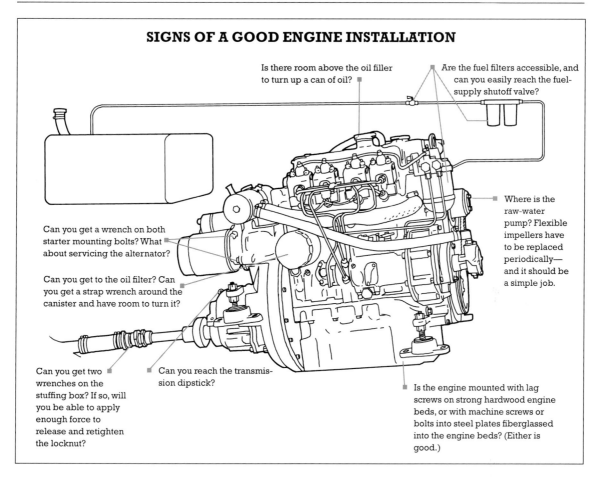

Is there room above the oil filler to turn up a can of oil?

Are the fuel filters accessible, and can you easily reach the fuel-supply shutoff valve?

Can you get a wrench on both starter mounting bolts? What about servicing the alternator?

Can you get to the oil filter? Can you get a strap wrench around the canister and have room to turn it?

Where is the raw-water pump? Flexible impellers have to be replaced periodically—and it should be a simple job.

Can you get two wrenches on the stuffing box? If so, will you be able to apply enough force to release and retighten the locknut?

Can you reach the transmission dipstick?

Is the engine mounted with lag screws on strong hardwood engine beds, or with machine screws or bolts into steel plates fiberglassed into the engine beds? (Either is good.)

in terms of degree. Yes, a Hinckley 40 is built with more expensive materials and more skilled man-hours (largely due to the hand-fitted wood interior) than the Beneteau 40, but three times more? Doubtful. To prove this true or false, however, you'd need access to records detailing every item installed, its cost, and the man-hours involved. No company will share those with a potential troublemaker! What I can tell you, however, is that as much as I admire Hinckleys, there are other builders offering comparable boats at significantly lower prices. In some cases, you do pay more for a name.

Where Can I Keep My Boat?

There are three basic choices:

- Marina dock
- Mooring
- Your driveway

In most marinas, slips are rented by the season or the month, depending on whether you live in the North, where the sailing season lasts from April—if you're lucky—to October or November; or in the South, where boats stay in the water year-round. Lest you envy the Floridians and Gulf Coasters, however, it is strange but true that people who can use their boats only part of each year often use them more because the months of absence build enthusiasm and discourage burnout. People in the South tend to grow jaded and just let their boats sit in the sun and decay. It's a major reason why boats between Florida and Texas have lower resale values. Blame it on . . . The Attack of the UV Rays!

The amount marinas charge for the sailing season is usually based on the length of the boat and figured by the foot: e.g., 30 feet × $18 = $540.

Some very beamy boats—catamarans and trimarans—may be charged extra because they occupy the space of two "normal" monohull boats. But don't ever tell a multihuller that his boat isn't normal; not unless you have all night to listen to his "shed the lead" diatribe!

Boats kept in slips must be tied to the dock in all directions with bow lines port and starboard (left and right), stern lines, and spring lines (see chapter 12).

In some parts of the world and the United States—such as New England and Catalina Island, California—boats also are tethered to moorings. These are large anchors, drills, or heavy objects embedded in the bottom of a harbor to which a heavy chain is attached and, on the surface, a buoy. One end of a strong rope is tied to the buoy, and the other end to the boat's bow cleat(s).

Prices for mooring rentals are less expensive than slips at docks. If you keep your boat at a mooring, however, you need some means of getting to it from shore. You might use your dinghy, or a launch service might be available from the harbor authority or the owner of the mooring.

Boats stored in your driveway or backyard on trailers don't cost you anything other than the aggravation of trying to mow the lawn around them. Towing a boat to and from the water for every outing can grow tiresome, though the trade-off in dollars saved may well be worthwhile. Road wear from dirt and gravel also takes a toll, but again this is at least partially offset by the convenience of having the boat at home to work on, not in a boatyard miles away.

Many owners of trailerable boats seem to go back and forth between paying for a slip or mooring and keeping it in the side yard between sails. It's a classic trade-off between cost and convenience, and you won't know which works best for you until you tote your beloved *My Way* down the highway for the first time, rig her in a parking lot, and then back her down the launch ramp (see chapter 11). If the mast hits a high-voltage electrical wire, or if you forget to unstrap the boat from the trailer, you'll probably wish you had anted up for the slip. But fear not. We've all made these and other mistakes, and most of us have lived to tell about them!

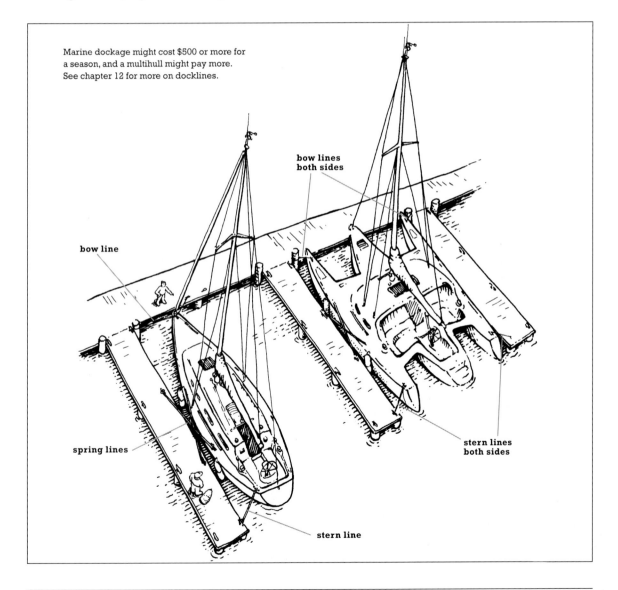

Marine dockage might cost $500 or more for a season, and a multihull might pay more. See chapter 12 for more on docklines.

bow lines both sides

bow line

bow line

spring lines

stern lines both sides

stern line

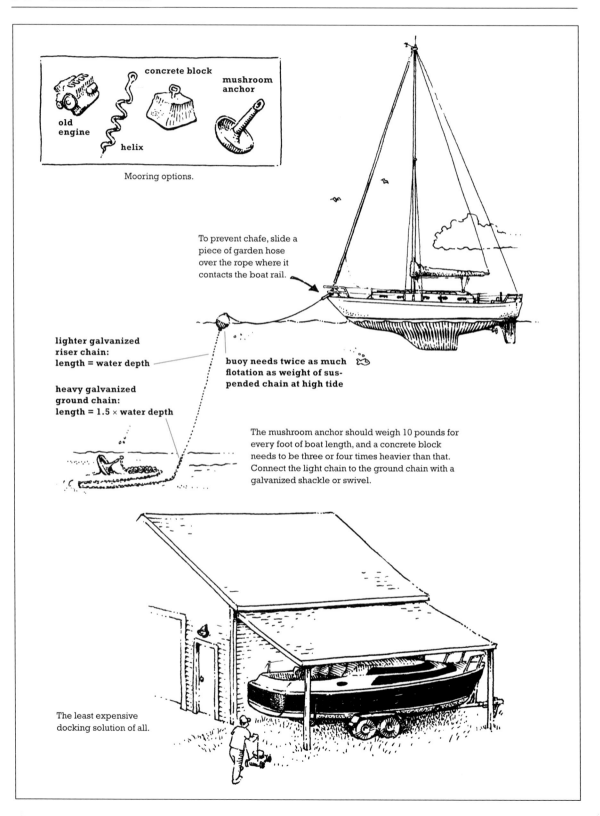

concrete block

mushroom anchor

old engine

helix

Mooring options.

To prevent chafe, slide a piece of garden hose over the rope where it contacts the boat rail.

lighter galvanized riser chain: length = water depth

buoy needs twice as much flotation as weight of suspended chain at high tide

heavy galvanized ground chain: length = 1.5 × water depth

The mushroom anchor should weigh 10 pounds for every foot of boat length, and a concrete block needs to be three or four times heavier than that. Connect the light chain to the ground chain with a galvanized shackle or swivel.

The least expensive docking solution of all.

What Will It Cost Me?

If you have to ask, you can't afford it."* Although this variation of jazzman Fats Waller's famous quote may be true for multimillion-dollar megayachts and superyachts, it certainly is not true of the millions of smaller boats and yachts in the world. Regardless of income, there is an affordable boat for every sailor. My first sailboat was a 15-foot Snipe I bought for a few hundred dollars. Aching for adventure, I filled the cockpit with camping gear and headed across Lake Michigan; I got run off one of the Manitou islands by a paramilitary goon in a jeep with a high-powered rifle, and was swept off course in a thunderstorm . . . but I digress.

Regardless of price, a boat is a major purchase for many people, often ranking right up there with their car and right below their home. Whether you are a college student spending your summer's earnings on a kayak or a middle-aged businesswoman financing a family cruising sloop, it's a transaction that deserves some prepurchase research.

The cost of owning most boats extends be-

yond the original purchase price. Exceptions might be a lightweight Snark that is transported on top of your Toyota 4Runner (don't forget to figure in the cost of a roof rack) and stored by the back door of your apartment when not in use. No loan interest, no insurance required, and maintenance is almost nil (still, the sail can rip and the hull can be gouged).

Here are the principal cost centers:

- **Loans.** Boat loans are available at roughly the same interest rates as automobiles. Start with your personal bank or credit union. If they look at you funny (see the introduction) compare rates with marine specialty lenders such as Essex Credit Corporation (see the resources section). If you have sufficient equity in your house, you can borrow against it, often at a lower rate, and the interest payments are tax deductible; home equity loans are smart choices. And the lenders generally don't care what you're buying with the money because they have your home in their clutches. You might fall into an owner-financed purchase, but with boats this is rare.

* "Lady, if you got to ask you ain't got it."—Thomas [Fats] Waller, when asked to explain rhythm.

- **Insurance.** Unless you have financed the purchase of your boat, insurance is not required by any other entity, including the long arm of any government. But it's relatively inexpensive and highly recommended. Policies for 30-foot sailboats may cost you less than $500 a year, depending on where you live, how you use the boat, and any past claims record you may have. Coverage includes collision, sinking, and personal liability. Policies differ regarding replacement values, so make sure you know what kind you're buying. Offshore policies are available, but world cruising coverage is harder to get. You'll probably need to work with a marine insurance agency to locate an insurer, although it's worth checking your homeowner's policy (assuming that you own a house) because some will cover boats below a certain size and value. If not automatically included, see if you can purchase a rider to cover your boat, which probably will be less expensive than a new marine policy.

- **Storage.** The least expensive form of storage is your backyard. This means you'll be trailering the boat to and from the water each time you use it. Marinas can charge for slip space daily (for transients), monthly, seasonally, and (in warm climates) annually. The cost might be one-third of what you'd pay for an apartment, so it's not inconsequential. Less costly (when available) are moorings located in the middle of a harbor or cove. Sometimes the mooring owner, especially a yacht club, provides launch service. Commercial owners may offer launch service for a fee. Of course, you can always use your own dinghy. In Florida and other warm locales, there is an increasing trend toward dry storage, a rather weird manifestation of future shock in which your boat is stacked like a corpse in a morgue and re-

trieved by a forklift, though to date it is mostly for powerboats. Whatever type of storage you choose, there are potentially significant costs and considerations. For further discussion, see chapter 8.

- **Additional Gear.** Few new boats come fully equipped. Most likely, you'll have to purchase certain safety items such as life jackets, anchor(s), flares, searchlight, and foghorn. All good stuff, and fortunately, most are one-time expenses. For a more complete list, see chapter 10.

- **Maintenance.** The bigger the boat, the more costly its annual maintenance. Taking care of a small daysailer may require little more than occasionally wiping it down with a clean rag, waxing the hull in the spring, and removing cushions before covering it for the winter. Boats that are left in the water for the season or year need antifouling bottom paint applied at least every other season. This means sanding the bottom, undoubtedly one of the most onerous tasks ever devised by man. By all means do it yourself, at least for a few years. It's a rite of passage. But at some point in your life, you'll want to pay a strongbacked kid who can hold a 5-pound sander at arm's length for eight hours. My friend Bill Seifert said he decided to refuse bottom work after age 50. I said, "That late?"

- **Upgrades.** Boatowners have expensive tastes. They like to keep spiffing up their vessels with electronic devices that tell them where they are, where they are going, and what they are seeing. A GPS (global positioning system), a fluxgate compass, and radar are just the beginning. How about an instrument to compute VMG (velocity made good)? An autopilot so you don't have to steer? A hoist so you don't have to lift the outboard from the dinghy to the deck? A refrigerator to keep the beer cold? New nonskid dishes so dinner doesn't always end up on the floor? New cushion fabric to replace the plaid that looks like it came from a bagpiper's kilt? A telltale compass so you can see which direction you're headed even while lying upside down in your bunk?

"My god," you cry, "is there no end to it?!" In a word, no.

"Is this penchant for acquiring boat gear as compulsive as buying barbecues and patio furniture for my home?"

More so.

But relax. It will give meaning to your life. Why? Because unlike your house, which is just a pile of concrete and two-by-fours rooted in the ground, your boat is a transcendent, extraspiritual, out-of-body, cosmic transporter that is going to transform your life. That's why.

The point here, however, is that even if you are ascending to a higher plane of existence, you still need to mind your dollars and sense: Consider all the costs associated with ownership before finalizing any purchase decision. By itemizing costs of items such as insurance, slip fees, and maintenance, you may discover that although you can afford to buy *Baby Lu*, you can't afford to keep her. Fortunately, the feeding of your soul doesn't depend on the cost of the boat. As cruisers Lin and Larry Pardey are famous for saying, "Go small, go simple, go now."

COST COMPARISON

	Trailer Sailer	Coastal Sailing	Cruiser
Purchase price	2003 Seaward 25—new $29,950	1979 Sabre 34 $34,000	1982 Tayana 37 $70,000
Loan interest	borrow $15,000 at 6% $4,983.60	borrow $24,050 $7,991.20	borrow $60,000 $19,951.60
Upgrades needed:			
sails	included	new mainsail $1,200	new mainsail $1,800
engine	$1,800 outboard	$3,000 rebuild	$10,000 new diesel
other		$2,000 refrigeration	———
Equipment needed:			
trailer	$2,500	———	———
safety (PFDs, horn, etc.)	$250	included	$4,000 life raft
ground tackle	$400	included	included
electronics	$1,200	$1,600 basic instruments	$3,500 radar
Total Cost to Buy	**$41,083.60**	**$49,791.20**	**$109,251.60**
Annual expenses:			
insurance	$400	$800	$1,600
yard work (e.g. bottom sanding)	do yourself	$400	$500
summer storage	trailer	$3,000	$3,000
winter storage	backyard	$650	$750
fuel and oil	$50	$120	$200
Total Cost to Operate	**$450**	**$4,970**	**$6,050**
Comments	small new boat: must buy all gear; save by trailering and storing in backyard	older boat with lots more room; needs electronics and engine rebuild	rugged world cruiser; needs reliable engine for world cruising, plus new sails and life raft

What Equipment Do I Need?

10

One advantage of buying a used boat is that very often the seller conveys much of the additional safety and navigation gear you'll need. Depending on the size of the boat, this can amount to a significant sum of money. A few builders offer basic equipment packages with a new boat as standard or at extra cost; Hunter Marine's CruisePac is one example.

Foremost in importance is safety gear. The U.S. Coast Guard mandates certain minimum requirements based on the size and type of boat (see www.uscgboating.org/safety.htm).

Required Safety Gear
The Coast Guard–required essentials include:

- A PFD (personal flotation device; otherwise known as a life jacket) for each person aboard. *$5–$50 from most basic to fancy vest*
- Fire extinguisher (not required on small boats without engines). *$30 to several hundred for automatic systems*

- Whistle or other sound-signaling device. *$6–$10*
- Bell or foghorn on boats larger than 39.4 feet (12 meters). *$10–$50, air horns to brass bells*
- Throwable cushion or other device (not required on boats under 16 feet or on canoes and kayaks of any length). *$10–$20*
- Visual distress signals such as flares (not required on open boats without auxiliary propulsion less than 26 feet in length). *$35–$150*

red hand-held flare (day/night)

- Navigation lights in accordance with U.S. Coast Guard Navigation Rules. *$100, but standard on most larger boats*
- Ventilation must be provided on any boat with an inboard engine, fuel storage areas, and enclosed living areas.
- Backfire flame arrester fitted to gasoline engines.

These essentials can be purchased relatively inexpensively. Special care should be

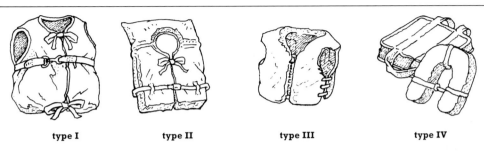

| type I | type II | type III | type IV |

Type I, Offshore Life Jacket. *Best when help may be delayed. Has at least 22 pounds of flotation and turns an unconscious wearer face up. Bulky and hard to swim in.* Type II, Inshore Life Vest. *Best when there is chance of a quick rescue. Has at least 15.5 pounds of flotation. Some models turn an unconscious wearer face up. Not as bulky as Type I.* Type III, Flotation Aid. *Same buoyancy as Type II. Made to be worn at all times, is comfortable, and easier to swim in. Will not turn an unconscious wearer face up.* Type IV, Throwable Device. *Meant to be tossed to someone or held onto when help is nearby. Horseshoe buoys have at least 16.5 pounds of flotation; cushions, 18 pounds.*

given to children's PFDs, however, because not all will automatically turn an unconscious child's face out of the water. There are five types of PFDs, and unfortunately, the most effective are also the least comfortable. This makes both adults and children less likely to wear a PFD, but remember, if you don't wear a PFD, it can't save you.

Inflatable PFDs are viable alternatives now that they are Coast Guard–approved, but only for persons older than 16 years of age. Some inflate automatically when immersed; others have manually activated CO_2 cartridges, and both types can be orally inflated if the mechanism fails.

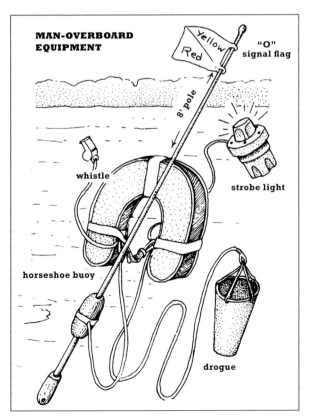

MAN-OVERBOARD EQUIPMENT

"O" signal flag

Yellow Red

8' pole

whistle

strobe light

horseshoe buoy

drogue

Additional Safety Gear

As noted, the U.S. Coast Guard requirements are a minimum. Other equipment may be important to have aboard, again depending on the size and type of your boat, and where you sail. Obviously, a boat crossing the Pacific Ocean needs a lot more gear than one routinely sailed on Lake Texoma or even Green Bay.

Here are my suggestions:

- Bilge pump, electric or manual or both. *$50–$500 manual, $20–$150 electric*
- Boat hook for picking up moorings and things in the water (such as hats), and for fending off docks and other boats (collapsible models often fail in this mode). *$25*

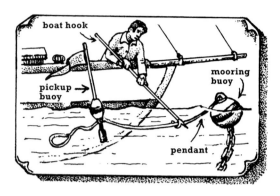

- Compasses: one for steering and, if cruising, a handheld model for taking bearings. *$30–$450, simple bulkhead to big binnacle mount; $30–$125, hand-bearing models*
- VHF radio for calling the U.S. Coast Guard, other boats, and shore stations. Range is limited to line of sight. *$150–$300*
- Anchor and rode. *$150–$650*
- Flashlight. *$10–$100, simple to powerful spotlight*
- Signal mirror. *$5–$15*
- Depth-sounder. *$150–$500*

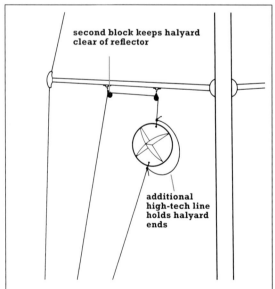

Radar reflectors suspended under a spreader will chafe conventional up-and-down halyards. Screw a pair of blocks to the underside of the spreader so the continuous halyard doesn't touch the reflector.

- GPS (global positioning system) or other position-fixing instrument. *$100–$300 handheld; $400–$2,000 fixed mount*
- Radar reflector (so ships with radar can "see" you). *$25–$200*
- Radar (in case ships miss "seeing" you, radar at least lets you "see" them). *$750–$2,000*
- Man-overboard devices, more sophisticated than a throwable cushion, include a horseshoe ring *($40–$60; with pole and light, $150)*, automatically inflated module, Lifesling *($200)*, harness and tackle to lift a person back aboard *($100)*, and so on.
- Life raft. *$2,000–$5,000*
- EPIRB (emergency position-indicating radio beacon). The best 406 MHz types transmit signals to satellites, which are in turn relayed to search-and-rescue stations on land. *$1,000–$1,400*

We're now out of the realm of "inexpensive." As you can see, a 406 MHz EPIRB costs about $1,200. Radar starts at a grand and goes up from there. A good life raft can cost $5,000 and more. Safety equipment for an offshore cruising sailboat can easily exceed $10,000.

Miscellaneous Gear

This catchall category can sure pile up fast! You'll learn soon enough what you need to use and care for your boat. Here are some clues:

- Docklines. *$60–$200 for four*
- Fenders to protect your boat from rubbing against the dock. *$20–$80 each*
- Cockpit cushions. *$10–$30 each (if custom-made, much more)*
- Awning or boom tent to keep off rain and sun when not sailing. *$200–$300*

A fender with eyes at both ends is more useful than a fender with an eye at just one end.

- Cleaning supplies: rags, mop, bucket, brush, boat soap, metal polish, vinyl cleaner, wax. Buy most at hardware store or supermarket.
- Glasses and plates, pots and pans. Nonskid tableware, *$50+; use home pots*
- Cook stove. *$65 (portable butane) to $1,200 (four-burner LPG stove/oven)*
- Refrigeration. *$600–$5,000*
- Flags (country plus signal). *$10–$35 for an ensign; $80 for a set of code flags*
- Windscoop for hatches to cool interior in hot weather. *$35*
- Windex (not the glass cleaner) or other masthead indicator of apparent wind direction. *$30*
- Boom vang to hold boom down when sailing off the wind. *$80–$300 for an all-rope tackle; $600–$1,500 for a rigid system*
- Preventer to keep boom from jibing when sailing dead downwind. *$75+*

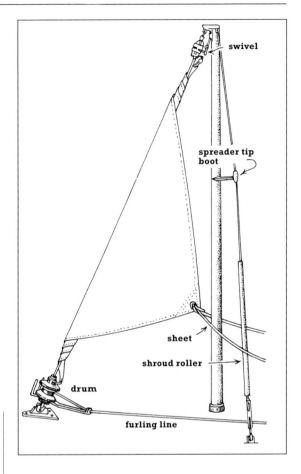

- Snuffer to collapse spinnaker efficiently and safely. *$100–$200+*
- Roller furling for headsail so you don't have to hank on jibs and genoas. *$900–$3,000 for keelboats; daysailer furlers are less*
- Jiffy reefing or other method of reducing mainsail area. *$100+*

Are You a Gearhead?

Sailing can be as simple or as complicated as you desire. I once worked for a man who had advanced college degrees and earned a handsome salary. His boat was a 12-foot O'Day Widgeon, and he never admitted to wanting anything larger, faster, or more luxurious. Certainly he could have afforded a big racing or cruising

GEAR COST COMPARISON BY BOAT SIZE

ITEM	ANCHOR	RODE	GENNAKER	REFRIGERATION
Catalina 22	$75 (6 lb.)	$70	$450	$50 cooler
Gemini 105	$100 (25 lb.)	$130	$1,200	$700 12-volt
Cabo Rico 38	$228 (40 lb.)	$240	$1,400	$3,000 engine driven

Note: The cost of some gear increases exponentially with boat size, whereas with others the relationship is linear. But generally speaking, larger boats require more sophisticated gear, and because manufacturers will sell far fewer, say, 200-pound anchors than 25-pound anchors, they have to charge a lot more to amortize the manufacturing costs.

sailboat. I suspect, however, that the simplicity of his little boat was much of its appeal. Over the years, I have come to better understand his thinking, having grown weary of fancy equipment that can be repaired only by factory technicians, if then!

Many sailors, however, take particular enjoyment in the gear that goes along with sailing. Who does not admire a recording barometer, slowly turning in its glass case? A precision gimballed and dampened compass faithfully pointing the way home? The strong clicking sound of a powerful sheet winch's gears and pawls as it trims the sail?

Passion for a hobby, pastime, or lifestyle usually involves more than just the activity; it involves the associated equipment, too. A fisherman loves his rods and lures; for fly fishers, fly-tying is an art form (my son once tied 86 flies in a row!). Same for the hunter, golfer, tennis player, woodworker, and needleworker. Good equipment should be admired, respected, and maintained accordingly. The sailor's life, more than most, may one day depend on it.

PART TWO

Handling Your First Sailboat

How Do I Get My Boat In and Out of the Water?

11

Trailerable boats are usually launched at ramps provided by your city or state's park service or department of environmental management. Many marinas also have ramps. Fees are sometimes charged, but are generally modest. A marina will launch a trailerable boat for you, but if you're going to be doing this regularly, you may as well learn how to do it yourself.

Here's a typical sequence:

- Load the boat onto its trailer with a winch cable holding the bow eye tight to the roller or padded stop. Cinch the *safety strap* tight, too (this is a length of nylon webbing that stretches from the trailer up over the boat and down to the other side of the trailer to hold down the back end of the boat).
- Park the car and trailer in a parking lot adjacent to the ramp. Let the car and trailer wheel bearings cool before submerging them in water.
- Step the mast. If the mast is too heavy for one or two persons to lift, there are mechanisms that can be rigged in which the boom or other spar is used for better leverage, and side stays keep the mast from falling to one side (see illustration). Tighten all stays.
- Insert rudder pintles into gudgeons on the transom. Insert the daggerboard, if there is one, partway into the trunk.
- Remove the safety strap.
- Tie a painter (a rope) to cleat or bow eye.
- Back the trailer down the ramp as your helper walks beside the boat with painter in hand. He or she should be prepared to get wet feet.
- Stop when water begins to support (lift) the stern of the boat. Hopefully, the water has not entered the car trunk or covered the exhaust. If you detect water in the backseat, you've gone way too far! A tongue extension for the trailer may be necessary.
- Have your helper undo the cable from the trailer winch to the boat's bow eye, and give the boat a shove backward off the trailer.
- Have your helper lead the boat away from the trailer and tie it to the dock.

- Pull the car forward, hauling the trailer out of the water. Park. Run—don't walk—back to the boat because you're occupying the dock space that a mean-looking dude at the helm of a 40-foot muscle boat wants!

Hauling Out

When the day is done and it's time to haul the boat out of the water and back onto the trailer, the procedure is more or less reversed:

- Tie the boat to the dock. Leave your crew to tend the boat while you get the car and trailer.
- Back the trailer down the ramp. Try not to hit anything. Avoid the dreaded jackknife (degree of difficulty: zero).
- Have your helper untie the boat from the dock and use the painter to pull it over the semisubmerged trailer. Positioning the hull correctly over the beds is made easier with a pair of guides; these can easily be made from $\frac{1}{2}$-inch-diameter PVC, fastened vertically to the trailer so that when the hull barely touches the guides on each side, you know it's aligned. This trick minimizes the number of times you try positioning the boat, which keeps you from looking stupid and is less annoying to the boatowners inevitably lined up behind you.
- Unreel some cable from the trailer winch and snap the hook through the boat's bow eye. Easy.
- Using the winch, reel the boat in until the bow is snug against the roller or stop. Now you've got it.
- Drive forward, hauling the boat out of the water. Do not proceed to the highway with the mast up! Instead, park well short of any nearby overhead electrical wires.

Sailors can and do get electrocuted by mast contact with electrical wires every year.

- Unstep the mast and secure it. Fasten the safety strap.
- Celebrate in an appropriate fashion while uttering some profundity, such as my old friend and sailing mentor Gene used to say: "Well, another day and we didn't drown."

Travelifts, Cranes, and Gin Poles

Boats too large to tow behind a car, minivan, SUV, or pickup are launched and hauled only at the beginning and end of the sailing season or when the bottom needs repainting with new antifouling paint. The boatyard usually performs this chore, though in some areas there are maverick transport companies with heavy-duty hydraulic trailers that will come pick up the boat from, say, your backyard, move it to a suitable location, and launch it for you.

Most boatyards use a device called a Travelift, the brand name for a big, mobile, steel frame in the shape of a cube that is open on one end (in case the mast is in the boat). Large canvas straps attached to both sides of the Travelift are draped under the boat's keel to support it. The operator, who stands in a small cage by one of the four vertical beams, can take up and let out on the straps, lifting and lowering the boat as desired. For the Travelift to lower the boat into the water, it must be driven out onto a pair of parallel piers, straddling the water between. Maximum speed is all of about 2 mph.

If you store your boat at the same yard, launching and hauling may be included in your winter storage fee. This is to make you feel like you're getting a deal. Other yard operators may charge a flat rate based on the size of the boat, or charge by the hour.

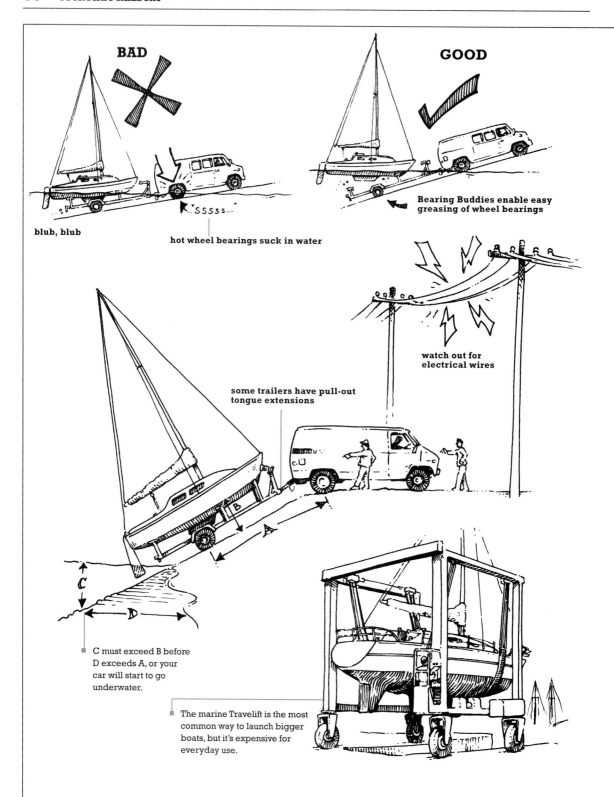

BAD

GOOD

Bearing Buddies enable easy
greasing of wheel bearings

blub, blub

hot wheel bearings suck in water

watch out for
electrical wires

some trailers have pull-out
tongue extensions

C must exceed B before
D exceeds A, or your
car will start to go
underwater.

The marine Travelift is the most
common way to launch bigger
boats, but it's expensive for
everyday use.

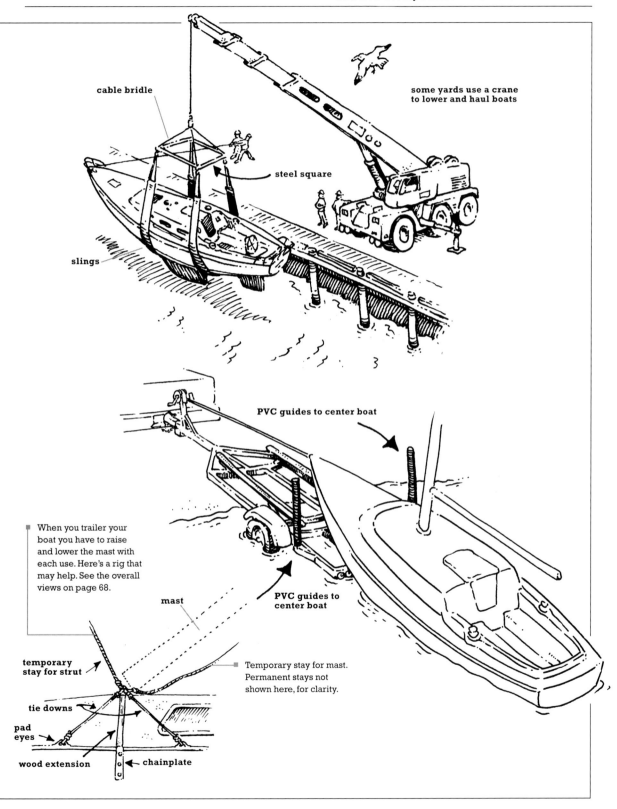

cable bridle

some yards use a crane
to lower and haul boats

steel square

slings

PVC guides to center boat

When you trailer your
boat you have to raise
and lower the mast with
each use. Here's a rig that
may help. See the overall
views on page 68.

mast

PVC guides to
center boat

temporary
stay for strut

Temporary stay for mast.
Permanent stays not
shown here, for clarity.

tie downs

pad
eyes

wood extension   chainplate

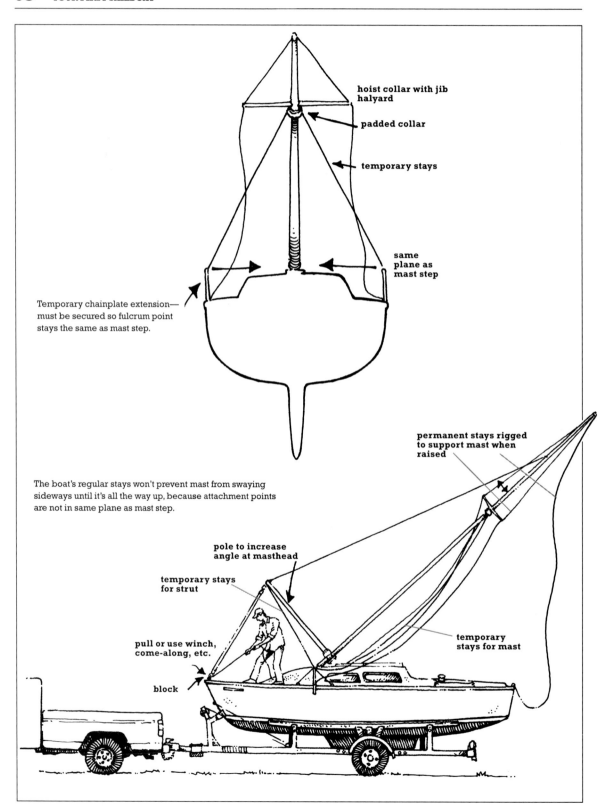

hoist collar with jib halyard

padded collar

temporary stays

same plane as mast step

Temporary chainplate extension— must be secured so fulcrum point stays the same as mast step.

The boat's regular stays won't prevent mast from swaying sideways until it's all the way up, because attachment points are not in same plane as mast step.

permanent stays rigged to support mast when raised

pole to increase angle at masthead

temporary stays for strut

temporary stays for mast

pull or use winch, come-along, etc.

block

Yards without a Travelift may use a crane like those you see at construction sites. The tackle includes a large steel square from which a pair of the same canvas straps can be fastened.

After the boat is in the water and made secure, the mast must be stepped. A gin pole often is used. This has nothing to do with alcohol, except that you may wish to knock down a shot of it while watching cavalier yard hands toss your mast around like the suitcase in the tender care of the gorilla "baggage handler" in that old Samsonite commercial. A gin pole looks a bit like a flagpole with a pivoting top section. A line from the end of the pole is taken around the mast, just under the spreaders. A ratchet winch on the gin pole takes in the line and allows the mast to be lifted to a vertical position. Workers hang onto the butt of the mast and guide it over the mast step on the boat, where it is then lowered. After the stays are secured, the line from the gin pole is released.

■ ■ ■

So there you have it. Launchings and haulouts tend to be slightly nerve-racking. Some owners insist that their boats never be touched unless they are present. Others can't bear to look and are more than happy to visit the yard after the operation is over and the boat is either sitting securely in its cradle or bobbing gently in its slip. Boats are made to be in the water, and the less handling out of the water the better. When 'tis done, celebrate! As Anacreon, the ancient Greek poet, said, "Bring water, bring wine, boy!"

How Do I Tie My Boat to the Dock?

12

On first thought, it seems that a dock is the safest place for a boat. When a storm threatens, you take it to the dock and tie it up and forget it. Everything's OK, right?

Most of the time, but not every time.

Docks often are safe because their locations are shielded from the full brunt of the wind, perhaps in the corner of a harbor with land, trees, or buildings around for protection. Waves, if they reach the dock unobstructed, are at least somewhat subdued by the pilings. As a further measure of safety, a boat can be tied off on all four quarters, keeping it from rubbing against the dock.

A nasty storm, however, will find and exploit the weakest link in the system. Wave action on the boat can be violent, causing it to jerk at its lines mercilessly. Lines chafe. Lines break. And should the boat come loose, it will be tossed against the dock structure time and again in relentless assault, damaging itself and possibly other boats and the dock, too.

Tying off the boat properly virtually guarantees protection from damage, and it isn't hard to do.

To make the most of available rental space, marinas usually give you just one side of a finger pier to tie up to (see illustration, pages 72–73).

Here's what you need for tying to a main dock and finger pier:

- **Two bow lines** led port and starboard to the main dock. These keep the boat centered in its slip. Centered is good, just as it is for your inner self.
- **One stern line** to the finger dock, to keep the stern from swinging out.
- **One or preferably two spring lines** led from the same midship cleat to the finger pier; one leading forward, one aft. These keep the boat from moving forward or aft.
- **Fenders placed between the hull and dock.** Fenders are soft vinyl cylinders filled with air to absorb the impact of the hull against the dock. (Do not buy the fenders shaped like topless mermaids because they are tacky.) A small line is tied to one end so that the fender can be secured to the boat and lowered over the side. Try to avoid tying fender lines to lifelines because sometimes a fender gets

caught on the dock, and the subsequent movement of the boat can result in the lifeline stretching or causing a stanchion to bend.

- **Chafe gear on all lines** where they rub against the boat. In the o-o-o-o-ld days (like 20 years ago and longer), leather was sewn to the lines. Today, a variety of polyester sleeves can be wrapped around lines at this critical juncture. Sections of garden hose work well, too, but tend to slide along the line unless tied to and through the line.

- **In tidal waters, allow sufficient slack in each of the lines** so that they don't come up short at high tide. A strong line can actually hold a boat out of the water, but a weak attachment point, like a poorly fastened cleat, can be wrenched right out of the boat. Ouch! Gauging the amount of slack may take some experimentation based on observations at different stages of the tide.

- Though there is no hard and fast rule, common practice is to throw a loop around the dock cleat or piling and then adjust the tension aboard the boat, cleating the line when satisfied.

When bad weather such as a gale or hurricane is predicted, double up on as many lines as possible. This means taking a second stern line across the stern of your neighbor to the piling at the end of his finger pier. And tie a second set of spring lines.

Unusually high tides can sometimes cause the loop in the end of a line to lift off a piling—not good! A boat loose in a marina is like Mike Tyson in a Victoria's Secret store. During a hurricane in Newport Harbor, Rhode Island, I once watched half a dozen boats pile up against the stone seawall in the northeast corner. The rending and splintering of wood, fiberglass, and metal was gut-wrenching. The forces acting on the boats were so powerful that there was nothing anyone could do until conditions abated. By the time that happened, half the boats were on the bottom of the harbor, and others were skewered on top of them. And it all started with one line parting on one boat.

Storm winds and storm surges will test your dock lines to the limit.

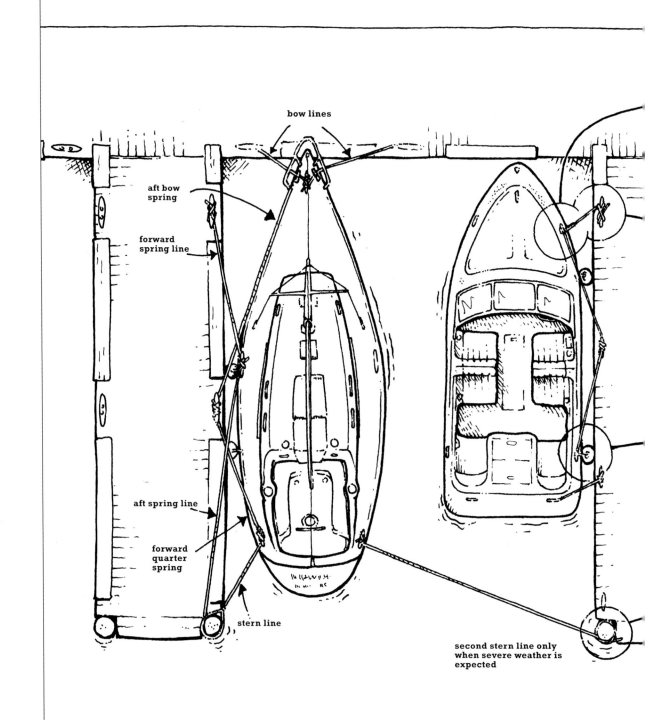

bow lines

aft bow
spring

forward
spring line

aft spring line

forward
quarter
spring

stern line

second stern line only
when severe weather is
expected

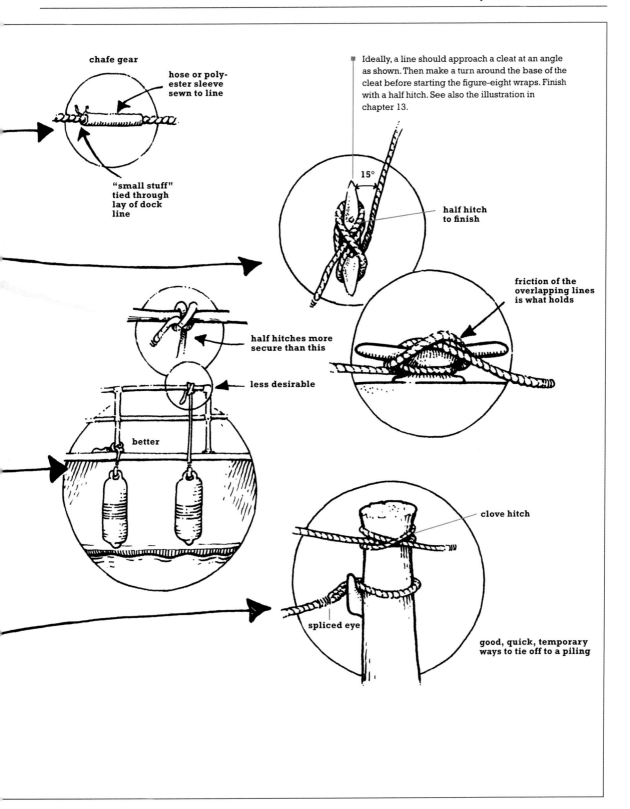

chafe gear

hose or poly-ester sleeve sewn to line

"small stuff" tied through lay of dock line

Ideally, a line should approach a cleat at an angle as shown. Then make a turn around the base of the cleat before starting the figure-eight wraps. Finish with a half hitch. See also the illustration in chapter 13.

15°

half hitch to finish

friction of the overlapping lines is what holds

half hitches more secure than this

less desirable

better

clove hitch

spliced eye

good, quick, temporary ways to tie off to a piling

All the Knots You'll Ever Need

13

Rope is nice stuff. It will be helpful if you develop at least a modest appreciation for it because rope is used for so many purposes on a sailboat: mainsheet, jibsheet, anchor rode, dinghy painter, halyards, and more. Some of the names may seem strange to you, but it's all just rope. The heft of a coiled rope in your hand can make you feel good, like, well, maybe a cowboy, an elephant trainer, or even a hangman. You'll learn to love rope that takes a lay and coils without a twist. And you'll learn to despise rope that, no matter how you work it, always revolts in kinks and responds to even a little abrasion with hockles.

The fibers used to make rope were organic for thousands of years, from plants such as hemp and manila. Today, most are synthetic: polyester (Dacron is the prevailing brand), nylon, and the newest aramid fibers such as Kevlar and Spectra. The most modern, high-tech ropes are much stronger and so can be thinner for a given job than the now widely accepted standards—nylon and Dacron. For example, New England Rope's T-900 Technora/Spectra braid, 6 mm, ¼-inch diameter, has a breaking strength of 4,400 pounds, about the same as ½-inch, three-strand polyester! The high-tech fibers differ in other ways, too. For example, they must not be bent as sharply over a masthead sheave or turning block, and they are more slippery. Slippery ropes make it more difficult to tie knots because they always seem to worm their way loose, like a fish in your hands. You may have to add extra turns to knots in slippery line.

Unless your first boat is a high-tech raceboat like the Melges 24, there's really no need to spend extra money on high-tech rope. Dacron (for low-stretch applications such as halyards and sheets) and nylon (for docklines and anchor rodes, in which a little stretch is helpful) will do just fine.

Knot nuts originate in childhood, maybe the Cub Scouts. They know how to tie dozens of strange knots for the most esoteric uses, usually involving mischief—like tying bags of sand for tree fort catapults.

Others just want to learn enough so they don't lose their boat. Page 77 illustrates all the ones you need. Learn others just for the joy of it, but these are the ones you'll use.

Bowline

This is the king of nautical knots. If you learn nothing else, learn the bowline (pronounced "bo-lin", not "bo-line" or "bow-line"). There are various ways to tie it, some faster than others. It was taught to me with this mnemonic: a rabbit comes out of his hole, runs around the tree, and goes back down the hole. The illustration on page 77 should make this exquisitely clear.

The beauty of the bowline is that it resists coming undone, can always be untied, and is reasonably strong (knots always weaken a line, but it retains about 70 percent of line strength). Bowlines are often used to fasten sheets to the clew of a sail and halyards to the headboard of a sail, and two bowlines tied through one another constitute a very strong way to tie two lines together. Probably the bowline's most valuable asset, however, is its capability to be untied even after having been heavily strained.

Round Turn and Two Half Hitches

This knot is most often used to attach a line to something else, like a line through a grommet or around a piling. It is quite simple and fast to tie and untie, and its strength is similar to a bowline. But half hitches do seem to slip and come undone more easily, so they are not recommended for use where safety is paramount.

Clove Hitch

You're standing on a dock. You've just had lunch harborside, and after key lime pie, a liqueur, and a cup of decaf, you step outside to take a look at the boats. Suddenly, a large boat approaches the dock. The wind is blowing it away, and the helmsman is gunning the engine in short bursts, trying to control the massive hulk. A man on the foredeck has some rope coiled in his hand. He looks panicky. There are whitecaps on the water and the rigging is whistling like a banshee. The skipper is trying to wedge this huge boat between two others, and there is little room to spare. Suddenly, the foredeck crew tosses you the rope and screams something that sounds like "Take the line!"

"The what?!"

A *line* is just a rope, which is just one more example of sailing's penchant for trying to make ordinary objects and actions seem mysterious through arcane language.

Your hands grasp at the air and find nothing. The line finds your face and neck, however, wrapping itself around you like a boa constrictor. In self-defense, your fingers find the rope. With both hands, you hold it away from your body; if it were alive, you'd strangle it.

The crew shouts again, "Tie it to something! Anything!"

The bow of the boat is blowing away from the dock in the wind. Any moment it will crunch into another boat. Tie it to anything, he says. Like what? Ah, the piling in front of you. It appears to be covered with creosote or some other gummy substance that is no doubt a preservative and a carcinogen. If you touch it, the substance may seep right through your skin and attack vital organs. Your liver will be dead in a week. But who cares at a moment like this, when a half-million-dollar yacht is in danger?!

You—the unlikely hero—rush forward, wrap the line around the piling, and hold tight.

"Tie it off!" yells the foredeck crew.

"Tie it off?" you ask yourself. "Like what I'm doing isn't enough?"

Do this: Take another wrap of the line on the piling, but instead of pulling the end taut, leave enough slack between the line and the piling so that you can pull the bitter end between the two. Then pull taut. All that's really holding is the friction of the line on itself, but it's amazing how well it holds. And it is easily undone.

Now you look like a pro. The onlookers who are always present at times like this—and hoping for the worst—think you really know what you're doing. And, hey, you do! Because you just tied a clove hitch.

Rolling Hitch

A rolling hitch is most often used to tie a small line to a larger fixed line or back to itself. Say you have loaded your dinghy upside down on top of your car. You lead the painter forward over the hood, around the bumper, and back up. You were intending to lead it back through the bow eye and tie it off, but the rope isn't long enough. What to do? Tie a rolling hitch. Like its half hitch cousin, a rolling hitch tends to loosen over time with loading, so don't use it for anything superimportant . . . or superexpensive.

Sheet Bend

Sometimes it's necessary to tie two lines of different diameter together. Two bowlines work, but a sheet bend is faster.

Square Knot

Last is the square or reef knot. Tie it like a granny knot (which the textbooks rightly call "useless on a boat"), but with each pair of ends coming out of the knot together. Under pressure, it holds well, but if tension is slack, it can loosen. As its alternate name implies, it can be used for reefing a sail, though short strips of canvas or webbing are usually used rather than line. Each strip is wrapped around the boom and through the gathered, disabled portion of the reefed sail (through a cringle, or reinforced hole, provided in the sail for this purpose), then the ends of the strips are tied together with a reef knot. In this use it's customary to leave a

bow in one end (as in a shoelace) so the knot can be untied quickly.

Cleating a Line

The illustration opposite also shows how to belay a line to a cleat. Take a complete turn around the base of the cleat, then take a turn around the far horn. Make one or two figure eights around the horns, then finish by making a loop in the line, turning it over so that the bitter end is down and then placing it over the near horn. That's a half hitch. Pull tight.

Not all knots are easily untied, especially after being placed under load. It's one important reason why you should always carry a sharp knife. Suppose you're working the foredeck in a race, and when the spinnaker is hoisted you find that the *sheet* (the line used to control one corner of the sail) is under the tether to your safety harness (worn in bad weather to keep you connected to the boat). You are at risk of being lifted off the deck and dumped unceremoniously in the water. The skipper will have to stop the boat to retrieve you, and the crew will be ripped. How could you?! But if you can grab the knife from the sheath on your belt and cut the tether, the race is saved, and you are still dry. (Cutting the spinnaker sheet also saves you, but lets the sail go. Despite the apparent importance of the race, if there is any doubt as to your safety, cut the sheet and not your tether.) In such situations, there is obviously no time to try untying a knot, so do as Alexander the Great did in 334 BC. When he was unable to untie the Gordian knot (diabolically tied by King Gordius of Phrygia and able to be untied only by the future ruler of Asia), he decided instead to sever it with his sword. Clever fellow, that Al.

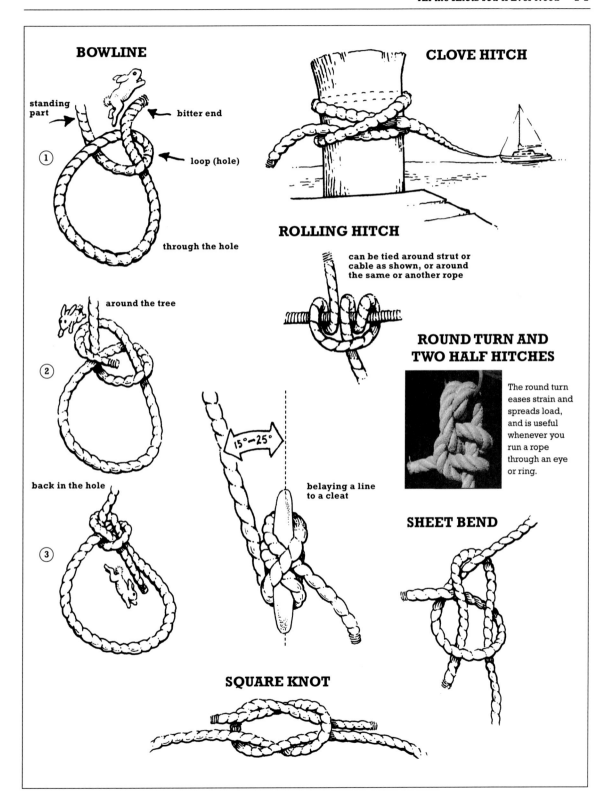

BOWLINE

standing part

bitter end

loop (hole)

① through the hole

② around the tree

back in the hole

③

CLOVE HITCH

ROLLING HITCH

can be tied around strut or cable as shown, or around the same or another rope

ROUND TURN AND TWO HALF HITCHES

The round turn eases strain and spreads load, and is useful whenever you run a rope through an eye or ring.

15°–25°

belaying a line to a cleat

SHEET BEND

SQUARE KNOT

How Do I Attach the Sails?

I f the sails are not connected to the boat, there is no way for the energy of the wind to transfer to the boat and make it move. Headsails (the sail or sails ahead of the mast, in the bow of the boat) attach to a wire stay, whereas the mainsail attaches to the mast, so we'll look at these separately.

Headsails

Headsails include *jibs* and *genoas* (which are big jibs, measured as a percentage of the fore-triangle area; that is, the triangle formed by the forestay, mast, and deck). There are three basic ways to attach a headsail to the boat:

■ It can be fastened to the forestay with a series of *hanks*, which look a lot like the snap shackle used at the end of dog leashes. The bottom, or *tack*, of the sail is shackled to a fitting on deck, usually the stem fitting itself. The halyard is shackled to the top, or *head*, of the sail. Pulling on the halyard raises the sail and draws it taut along the forestay.

■ When it's time to douse the sail, releasing the halyard drops the sail to the deck . . . unless it's windy, in which case crew might have to go forward and pull down the sail.

■ If you plan on rehoisting the sail later that day or the next, it can be stuffed in its bag and left on deck, still hanked to the forestay.

■ Hanks cause a teeny bit of wind resistance, and the slight sag in the sail between each hank disturbs the air flow over the sail. For a smoother leading edge, racers install a *luff foil* over the forestay. This is usually a thin extrusion of aluminum or plastic with one or more grooves in it. The sail's bolt rope is fed into the groove as it is hoisted. This system creates a continuous connection between the sail and foil, which causes less turbulence than hanks.

■ Luff foils are impractical for cruisers because when the sail is lowered, it is free to blow around on deck and over the side. Several crew may be needed to wrestle it into a bag or stuff it through a hatch into the forward cabin.

- A variation of the luff foil is the *roller furler*, which is practical for cruisers. It also uses a luff foil over the forestay, but at the top and bottom are bearings that allow it to be rotated—even with the sail in the groove. A control line led aft to the cockpit enables crew to unroll the sail and later to roll it up. With this arrangement, the sail never needs to be lowered, which means that the crew of a shorthanded cruising sailboat need not leave the safety of the cockpit each time the headsail has to come down. The biggest headsail for roller furling is usually about a 135 percent genoa, which means the sail is larger than the area of the foretriangle by 35 percent. It can be partially rolled up when the wind strengthens, but usually only about a third before it starts to lose its shape and efficiency.

Most sails are triangles. Each corner has a name: clew, head, and tack. When stuffed in the bag, identifying the corners can be difficult. A common practice is to label each corner with an indelible marker.

But even knowing which corner was which didn't help me on my first solo sail. When I was a kid, my father bought a used wooden Rhodes Bantam. One day soon after, I invited a friend to go sailing. I figured the main out and got it hoisted. But the jib's corners confused me, and I raised it upside down, with the head and tack reversed.

As it happened, there was a very knowledgeable woman named Mrs. Stewart who sailed Barton Pond. Her husband was an invalid, so she had taught their collie to crew. The dog gripped the jibsheet in his teeth and was able to do a modest amount of trimming, as instructed by his indomitable mistress. On this particular day, she saw me floundering around the pond, jib upside down, and immediately assailed us. Her indignation was virulent. I might as well have spat on the American flag. She told the collie to tend the sheets (see chapter 15 for attaching sheets) and helm and then boarded our boat. Remonstrating with a scolding tone, she let down the jib, righted it, and rehoisted it. "Don't ever let me catch you with your jib upside down again!" she called, sailing away.

After that humiliation, I never forgot the difference between clew, head, and tack. In fact, I can recognize each by its angle, even crumpled in a sailbag.

Mainsails

Mainsails are nearly always run up an external track or internal groove on the aft side of the mast. A track accepts slides, which are sewn at intervals along the *luff*, or forward edge, of the sail. A groove usually accepts *slugs*, which are short, dowel-like, plastic fittings along the luff. The slides or slugs substitute for the hanks used on headsails and have the same drawback—scallops caused by inadequate halyard tension—though disturbance of the air flow caused by slides or slugs isn't as big a deal because they are hidden behind the thick mast.

Sometimes a mainsail is loose-footed—that is, attached only at the forward and after ends of the boom—but this is rare. Usually, slides or slugs like those used at the mast are also used to attach the sail to the boom.

For the same reasons that racers use luff foils for jibs, mainsails can be connected continuously to both mast and boom. The usual way to accomplish this is to sew ropes into the *foot* (bottom edge) and *luff* (leading edge) of the mainsail. These bolt ropes are then inserted into grooves in the boom and mast, respectively. A bolt rope seldom runs freely, however, which means that the sail has to be pulled down, sometimes with force. This can be dangerous if you need to drop the sail quickly (as for an approaching thunderstorm, or some

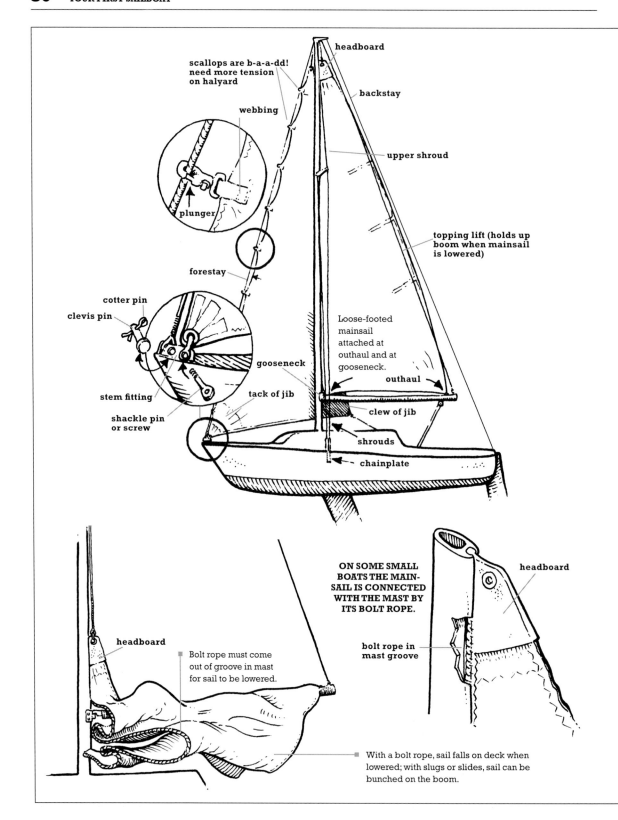

headboard

scallops are b-a-a-dd!
need more tension
on halyard

backstay

webbing

upper shroud

plunger

topping lift (holds up
boom when mainsail
is lowered)

forestay

cotter pin

clevis pin

Loose-footed
mainsail
attached at
outhaul and at
gooseneck.

gooseneck

outhaul

stem fitting

tack of jib

clew of jib

shackle pin
or screw

shrouds

chainplate

headboard

ON SOME SMALL
BOATS THE MAIN-
SAIL IS CONNECTED
WITH THE MAST BY
ITS BOLT ROPE.

headboard

Bolt rope must come
out of groove in mast
for sail to be lowered.

bolt rope in
mast groove

With a bolt rope, sail falls on deck when
lowered; with slugs or slides, sail can be
bunched on the boom.

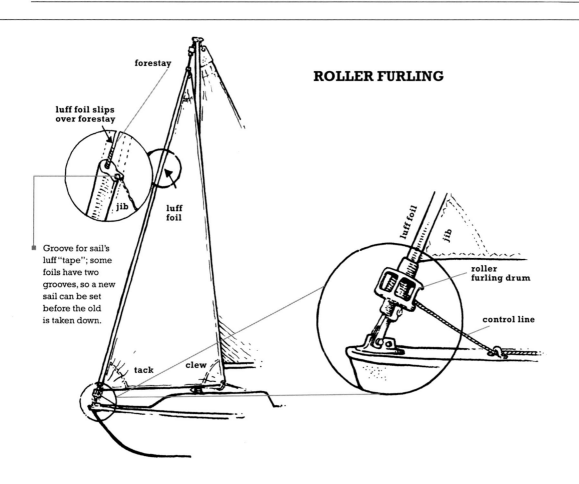

ROLLER FURLING

forestay

luff foil slips over forestay

jib

luff foil

Groove for sail's luff "tape"; some foils have two grooves, so a new sail can be set before the old is taken down.

luff foil

jib

roller furling drum

control line

tack

clew

OTHER BOATS—INCLUDING ALMOST ALL ABOVE 20 FEET LONG OR SO—ATTACH THE MAINSAIL TO THE MAST WITH SLIDES OR SLUGS.

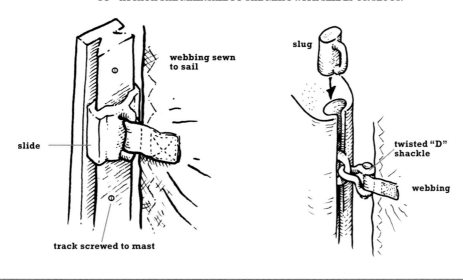

webbing sewn to sail

slug

slide

twisted "D" shackle

webbing

track screwed to mast

such). Also, as you pull the sail down, the bolt rope exits the mast groove, and the entire sail ends up loose on deck. Thus, this method is confined to small boats.

Two other notes on attaching sails:

On dinghies, the mainsail is usually removed after each outing and stowed in a bag. On larger boats, the mainsail is flaked on top of the boom and secured with *sail ties* (long narrow strips of cotton or elastic cord); a sail cover protects it from the thread-eating ultraviolet rays of the sun.

And there is a proper sequence for the steps involved: Mainsails should be attached to the boom before the mast. If there are slides or slugs on the foot of the sail, attach them one by one to the track, pulling toward the end of the boom. When all slides are on the boom, secure the tack at the forward end of the boom. Then attach the outhaul, which is usually adjustable, and tension it to take the scallops out of the sail's foot. Now you can attach the slides to the mast. It may help to attach the halyard and raise it slightly, just so you don't have to hold up the entire weight of the sail as you feed slides onto the track.

This same trick may help with the jib—that is, hoisting the head of the sail 4 or 5 feet in the air so you have more room to attach the hanks below it. Be careful if it's windy, though, because a gust can pull the sail up the stay and get you under way sooner than you want! Fasten the tack to the stem fitting and then you're ready for the sheets.

In days of yore, there were yet other ways to attach sails, such as with a series of hoops known as *parrels*, but they now are obsolete . . . unless you own an antique boat and have a touch of Walter Mitty in you.

How Do I Attach Sheets and Halyards?
(And By the Way, What Are They?)

A *sheet* is a line used to adjust the angle of a sail to the wind. With rare exceptions (such as the bolt rope), any rope in use on a boat is no longer a rope—it's a line. A *halyard* is a line (sometimes a wire) used to hoist a sail.

In the old days aboard square-riggers, sails had to be *trimmed* (their angle to the wind adjusted) by crew who had to climb the rigging high above the deck and then scooch out on the footropes (there were more "ropes" in the old days) that were strung precariously along horizontal wooden spars called yards. This was dangerous work. Can you imagine clinging to a wet piece of wood 100 feet or more above a heaving deck, swinging through an arc of equal distance, the wind howling, the rain pelting your skin, your fingers numb with cold and fear? And the watch commander below is bellowing that you'd better step out on that yard or have your arse flogged? Then the shipmate next to you falls. Join the navy, see the world!

If you ever get the chance, watch Irving Johnson's early twentieth-century film about rounding Cape Horn (*Sailing Adventures: Around Cape Horn*) on the last of the grain ships. If you're at all prone to motion sickness, pop a couple of Bonine tablets first.

On modern, conventionally rigged sailboats, all sails are trimmed from the security of the cockpit. Trimming is accomplished by tying a sheet or sheets to the clew of each sail, and leading the sheet through one or more blocks (pulleys) to the cockpit. You need only one sheet to trim the mainsail on either tack, but modern headsails require two sheets—one leading aft to the cockpit on either side of the mast. Only one—the leeward one—is in use at any given time; the windward sheet is thus referred to as the "lazy" sheet. Each time you tack, the old leeward sheet must be cast off and the new one trimmed in, which usually requires crew to put down their books or sandwiches and do some grunting and heaving. After a little of this, they will thank you for minimizing the number of tacks. Meanwhile, the mainsail merely flops from one side to the other on each tack—much less labor intensive.

On very small boats, the crew simply holds the headsail sheet in his or her hand. To adjust the trim, he pulls the sheet in or pays it out. On larger boats, the sheet is wrapped around a winch, which provides considerable mechanical advantage. The crew turns the winch by cranking a handle inserted into the top. Some headsail sheet winches have two or three "speeds," which means they have different gear ratios in their guts. Slower speeds provide greater mechanical advantage for those last few inches of trim.

On ordinary winches, a crew must *tail* the sheet by keeping tension on the bitter end peeling off the drum. The *grinder*, or person turning the handle, often has a hard time tailing at the same time, especially if he needs both hands to grind. Self-tailing winches have a mechanism that grips the bitter end of the sheet as it comes off the winch drum, then lets it go without the line losing tension.

It's a good idea to tie a figure-eight knot in the end of each sheet so that it can't be pulled through a fairlead or block if it comes off the winch and the sail starts flapping. Otherwise, the sheet could go airborne, and trying to retrieve it would be both dangerous and difficult.

Self-tailing winch. Note that a line always wraps clockwise around a winch.

Attaching Sheets

Jib and genoa sheets should be attached to the clew without any metal hardware because otherwise, when the sail flaps back and forth over the foredeck (which happens when you tack or come into the wind to anchor or intentionally stall the boat), any person forward could be injured. Despite such admonitions, some people insist on using snap shackles or other hardware because it seems simpler. Snap shackles will not only give you a good rap on the skull, they are notorious for popping open without warning and letting the sail fly free.

An easy, safe way to attach headsail sheets is simply to tie a bowline through the clew, one for each sheet. Bowlines are easy to tie (see chapter 13) and won't hurt (much!) if they hit you on the noggin. The knot might lay an egg on you, but it won't fracture your skull.

Mainsheets are different. Because the mainsail is secured to the boom, the mainsheet attaches to the boom rather than the sail. And because the boom is metal, usually aluminum, the attachment of the sheet can be metal also, usually a D shackle with either a threaded or captive pin. This shackle is connected to the sheet by a spliced eye. Learning to do splices is a surefire way to connect yourself spiritually with the thousands of dead sailors stretching back to ancient Phoenicia, Greece, and Egypt.

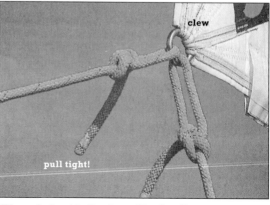

Tie each sheet to the clew with a bowline.

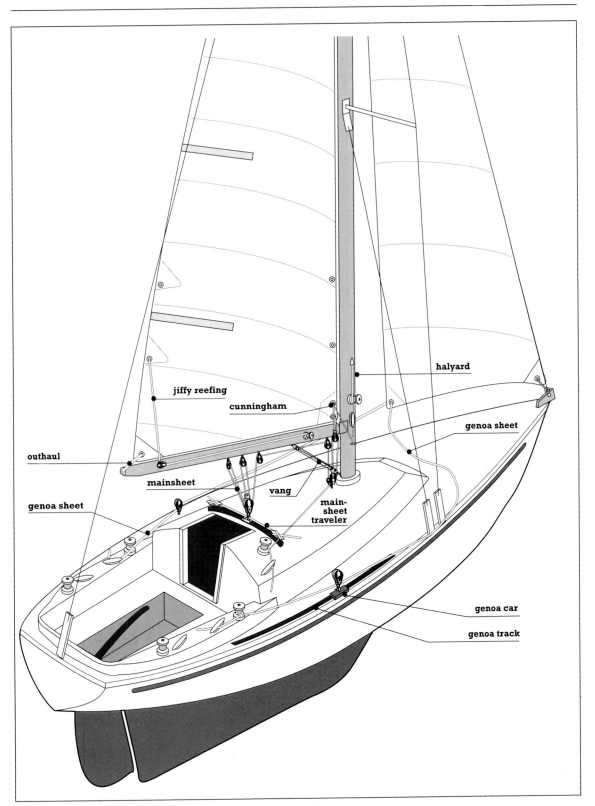

jiffy reefing

cunningham

halyard

outhaul

genoa sheet

mainsheet

vang

genoa sheet

main-
sheet
traveler

genoa car

genoa track

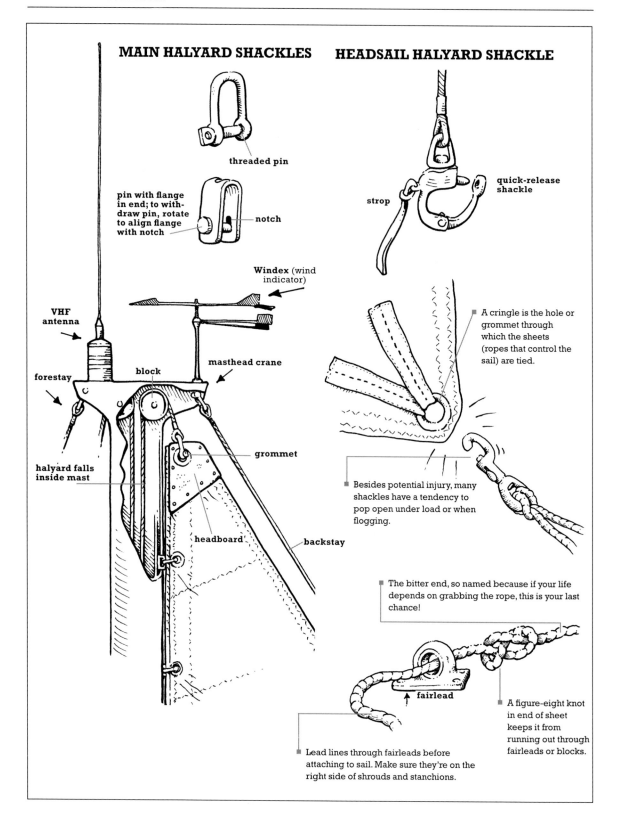

MAIN HALYARD SHACKLES

threaded pin

pin with flange in end; to withdraw pin, rotate to align flange with notch

notch

Windex (wind indicator)

VHF antenna

masthead crane

forestay

block

halyard falls inside mast

grommet

headboard

backstay

HEADSAIL HALYARD SHACKLE

quick-release shackle

strop

A cringle is the hole or grommet through which the sheets (ropes that control the sail) are tied.

Besides potential injury, many shackles have a tendency to pop open under load or when flogging.

The bitter end, so named because if your life depends on grabbing the rope, this is your last chance!

fairlead

A figure-eight knot in end of sheet keeps it from running out through fairleads or blocks.

Lead lines through fairleads before attaching to sail. Make sure they're on the right side of shrouds and stanchions.

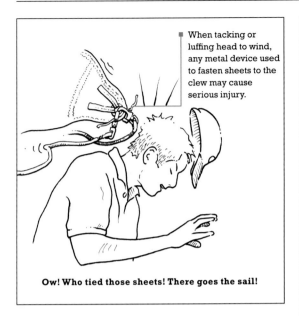

When tacking or luffing head to wind, any metal device used to fasten sheets to the clew may cause serious injury.

Ow! Who tied those sheets! There goes the sail!

(See the resources section for suggested books on splicing.)

But if marlinspike seamanship isn't for you, pay a rigger, who will gladly accept your payment.

Attaching Halyards

Halyards, as we've already noted, are the ropes, or lines (or wires), used to hoist sails. Each halyard must be at least twice the length of the hoist because it must start at deck level, run up the mast through a block, and run back down to the head of the sail to which it is attached.

How do you attach it?

You could use a bowline, but because there is no danger of hurting anyone, and there is the possibility of chafe, a metal fitting is best. There are special shackles designed just for this purpose; interestingly, they differ for jib and mainsail, though both are available for wire or rope.

For attaching mainsail halyards, a headboard shackle with a double-threaded pin is often used. Use a pair of pliers to gently tighten the pin. Alternatively, mainsail halyards are sometimes equipped with captive pin shackles that have little arms at the end which, when twisted 90 degrees lock in small detents in the shackle body.

For headsails, quick-release shackles are common and generally won't open accidentally as long as the tension on them remains constant.

Shackles are mostly made of stainless steel and can be cast, stamped, or forged; forged is the strongest. We could talk now about the different grades of stainless steel—such as 316, which is the most corrosion resistant, and 304, which tarnishes more easily but is stronger—but because your eyes are no doubt glazing over, I won't tell you about how to passivate stainless, about grades with varying amounts of nickel and molybdenum, or about the crystalline structure of stainless that, if magnified a thousand times, would look like a diamond as big as the Ritz. See chapter 23 for more on stainless steel.

How Do I Leave the Dock?

16

Leaving. It's something we do every day, in varying orders of magnitude: leaving the house, leaving the state, leaving the job, leaving the marriage, leaving the past. Sad, terrifying, exhilarating, liberating: leaving conjures all these emotions and more.

Symbolically, leaving the dock is little different. You're giving up a safe haven for an experience less certain. If you feel apprehensive about shoving off for the first time, don't worry—it's a normal reaction. But don't procrastinate too long because anxiety will mount and only make the leave-taking more difficult. As someone told me many years ago, "Leave while you still look good."

OK. You've rigged the mast, launched the boat, tied it to the dock, and attached the sails to the boat and the sheets and halyards to the sails.

If your boat has an engine, leaving the dock under ordinary conditions is comparatively easy. Start up the engine, cast off the spring lines, wait for the right moment (no big wind gust pushing you into the dock, and no boat traffic passing by), take the bow line aboard,

have your crew or dock attendant push the bow out, then let your crew board aft with the stern line as you power away from the dock. Easy as 1-2-3-4-5-6. Find an uncrowded piece of water and then hoist the sails (see chapter 17).

For the moment, however, let's assume you're in a dinghy or daysailer without an engine.

If leaving under sail, you should already have figured out where the wind is coming from. Knowing the wind direction is fundamental to sailing. At first, you'll have to look for the visual clues that are all around you. Wave direction is one such clue, especially if the waves are large enough to see easily. Whitecaps help. But waves often are driven at an angle to the wind, so this method isn't always entirely accurate.

You might also look to see which direction any smoke plumes or flags are moving.

Or, if your boat is stationary, study the Windex, or wind indicator, on top of your mast or that of another boat, or glance at the *telltales* (strips of nylon or yarn) that you might have tied to your boat's *shrouds* (the wires on the port and starboard sides of the mast) for just this purpose.

After a while, you won't have to look, you'll just feel it on your skin and clothes. When the wind is faint and I'm not quite sure of its directon, I turn my head until the sound and pressure on my ears is equal. Con your head left and right. (We should start saying port and starboard; remember this mnemonic—"port" and "left" have the same number of letters, "right" and "starboard" don't.) As you turn, you will feel the difference: the pressure first on one side of your face and ear, then on the other.

Knowing wind direction is vital to clearing the dock and returning safely, not to mention steering the boat into the wind and tacking.

What this all boils down to at the moment is determining which way to leave the dock . . . which brings us to this rule:

Heading into the wind stops the boat.

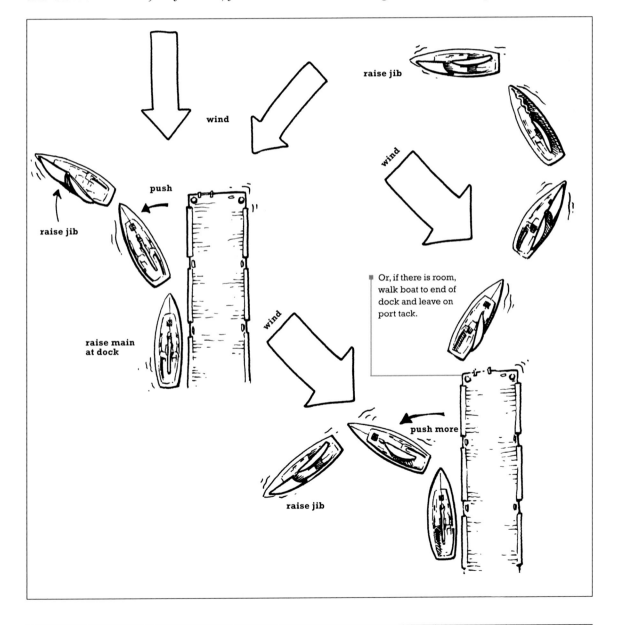

OK, you're already stopped, but you want to gain speed slowly while you're getting away from the dock so that you can maintain control. If you take off downwind, the boat will gain speed quickly, and this could be tricky if there are other boats nearby. The boom may jibe, which is at the least distracting and at the worst dangerous, should you or your crew be hit by it. Controlling the boat during a jibe requires experience, and the close quarters around a dock are neither the time nor place to start practicing.

OK, let's assume that the wind is parallel with the dock, or coming from the far side of the dock so that the wind is pushing your boat off the dock (see left-hand illustration on page 89). If either of these are the case, and there are two of you, do this:

- Have your crew sit forward.
- Seat yourself aft where you can hold the tiller in one hand and the mainsheet in the other. Be ready to switch sides quickly.
- Check that the halyards aren't wrapped around the spreaders or otherwise fouled. Then have your crew raise the mainsail (see chapter 17). Hold the mainsheet loosely so that it can swing to either side, but not violently. Because the sail behaves

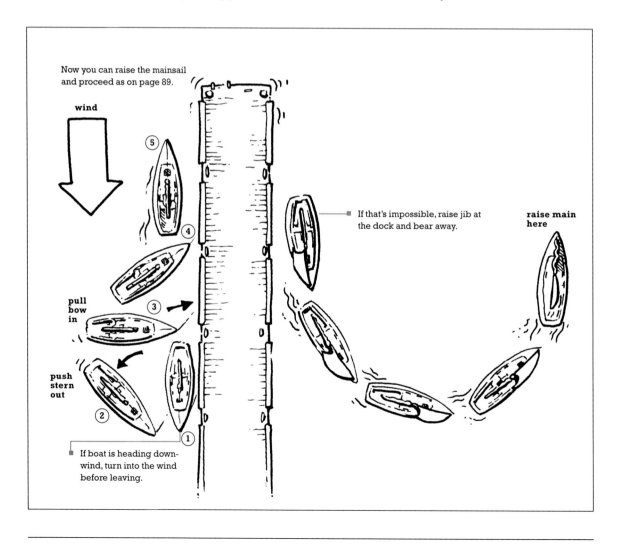

Now you can raise the mainsail and proceed as on page 89.

wind

⑤

④

pull bow in

③

push stern out

②

①

If boat is heading downwind, turn into the wind before leaving.

If that's impossible, raise jib at the dock and bear away.

raise main here

like a big weathercock, this gives you a good chance to confirm your earlier estimate of wind direction.

- Have your crew push the bow away from the dock far enough so that the wind pushes the sail to the side of the boat away from the dock. This guarantees that the wind will push the boat away from the dock, not back into it. Make sure that the mainsheet hasn't managed to wrap itself around a dock cleat—mainsheets just love to embarrass sailors with this little trick.
- Get your crew aboard and let the mainsail start to pull so the boat begins to gain speed.
- If there is a jib, your crew can now raise it. The wind will blow it to the same side as the mainsail.

- Once your crew makes the end of the jib halyard fast on a cleat, he or she takes the jibsheet in hand and pulls until the sail is at about the same angle as the mainsail.

Guess what? You're under way!

If the wind is pushing you onto the dock (see right-hand illustration on page 89), you must either push the bow out extra hard so that the wind catches the sail on the opposite side, or walk the boat to the end of the dock where there might be more room to maneuver. The illustration shows both possibilities.

Enjoy your sail. Savor it. Soon you'll realize that one of the best things about leaving is NOT returning. Push it to the limit. Push it until the sun sets, but do come back before dark. Night sailing, as we'll see in chapter 30, is a whole other bag.

How Do I Raise the Sails?

How do I raise thee? Let me count the ways. Well, if you're in an engineless dinghy or daysailer, you've already got your sails up by now, and I'm sure it went just fine. But maybe you have a bigger boat with auxiliary power—an outboard motor or inboard engine (you hot ticket!)—and so you motored away from the dock. Now you have the luxury of raising the sails away from other boats and structures, which certainly is less stressful.

Here are some tips and techniques to aid what is actually a very simple operation:

- You should already have removed the sail cover and attached the halyard to the headboard. (You want to be able to quickly set the sail should the engine fail. If you take this precaution, the engine will never fail; if you don't, it will.)
- Steer the boat slowly into the wind. Directly into the wind. Check the wind indicator on the masthead if necessary.
- Always set the mainsail first.
- Remove the sail ties.

- Uncleat or unfasten the mainsheet, and make sure the line is free to run.
- If there is a winch on the mast, wrap the halyard around the winch (clockwise, when viewed from the side) one or two times.
- When the helmsman gives the signal that all is clear, the crew pulls on the halyard to raise the sail as quickly as possible, looking up periodically to make sure that the halyard isn't wrapped or tangled aloft.
- When the effort becomes too great, insert the winch handle into the winch.
- If the winch is self-tailing, jam the halyard into the self-tailer groove. If it's not self-tailing, either use one hand to tail and one to grind, or if there is a third crew member, have him tail.
- Take the halyard up taut but not excessively so. Winches are powerful, and it is possible to rip the headboard out of the sail.
- If there is no winch, take up the halyard as taut as you can, and then lead the line around a cleat and pull up with one hand at waist height while pulling the halyard

away from the mast with the other hand. (This is called *swigging*, but is not to be confused with what a thirsty mate does with a tall glass of ale.)

- Make the halyard fast to the cleat (see chapter 13).
- Coil the halyard and hang it on the cleat (see next page).
- With the mainsail set, bear off slightly so that the wind catches the sail on one side.

Now set the jib in the same manner. If the helmsman cannot reach the jibsheets, be prepared to hop back to the cockpit quickly so the jib doesn't flap in the wind too long. Flapping (sailors call it *luffing*) damages the threads that hold the sail's panels and other parts together. Plus the noise and action is annoying, sometimes even nerve-racking. So trim that headsail in until it stops flapping and starts pulling. Ah, that's more like it. The boat picks up speed, you shut down the engine, and now you can enjoy the silent powerful pull of the sails. Now you're sailing!

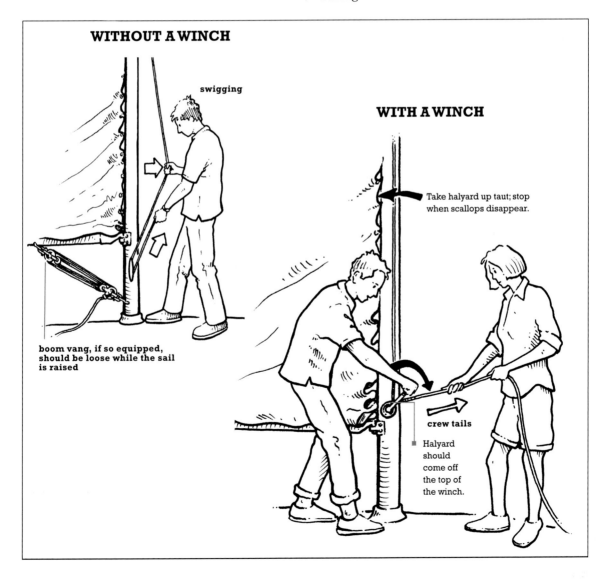

WITHOUT A WINCH

swigging

boom vang, if so equipped, should be loose while the sail is raised

WITH A WINCH

Take halyard up taut; stop when scallops disappear.

crew tails

- Halyard should come off the top of the winch.

STOWING A HALYARD ON A CLEAT.

(Clockwise from top left): *Coil halyard in loops. Pull standing end through loops, twist, pull over loops, and hang on top horn of cleat.*

How Do I Turn?

18

The way to change direction in a sailboat is to turn its rudder. There are several mechanisms by which a rudder can be turned, including a tiller, a steering wheel with connecting wires, a steering wheel connected to a solid metal rod, a steering wheel with gears, and a steering wheel with hydraulic hoses.

As the illustration on page 96 shows, there are four basic points of sail: close-hauled, reaching, broad reaching, and running. Changing direction anywhere between close-hauled and running requires only moving the tiller or wheel and adjusting the angle of the sails to the centerline of the boat. Tacking or jibing—shifting the sails from one side of the boat to the other—is not necessary.

- When tiller steering, push or pull the tiller in the opposite direction from which you want to turn. The first few times you try this it will feel odd, but you'll soon get used to the relationship between tiller and rudder.
- When wheel steering, turn the wheel in the same direction you want to turn. Just like a car.

- Note the relationship of sail trim to point of sail: The more close-hauled the boat, the more the sails are pulled in toward the boat's centerline. But they are never brought in all the way, because sails need some shape to generate lift.
- The more the boat is aimed away from the wind—reaching and running—the more the sails are let out. You might think when sailing dead downwind that the sails should be let out to a 90-degree angle to the boat's centerline, but for several reasons this is not as effective as trimming them to a lesser angle, maybe 65 to 70 degrees.

When the boat's bow is turned through the wind, say from being close-hauled on port tack (wind coming over the port side) to close-hauled on starboard tack, the maneuver is called *tacking*. This requires letting go of the jibsheet until the sail flops over onto the other side, then pulling in (or trimming) the formerly "lazy," or slack and unused, sheet and making it fast. The mainsail flops over to the other side automatically and doesn't need adjustment as long as the same point of sail is pursued.

When the boat's stern passes through the wind, from a broad reach with the wind over the port side to a broad reach with the wind over the starboard side (or vice versa), the maneuver is called *jibing*. This also requires letting go of the jibsheet until the wind pushes the jib through the space between the mast and forestay to the other side. Unlike when tacking, the mainsail may require assistance flopping over to the other side. Because tremendous forces can be generated during a jibe when the wind finds what has been the "back side" of the mainsail and tries to fling it across the cockpit, it is wise to sheet in the boom prior to jibing.

Do this:
- The helmsman calls out, "Ready to jibe!"
- The crew prepares to free the jibsheet by removing the top wrap of line on the cleat or winch.

- The helmsman or other crew unfastens any *preventer* (a line from the bow to the end of the boom) that might have been set up to "prevent" accidental jibes, and begins to haul in the main close to the boat's centerline.
- The helmsman calls out, "Jibe-O!"
- The crew lets go of the jibsheet (but not entirely, because this might allow the sail to blow straight out in front of the boat rather than pass through the foretriangle).
- The helmsman turns the boat onto the new point of sail.
- The crew sheets in the jib on the new side.
- Simultaneously, the helmsman or other crew quickly lets out the mainsail. A preventer can be set up at your leisure, if desired.

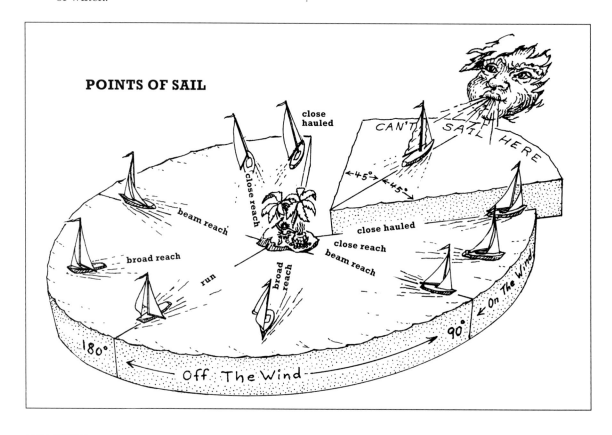

POINTS OF SAIL

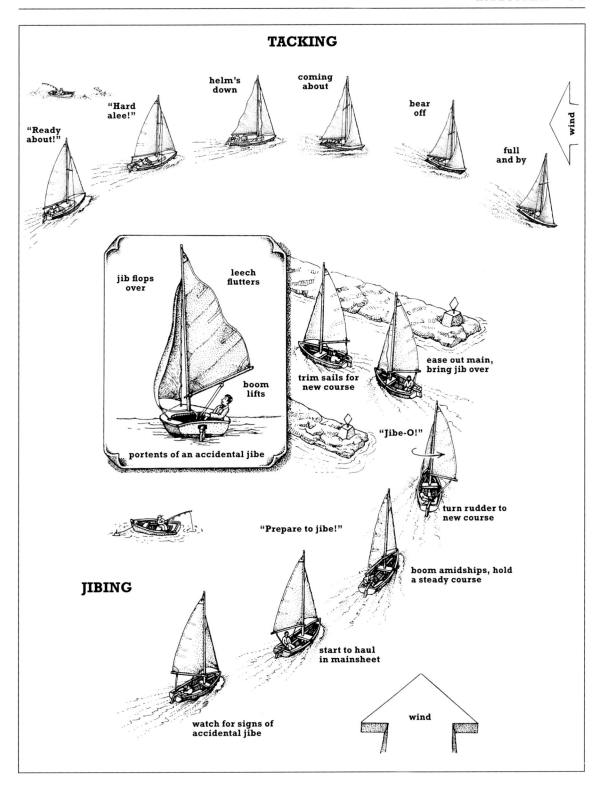

TACKING

"Ready about!"

"Hard alee!"

helm's down

coming about

bear off

full and by

wind

jib flops over

leech flutters

boom lifts

portents of an accidental jibe

trim sails for new course

ease out main, bring jib over

"Jibe-O!"

turn rudder to new course

JIBING

"Prepare to jibe!"

boom amidships, hold a steady course

start to haul in mainsheet

watch for signs of accidental jibe

wind

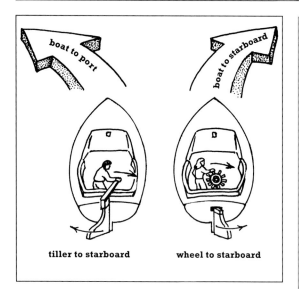

tiller to starboard   **wheel to starboard**

ther scenario, make sure that all crew stay in the safety of the cockpit. And when jibing, make sure that no one stands up unless the boom is so high that it is impossible for anyone to be hit in the head. Too many sailors have been either knocked overboard and drowned or seriously injured by jibing booms. Let's repeat the warning: When jibing, DON'T STAND UP!

The safe way to jibe is to bring the mainsail in before you start turning, then ease the mainsail out after the turn. This way, no one gets hurt, including the boat, which can be damaged (usually at the gooseneck fitting that attaches the boom to the mast) by the shock of the boom slamming over.

It is possible to avoid jibing by heading into the wind and tacking instead. Do this if conditions are rough and you aren't confident in your jibing skills. But heading into the wind in rough conditions poses its own set of problems. In ei-

How Do I Stop?

19

It is, perhaps, unfortunate that boats do not have brakes. Your engine (if you have one) can be set in reverse and revved up like an airplane's jet engines, but the technique is not as effective as braking an automobile, which is well connected to terra firma. Like a ship or train, it takes awhile for a boat to stop. The heavier it is, the longer it takes. Physics, dear Watson. Mass and momentum.

- Under sail, the only way to stop completely is to head the boat directly into the wind so that there is no force on the sails. There will be both wind and wave forces on the hull, however, which slow it. The heavier the boat, the greater its momentum. The mainsail can be left in tight because it is aft of the center of effort, and any force on it, from either side, will only turn the boat back into the wind. The jibsheets, however, should be freed. Not for long, though. If you intend to stay in this position for long, drop the jib.
- The other thing you can do to slow the boat when close-hauled is to simply let go of the sheets. The sails will align themselves parallel with the direction of the wind so that the driving force is removed. The boat may continue to move forward ever so slowly because the hull and rig continue to receive the force of the wind. Releasing the sheets doesn't work with the wind behind you, however, because the boom can't go forward of the shrouds (side stays), so it (plus any exposed sail area) will continue to "catch the wind."
- If you want to stop for any length of time, try heaving-to. This strange-sounding maneuver is a great technique for making the boat stay in one place as much as possible. Here's how you do it:
  - Turn into the wind until the angle between the wind and the centerline of the boat is about 30 degrees. Sheet the mainsail and jib in tight if they aren't already.
  - Tack, but don't touch either of the sheets. The jib will backwind. The boat will momentarily heel.
  - Here's what's happening: Wind on the mainsail, because it is aft of the center

of effort, is trying to push the bow toward the wind. At the same time, the jib, because it is forward of the center of effort, is trying to push the bow away from the wind. With a little experimenting with sail trim, the two will cancel one another and the boat will lie about 30 to 40 degrees off the wind, loping along at a knot or two, riding comfortably over the waves. Single-handed sailors sometimes use this technique to rest or sleep for a while. Even for fully crewed boats, heaving-to is useful when you need to collect yourself after an incident, to wait for another boat to catch up, or just to have lunch.

For stopping the boat at a dock, see chapter 22.

As with sports cars, sometimes being able to stop is just as important as speed.

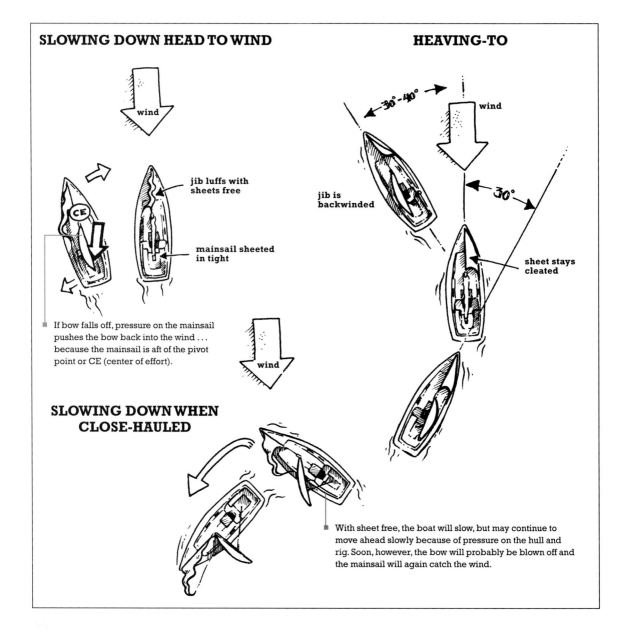

SLOWING DOWN HEAD TO WIND

wind

jib luffs with sheets free

mainsail sheeted in tight

If bow falls off, pressure on the mainsail pushes the bow back into the wind . . . because the mainsail is aft of the pivot point or CE (center of effort).

SLOWING DOWN WHEN CLOSE-HAULED

wind

HEAVING-TO

30° - 40°

wind

jib is backwinded

30°

sheet stays cleated

With sheet free, the boat will slow, but may continue to move ahead slowly because of pressure on the hull and rig. Soon, however, the bow will probably be blown off and the mainsail will again catch the wind.

What If the Boat Heels?

All boats heel. It's the nature of the beast. Catamarans, due to their wide beam, heel least, but they still heel—maybe just 5 to 10 degrees. Trimarans heel more, about 15 degrees. Monohulls heel more than multihulls.

Fear of heeling is common, so don't feel embarrassed if you get a feeling of dread as the boat begins to shift.

"What if it tips over?!" you yell.

Ballasted boats in anything but the most extreme conditions will not tip over.

Unballasted boats may tip over. My advice? Wear a life jacket, read chapter 21, and don't worry, be happy.

Here are the facts:

- The amount of heel depends on hull shape. Flat-bottomed boats don't heel as much as round-bottomed boats, but they pound more and are not as comfortable.
- Your point of sail affects the heel angle. Boats heel most sailing upwind and least when pointed downwind.
- The deeper and heavier the ballast, the less heel.
- Moving crew weight to the windward side of a boat reduces its heel.
- Keeping fixed weight inside the boat low and near the centerline reduces heel.
- Baggy sails increase heel.
- Heeling can be decreased by easing (letting out) the sheets. Obviously, if you ease the sheets too much, the sails will luff and lose driving power. Experiment.
- Heeling also can be decreased by heading up closer into the wind, which presents less sail area to the wind. This is called *pinching*; that is, heading up just until the sails begin to luff and then falling off slightly to fill the sails again. Head up too far, however, and you risk flogging the sails and possibly passing through the eye of the wind so that the wind is now on the opposite side, with the jib backed.

The best way to overcome a fear of heeling is to go sailing. The more you see that heeling is not a near-death experience, the sooner you will relax and start enjoying yourself. Short of hiking out on a trapeze on a small catamaran, I can think of no sailing experience more exhilarating than rushing to windward with the sails taut, the hull neatly slicing through the waves, the resistance of the helm reassuring in your hand, the water rushing by the leeward rail, and the boat heeled 30 degrees.

Eventually, you'll learn to love that heeling feeling.

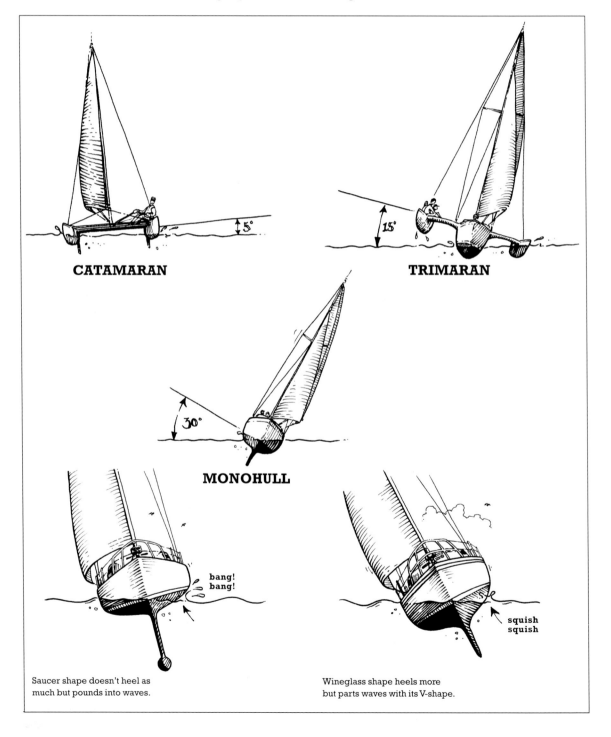

CATAMARAN

TRIMARAN

MONOHULL

Saucer shape doesn't heel as much but pounds into waves.

Wineglass shape heels more but parts waves with its V-shape.

What If the Boat Flips?

L et's be honest. Sailboats can and do capsize or roll over, though it is rare and can be prevented. In worst-case scenarios, here's what can happen:

- **Knockdown.** This happens when a burst of wind hits the sails and knocks the mast into or near the water. Boats with ballasted keels will right themselves unless sufficient water enters the interior through the companionway and hatches to prevent self-righting. In such a circumstance, a ballasted boat might sink (see chapters 34 and 35), but the odds of this ever happening to you are extremely remote. Boats without ballasted keels may stay knocked down until the crew rights them, or they turn upside down (turtle), or they sink. Boats with positive foam flotation and without ballast, however, will not sink.

- **Rollover.** In rare circumstances, a boat sailing in the open ocean may experience extremely violent weather that causes it to roll through a 360-degree circle. The wind seldom causes such dramatic events;

rather, it is a giant wave that simply rolls the boat like a beach ball. The rig may be broken and the interior made a mess by flying books and plates and clothing, but the boat and crew can survive if water is kept out of the interior.

- **Pitchpole.** In even rarer circumstances, a boat moving too fast before giant waves may "trip" and somersault head over heels. This occurs when the boat races down the face of a wave and buries its bow in the wave in front of it. The water coming from behind lifts the stern and throws it over the bow. Sailors finding themselves at risk of pitchpoling can successfully avoid doing so by streaming *warps* (ropes that may have things tied to them, such as car tires) behind the boat to slow down, or by turning the bow into the waves and setting a parachute anchor.

Now that you're scared to death, let's be realistic. For 99.9 percent of all sailors, their most dramatic event will be getting knocked down on a small unballasted daysailer. If it's a nice warm day, they may actually enjoy the experience. The most fun my son Steve had in his junior sailing program was capsizing his Optimist and righting it.

Here is the technique, assuming that the boat is lying on its side, with the mast horizontal and not upside down (therefore, it is technically not a capsize, though the word is often used to describe both knockdowns and rollovers; in other words, the boat has not "turned turtle"):

- Get out from under the sail and make sure that no one else is underneath.
- Free yourself from any lines you might be tangled in.

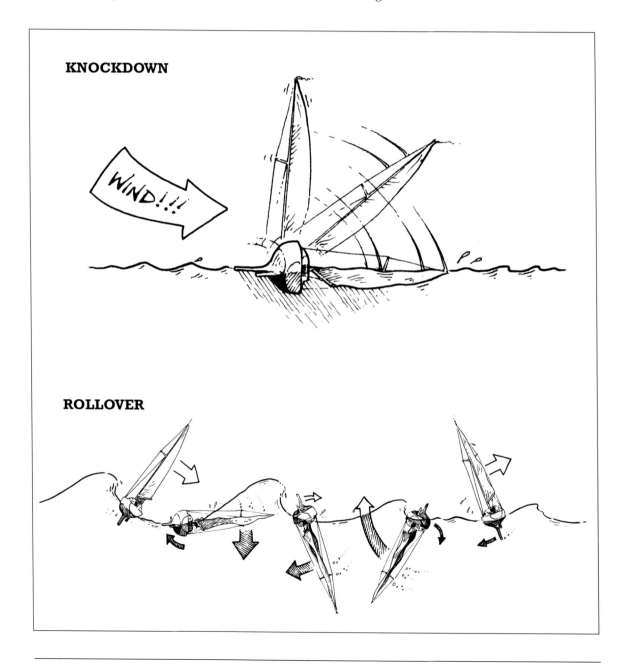

KNOCKDOWN

WIND!!!

ROLLOVER

- Do not let go of the boat at any time or risk getting separated from it.
- Unfasten the halyard(s) and lower all sails as best you can.
- With halyard in hand, move to the other side of the boat, so that the bottom of the hull faces you.
- Place your feet on the centerboard and, holding the halyard with both hands, pull yourself up. The boat should come upright.
- Grab the rail as it comes down to you.

The boat will have a lot of water in it. If there are two of you, position yourselves on either side of the boat so that one counteracts the weight of the other while climbing in. The crew in the water should stay there and keep the boat as steady as possible while the person in the boat bails. When clear, the other crew can climb in, you can rehoist the sails, and off you go—wet, but no worse for wear. Indeed, mastering the small-boat capsize instills tremendous confidence that will stay with you the rest of your boating life.

TURNED TURTLE

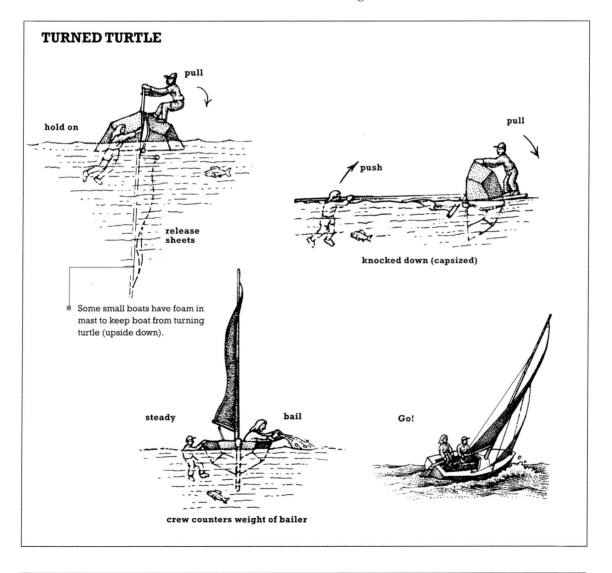

pull

hold on

release sheets

■ Some small boats have foam in mast to keep boat from turning turtle (upside down).

pull

push

knocked down (capsized)

steady   bail

Go!

crew counters weight of bailer

How Do I Come Back to the Dock?

Docks and moorings are always approached from downwind, if possible. As you learned in chapter 19, a boat is stopped by heading into the wind.

When I was learning to sail, I took a friend out one day on a small lake. At the end of the sail, I struck the jib and released the mainsheet so that we glided slowly toward the dock. My inexperienced friend sat on the bow with a dockline in hand. His instructions were to hop onto the dock and make the line fast on a cleat or piling. Worried that we were coming in too fast, he instead extended his leg and placed his foot against the end of the dock. Despite the small size of the boat, its weight and momentum were sufficient to really shock my friend's leg. He hobbled around for weeks, and I felt terrible that I hadn't known enough to caution him against trying to stop the boat in this manner. It's much better to use a line on a secure part of the dock.

Momentum, as noted, plays a big role in docking. With experience, you'll learn how far your boat will continue to glide (make way) after all power is cut (engine off or sails down).

That reminds me of another story in which a Michigan family decided to buy a heavy, Taiwan-built, 54-foot ketch and go world cruising. None had any serious sailing experience to speak of. The salesman promised to teach them, and a cruise on Lake Huron was planned. At the end of the first day, the boat was anchored. The salesman got himself ashore somehow, making some flimsy excuse about needing to call his wife. In any case, he did not return, which left the family alone at anchor. The father was anxious to dock the boat so they, too, could get ashore. Wisely, he decided he needed to practice maneuvering the boat under power before attempting to dock. Again wisely, he ordered the dinghy tied to the anchor line, then cast off and motored in a big circle. His idea was to pretend the dinghy was the dock. As he approached, he placed the engine in neutral and glided toward the dinghy, which he expected to come alongside just as the boat came to a stop. Unfortunately, he grossly underestimated the momentum of such a large boat. The kids screamed a warning, but too late. Dad ran over the dinghy and sank it. Not only had they lost the dinghy, but the anchor, too. And then darkness fell. Happily, the family survived this rugged initiation and eventually completed a successful circumnavigation.

Here's the proper docking sequence under sail, assuming that the wind is parallel to the dock:

- Sail toward the dock at a right angle and well downwind of the place you want to stop.
- Drop the jib.
- Ease the mainsheet to slow the boat.
- As you near the dock, turn up into the wind.
- Let the mainsail flap (luff).
- Grab the dock. Have your crew take the after spring line (a line cleated to the bow but led aft) onto the dock and make it fast.

This stops the boat, whereas a line led forward, with the boat moving forward, does no good.

- Tie your stern to the dock, then tie the bow. If necessary, add a forward spring.
- Drop the mainsail.

If the wind is not exactly parallel to the dock, but blowing toward it at an angle, your landing is likely to be a little rougher. If you have fenders, drop them over the side while there's still plenty of distance between you and the dock. Stop just upwind of the dock and let the wind blow you down on the dock.

If the wind is coming from the inland side of the dock and tending to blow you away from it (which means you are approaching from the leeward side), you will have to keep the bow

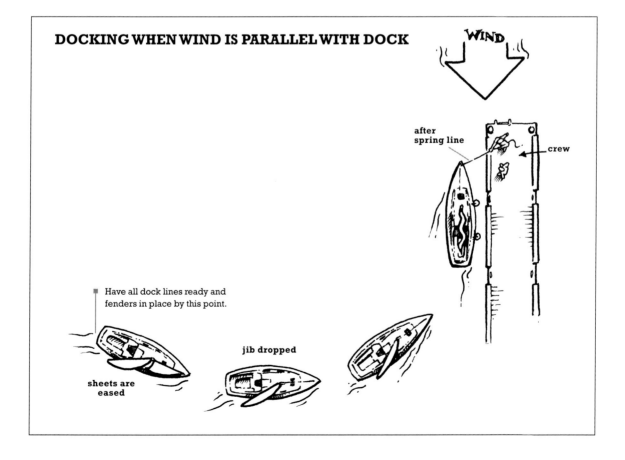

DOCKING WHEN WIND IS PARALLEL WITH DOCK

WIND

after spring line

crew

Have all dock lines ready and fenders in place by this point.

jib dropped

sheets are eased

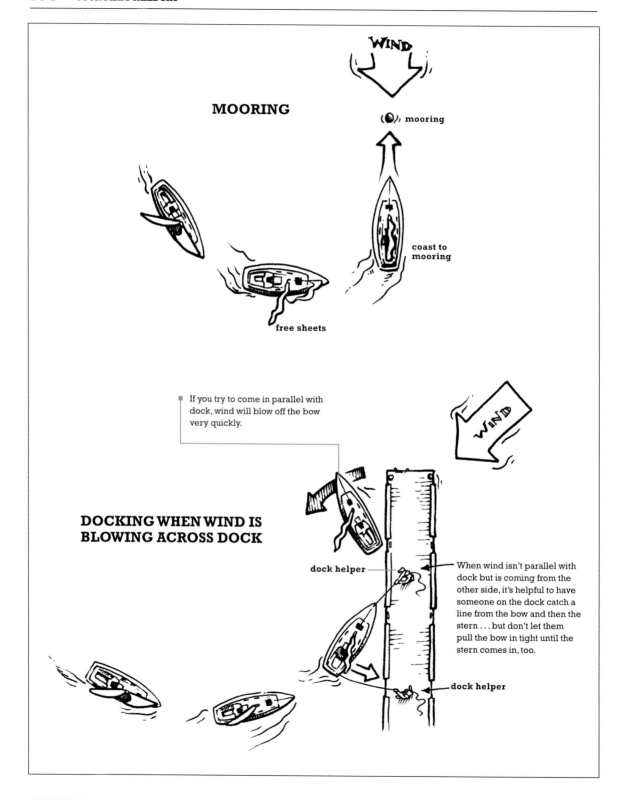

WIND

MOORING

(◉), mooring

coast to
mooring

free sheets

If you try to come in parallel with
dock, wind will blow off the bow
very quickly.

WIND

DOCKING WHEN WIND IS
BLOWING ACROSS DOCK

dock helper

When wind isn't parallel with
dock but is coming from the
other side, it's helpful to have
someone on the dock catch a
line from the bow and then the
stern . . . but don't let them
pull the bow in tight until the
stern comes in, too.

dock helper

more into the wind, which means arriving at the dock bow first. When the after spring is made fast, the wind will keep the stern off, so you may have to toss the stern line to your crew on the dock. Then pull in the stern, after which you can tie a bow line and perhaps a forward spring at your leisure.

Of course, if your boat has an engine or outboard motor, you can douse sails before approaching the dock and motor in. Docking a boat under power requires additional skills, but none as difficult as maneuvering in close quarters under sail. Most sailboat engines don't deliver a lot of power in reverse, so you must still approach slowly. Make fast the after spring and then turn the rudder toward the dock while reversing to bring the stern in. Secure the stern line and then the bow line, and you're basically set.

If you keep your boat on a mooring, make your initial approach from downwind or a reach. When you get close, free the sheets and head upwind toward the mooring. Your momentum should carry the boat to the mooring and just past, but not by much. Gauging when to free the sheets and learning how far your boat makes way without power takes practice! So practice.

■ ■ ■

Now, congratulate yourself that you've completed the day's sail without any major problems! You launched the boat, rigged it, left the dock, sailed through several tacks and jibes, and returned to the dock. Haul out, and while driving home begin to formulate an account of your day: "There I was, a freighter on one side of me, while the biggest wave I've ever seen was bearing down on the other side. And just when I thought it couldn't get any worse, what do I see come screaming over the horizon but a damn waterspout! Well, let me tell you . . ."

Now go read your Tristan Jones book (see the resources section) and go to bed! The famous sailor and teller of tales has nothing on you.

PART THREE

Maintaining Your First Sailboat

How Do I Take Care of This Thing?

23

The exterior of your boat consists of three principal materials: fiberglass, metal, and possibly some wood (upkeep of the latter being the most labor intensive). Not so many years ago, the more teak on deck, the classier the yacht was considered to be. You paid a princely sum for extra teak. Then a funny thing happened: people got sick of maintaining it, even though teak requires very little care compared with other woods.

Wood

Left untouched, teak weathers to a silvery color. But most people prefer varnished *brightwork* (the nautical name for wood trim on deck). Varnish is particularly vulnerable to the sun's ultraviolet (UV) rays, so in many regions it must be reapplied more than once a year. If you fail to do this, the varnish first loses its gloss and then splits over joints in the wood. General checking and erosion of the finish follows, along with lifting of the split edges and black discolorations in the wood where the finish has worn away. When this happens, you need to sand all the varnish down to bare wood and reapply the many recommended coats.

To avoid the tedium of hours spent sanding, some people opt for oiling teak instead. The early oils didn't last a long time, either, but at least they didn't have to be sanded before reapplication—though any time wood is allowed to weather and turn gray, it must be sanded or bleached to restore its rich brown color. And exterior oil finishes require frequent—perhaps even monthly—refresher coats, so in the end, an oil finish is no easier to maintain than a varnished one.

Beginning in the early 1990s, pigmented stains were developed that have much greater resistance to UV attack. The first of these was probably Sikkens Cetol, a house and deck stain that—after the addition of extra UV inhibitors—was offered in a marine version, at a higher price, of course. In northern latitudes, several coats of Cetol will last a season; three or four coats should last a year.

Fiberglass

Fresh out of the mold, a new boat is glossy. The surface of a fiberglass boat is not fiberglass at all,

ISLAND PACKET 38

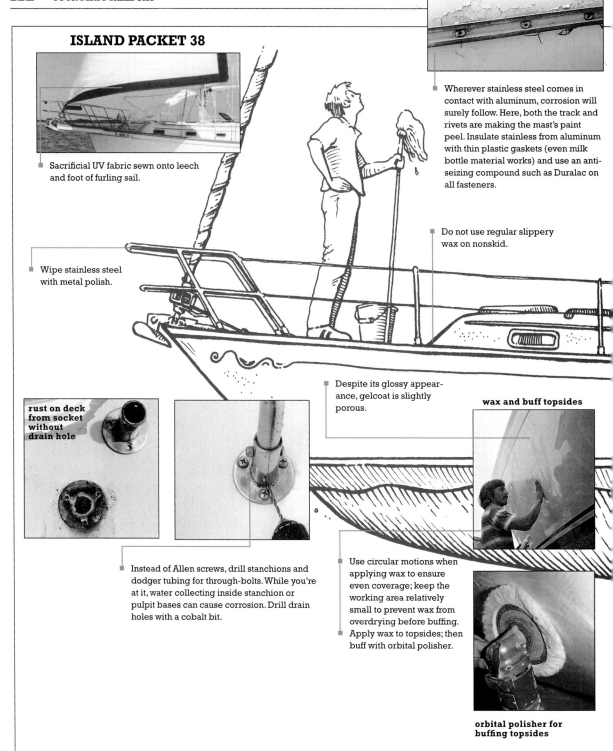

Sacrificial UV fabric sewn onto leech and foot of furling sail.

Wherever stainless steel comes in contact with aluminum, corrosion will surely follow. Here, both the track and rivets are making the mast's paint peel. Insulate stainless from aluminum with thin plastic gaskets (even milk bottle material works) and use an anti-seizing compound such as Duralac on all fasteners.

Do not use regular slippery wax on nonskid.

Wipe stainless steel with metal polish.

Despite its glossy appearance, gelcoat is slightly porous.

wax and buff topsides

rust on deck from socket without drain hole

Instead of Allen screws, drill stanchions and dodger tubing for through-bolts. While you're at it, water collecting inside stanchion or pulpit bases can cause corrosion. Drill drain holes with a cobalt bit.

Use circular motions when applying wax to ensure even coverage; keep the working area relatively small to prevent wax from overdrying before buffing.

Apply wax to topsides; then buff with orbital polisher.

orbital polisher for buffing topsides

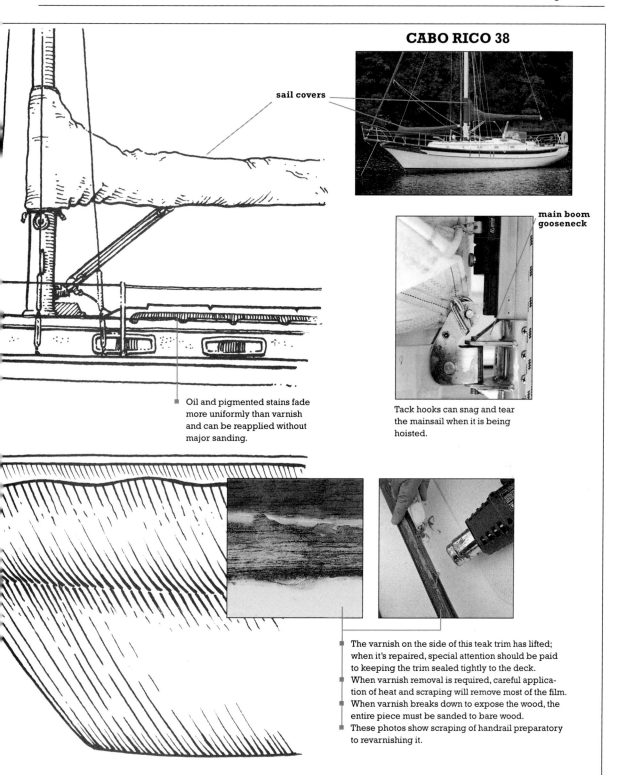

CABO RICO 38

sail covers

main boom
gooseneck

Oil and pigmented stains fade more uniformly than varnish and can be reapplied without major sanding.

Tack hooks can snag and tear the mainsail when it is being hoisted.

- The varnish on the side of this teak trim has lifted; when it's repaired, special attention should be paid to keeping the trim sealed tightly to the deck.
- When varnish removal is required, careful application of heat and scraping will remove most of the film.
- When varnish breaks down to expose the wood, the entire piece must be sanded to bare wood.
- These photos show scraping of handrail preparatory to revarnishing it.

but a polyester gelcoat. It is the first material applied to the mold during layup. Gelcoat is a thin film, about 20 mils (0.020 inch) thick. Though it looks mirror-smooth, it is slightly porous. Over time, UV rays dull the finish. To stave off dullness, fiberglass should be waxed. The best waxes require the most work, wouldn't you know. Paste wax generally lasts longer than liquid wax, but anything is better than nothing. And it doesn't really matter where you buy it—Wal-Mart or West Marine—though there are differences in performance. *Practical Sailor* magazine regularly tests wax, so my advice is to check there for current recommendations (see the resources section). Anyway, as part of your spring regimen, wax the hull topsides, sides of cabin, and any other surface that is not walked on.

Until recently, there was no nonslippery wax or coating for the nonskid areas of the deck, so these areas tended to degrade more quickly than other parts of the boat. A few years ago, Aurora Boat Care Products introduced Sure Step, a nonskid deck polish that protects the gelcoat and may actually enhance traction.

Chalked or hazy gelcoat can be brought back with a rubbing compound and buffed with an electric hand tool. As noted above, however, gelcoat is thin, and it is easy to rub or sand right through to the underlying laminate.

There comes a time in the life of every boat, however, when its gelcoat can no longer be resuscitated, and painting is the only answer. The most durable paints today are polyurethanes. One-part polyurethanes are easy to work with and impart a high gloss, but two-part polyurethanes are much more durable in their resistance to scratches, scuffs, and general abrasion. They are the paint of choice for chalky topsides. They are too glossy for decks, though you can add dulling agents as well as granules to improve ailing nonskid. Alternatives include special nonskid paints and rubberized mats that are cut to the desired shape and laid over the old deck with special glue or epoxy resin.

Spray application of two-part polyurethanes should be left to professionals, if only because the stuff is highly toxic. But despite what many experts will tell you, it is perfectly possible to get a professional-looking two-part finish on topsides by rolling on the paint and then tipping it lightly with a brush. If you're working inside, wear a respirator to protect yourself from the fumes.

Metal

Masts and booms are usually made of aluminum, and hardware is most often stainless steel. Although better suited to the marine environment than most other metals, neither aluminum nor stainless steel is without shortcomings.

Aluminum oxidizes and becomes quite dirty. For years, the standard protection was *anodizing*, which involves placing the entire spar in a chemical bath and then subjecting it to an electrical charge. The wastewater, however, is hazardous, and the cost of proper disposal has prompted some spar makers to start painting instead of anodizing. Linear polyurethane paint is glossy and reasonably long lasting, but it can be nicked. Touch-ups always look like, well, touch-ups.

The most serious danger with aluminum is corrosion. Unlike steel and iron, aluminum has no telltale rust. Instead, it begins turning to white powder. Corrosion can eat through the thin wall of a mast in no time. To corrode, however, aluminum must be starved of oxygen; otherwise, a layer of aluminum oxide protects the underlying metal from corrosion. That is why aluminum always corrodes where you can't see it: at the base of a mast sitting in salt water under the cabin sole, the casing of a windlass under a vinyl cover, and spreader tips covered by a rubber boot.

There are various grades of stainless steel. The most common ones used on boats are 304 and 316. The latter is more corrosion resistant, but not as strong as 304. Nickel and chromium are added to each in differing amounts to improve corrosion resistance. Nevertheless, all stainless steel alloys tarnish in a saltwater environment. This tarnish can be removed by rubbing with a metal polish, and future tarnishing can be retarded if a good protective film is left on the surface.

The basic idea is to coat the boat and everything on it with some sort of protection. Besides the hull, wood, and metal, the main- and mizzensails left on the boom should have canvas covers, and furling headsails should have UV strips sewn onto the leech. On some fancy yachts, you'll see custom canvas covers fitted over varnished teak handrails and other trim. Canvas covers also are available for stainless steel barbecues left on the stern rail. The compass and electronic cockpit instrument displays come with plastic covers to protect them when not in use. Old Sol is relentless, even on cloudy days. You can't beat him, but you can forestall his attack on your possessions.

What If I Hit Something?

24

Fiberglass is a marvelously tough and resilient material. It is reasonably abrasion resistant, quite stiff (especially when laminated on both sides of a core material such as end-grain balsa or foam), flexes just enough to absorb small impacts without fracture, and is surprisingly strong. Perhaps its most remarkable property, however, is the ease with which holes and cracks can be repaired. Some repairs you can do yourself; others are best left to professionals.

Groundings

Everyone runs aground sooner or later. Usually sooner. Damage is usually below the waterline, so one of the first things you must do—and quickly—is check the bilge (under the cabin or cockpit sole) for signs of water leaking in. Stuff or squeeze anything you can into the crack to slow the ingress, and get yourself to shore as quickly as possible.

The first time I ran aground was when sailing my Snipe along the shore of a freshwater lake in Michigan. The ice had barely melted. We were hiking out, and the boat was screaming. What a thrill! Suddenly the boat came to a grinding halt, and the stern bucked up in the air like a bucking bronco. The boat twisted and then the wind slammed the sail down into the water. My friend and I were thrown overboard. The water was ice cold. Fortunately, we could stand up. Sometimes that is the saving grace of running aground—terra firma isn't all bad, especially if you can't swim.

The reason the boat stopped so quickly was because it had a daggerboard, which doesn't pivot like a centerboard (see chapter 1). A grounding puts a lot of load on the trunk into which the daggerboard slides, and it is not uncommon to crack it.

If you do crack a fiberglass daggerboard or centerboard trunk or other part of the hull, here is the basic repair procedure. If you're comfortable with basic hand tools, you can do this work; there's nothing magic about fiberglass. The skills to work it are cruder than those required for wood.

- Grind the crack and the area all around it until you reach solid laminate. If the crack penetrates all the way through, grind half the thickness of the hull on one side and half on the other. The proper tool is a high-speed grinder, but you might get by with an electric drill fitted with a grinding wheel. Wear safety glasses and gloves.

- The area to be ground depends on what is called the *scarf ratio*—the recommended taper of the grinding. A larger ratio means a gentler taper, and thus a larger area of contact for the fresh resin of the repair. A fiberglass repair requires a minimum of a 12:1 ratio. This means that if you have to grind into the laminate to a depth of ¼ inch to reach the base of the damaged layers of laminate, the repair must extend at least 3 inches outward on all sides; 6 inches would be better.

- Feather the repaired area as evenly as you can from the deepest point (the crack) out to the untouched laminate.

- Wipe the area with acetone to remove any dirt, wax, or other contaminants that might prevent a good bond. Acetone is available at most hardware stores; it's also extremely flammable, so treat it with respect.

- Buy and cut some fiberglass mat into patches the same shape as the repaired area. Depending on the depth of the repair, you'll need maybe three to five layers. The first should just cover the deepest area. Each successive layer should be 1 inch or so larger in diameter than the one beneath it, so that each layer has direct contact with the hull around its perimeter. The last layer should come close to the perimeter of the ground-down area. The top of the last layer should be ever so slightly below the desired finished height. To determine this, you have to eyeball the surrounding area or pass a batten over the repair.

- The last layer can be cloth rather than mat, if you like. Fiberglass cloth presents a neater, smoother appearance.

- If the crack penetrated all the way through the hull and you've ground down both sides, your repair will have be made on both sides, too.

- Once you've cut out and dry fitted your patches, buy some two-part polyester or epoxy resin, and mix up a batch. Polyester is cheaper, but epoxy adheres better. Both are available at hardware stores, marine stores, and via mail-order from sources such as West Marine and Defender Industries. Use a disposable paintbrush to "wet out" each layer of fiberglass. Generally, this is done in situ. Avoid overbrushing because mat has a tendency to come apart.

- After the patch has cured, mix up another small batch of resin and mix in some fairing compound. This is a fine powder that will thicken the resin. Add the compound gradually until the resin is the consistency of peanut butter.

- Using a wide putty knife or plastic scraper, apply the goop to the repair. Fill the weave of the fiberglass fabric completely and then some. The smoother you make the repair now, the less sanding you'll have to do later.

- After the goop has cured, sand fair the surface. A random-orbit sander is a good tool for this job. Be careful not to let the sander stay in one place; keep it moving. If the area is curved, try to follow the curve with the motion of your hands and arms. A longboard (a piece of wood 2 to 3 feet long with sandpaper on one side and handles on the other at either end) is good for fairing the patch, but does scuff up the surrounding area.

- Paint or gelcoat the patch to match. Matching colors isn't easy. If you can obtain a sample of the hull color, many paint shops can perform a spectrum analysis and mix a matching color.

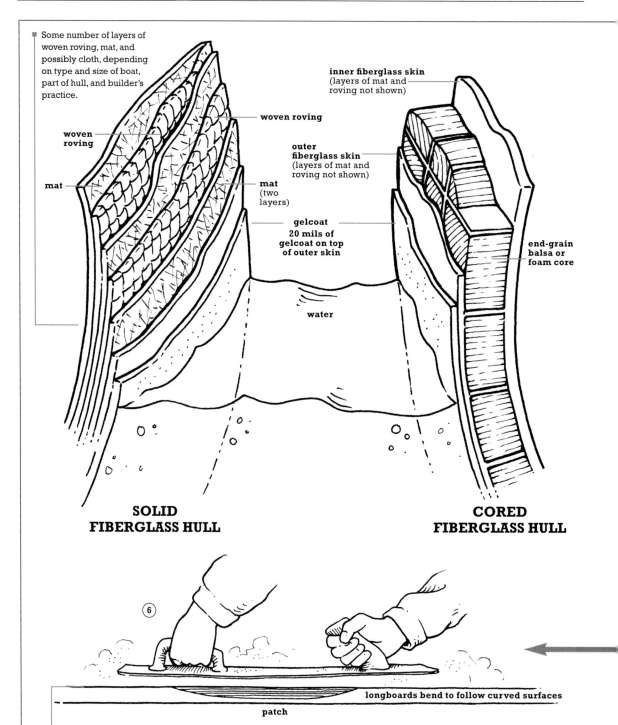

■ Some number of layers of woven roving, mat, and possibly cloth, depending on type and size of boat, part of hull, and builder's practice.

inner fiberglass skin (layers of mat and roving not shown)

woven roving

woven roving

outer fiberglass skin (layers of mat and roving not shown)

mat

mat (two layers)

gelcoat 20 mils of gelcoat on top of outer skin

end-grain balsa or foam core

water

SOLID FIBERGLASS HULL

CORED FIBERGLASS HULL

⑥

longboards bend to follow curved surfaces

patch

■ Sand fair. The surrounding area is likely to get scuffed; try to minimize. When using an electric sander, keep it moving and try to follow curvature of hull with your arm motion. Once the repair is flush and fair, apply paint as described in text.

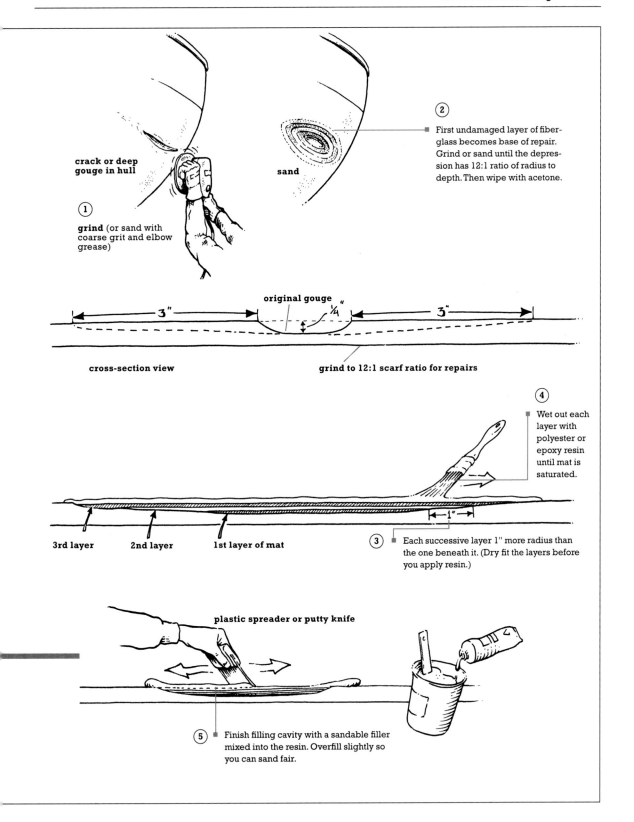

crack or deep gouge in hull

sand

① grind (or sand with coarse grit and elbow grease)

② First undamaged layer of fiberglass becomes base of repair. Grind or sand until the depression has 12:1 ratio of radius to depth. Then wipe with acetone.

original gouge

¼"

3"

3"

cross-section view

grind to 12:1 scarf ratio for repairs

④ Wet out each layer with polyester or epoxy resin until mat is saturated.

1"

3rd layer

2nd layer

1st layer of mat

③ Each successive layer 1" more radius than the one beneath it. (Dry fit the layers before you apply resin.)

plastic spreader or putty knife

⑤ Finish filling cavity with a sandable filler mixed into the resin. Overfill slightly so you can sand fair.

- Gelcoat kits are available in marine stores. Some come with pigments to mix and match colors, but in the hands of us amateurs the results often leave a lot to be desired. You'll be surprised how many shades of plain white there are. Because gelcoat is thicker than paint, you'll want to finish your repair with a slight depression, so that the gelcoat brings it up to the same level as the surrounding area—actually, a little higher so you can sand flush. Also, note that gelocat is a polyester and it doesn't adhere well to epoxy. It's a one-way street, because epoxy adheres very well to cured polyester. Go figure, or better yet, ask your chemistry professor, because it's all about linking molecules.

STRIPPED SCREW HOLES

Some manufacturers use self-tapping screws to hold hardware to the deck, or even the deck to the hull. This is less secure than using bolts that go all the way through, with washers and nuts on the other side, but the only way to fight economy is by opening your wallet wider. Screws don't sit as well in fiberglass as in wood because fiberglass is not as elastic. If a fiberglass screw hole gets stripped, you have two choices: use a larger screw (if it will still fit through the hole in the hardware), or fill the hole with epoxy resin and then drill a new pilot hole.

When sizing screws for use in fiberglass, the pilot hole must be at least as large as the screw body, which leaves only the threads to grip the material. But if you make the pilot hole any smaller, the screw will fracture the glass around it. Work slowly, and don't use a lot of force driving a screw into fiberglass because it's sure to jump back and bite you!

Groundings on keelboats usually affect the keel because that is the deepest part of the boat. Most keels are made of lead, which is fairly soft and easily dented by a rock. If the dent is deep, you can buy a chunk of lead, hammer it to fit, and use screws to fasten it in place. Boats with full keels usually have internal ballast, which means that the keel is part of the fiberglass hull, and the ballast is molded to drop down inside the keel cavity. It is then covered with fiberglass. When a boat with internal ballast grounds, there is usually damage to the fiberglass molding surrounding the ballast. Repairs are made for crushed or fractured fiberglass just as described above for cracks.

Collisions

When two boats collide, the damage to the fiberglass generally will be in the form of a *fracture*, an unclean break that may or may not penetrate all the way through the hull laminate. Sometimes, however, the fracture can occur internally and will not be visible on the surface. This is especially possible on cored hulls, in which the force of impact causes a delamination of the inner and outer skins from the core. A surveyor tapping the hull with his special hammer can detect the area of delamination. This should be repaired, but because it involves removing one of the skins and possibly replacing coring, get estimates from several boatyards. Hopefully, you have insurance.

PART FOUR

Navigation

How Do I Know Where I Am?

25

Like Dr. Seuss's Who Bird, you could sail backward to see where you've been, and thereby deduce where you are and where you're going.

The Who Bird isn't as silly as he might seem. As you sail along a coastline, the topography changes with the angle of your viewing. Familiar landmarks may suddenly become unrecognizable, especially when you're returning and are heading in the opposite direction. So if while heading out you occasionally turn around to see where you've been and note what the land looks like, you'll have a better chance of recognizing your whereabouts on your return.

Navigation may seem like a baffling subject—some sort of black magic that only airplane pilots understand—worked with hundreds of toggle switches, blinking lights, and an incomprehensible vocabulary. Although nav freaks like William F. Buckley can delight in the more esoteric aspects of it, the basics are really quite simple. This chapter and the next three distill the essentials.

There are a few tools you need to practice navigation. Start with a nautical chart, a compass, parallel rules, and dividers, all of which we'll discuss in the following sections. The rest can wait . . . if you're still interested.

The Chart

The nautical chart is no different, really, than a road map—that is, a bird's-eye view of a section of water and adjacent land. But instead of roads (those may be shown, too, though probably not in any great detail), you'll find other features, such as depths of water, heights of coastal features, locations of rocks, navigation aids such as buoys and lights, and a compass rose, which points to north. The rose is essential in helping you determine where you are on the chart; more on that shortly.

Charts also have lines of *latitude* and *longitude* marked on them. The latter, also called *meridians*, are the lines running from the north pole to the south pole. By a centuries-old convention, cartographers place the zero or prime meridian so it runs through Greenwich, England, where there is an astronomical observatory. Meridians are numbered west and east from there until, on the opposite side of the world, the west and east lines of longitude meet each other again at 180°.

Cartographers next imagined lines crossing the meridians at right angles. These are the lines of latitude, and they increase by degrees north and south from the equator, which is 0° latitude. Because each line of latitude is parallel with every other line of latitude (unlike meridians, which converge at the poles), lines of latitude are also called *parallels*.

Any spot on earth can be defined by its latitude and longitude. For example, 45° N by 115° W is just about Las Vegas, Nevada. More precise locations—say, a certain wedding chapel in Las Vegas—can be given by dividing degrees into minutes and seconds. Each degree consists of 60 minutes, and each minute consists of 60 seconds.

The Compass

True, or geographic, north is in the direction of the north pole, where the lines of longitude converge. But a compass, as most people know, points not toward true north but toward the earth's magnetic north pole, which wanders around from decade to decade somewhere in the high Canadian arctic. Your magnetic north will be either west or east of true north, depending on where in the world you are. The difference is called *variation*, and although usually modest, in many places it exceeds 20°. Some navigators derive pleasure from the esoterica of converting back and forth between true and magnetic directions (for which they have their reasons), but the far easier thing to do is to confine all your observations to degrees magnetic.

Check out the compass rose in the illustration. Its outer circle is demarcated in degrees true, whereas the inner circle—the one we care about—shows degrees magnetic. North on either circle is either 0° or 360°, depending on whether you want your glass full or empty; east

is 90°, south is 180°, and west is 270°. North on the outer circle is, logically, straight up because this is geographic north. Magnetic north on the inner circle is offset from true north by an amount equal to local variation (assuming that your chart is reasonably up to date).

There should be a compass on every boat; if yours isn't permanently mounted, have it in your pocket. To be useful for steering, however, the compass must be aligned with the centerline of the boat, and a well-installed fixed compass is by far the best option for this. A handheld compass can be used to take bearings on features found on the chart, as you'll see in the next section.

Plotting a Position on a Chart

There are several ways to determine your position on a chart. The easiest, using information from an electronic instrument such as a GPS, we'll consider last. First, the old-fashioned methods.

Besides the chart, you'll need a pencil, a handheld or hand-bearing compass, as mentioned previously (an ordinary compass, but designed so that you can sight an object and read the number of degrees on the compass card at the same time), and a set of parallel rules. *Parallel rules* are two pieces of wood or plastic linked together by pivoting arms so that their edges are always parallel. By holding one rule firmly in place, you can "walk" the other until its edge bisects a point of interest you're using for reference, such as the water tower in the following example and in the illustration.

Assuming that you can see charted landmarks along the coast, it is possible to plot bearings with the hand-bearing compass from two or three of these landmarks. Your position will be somewhere inside the triangle formed by the three lines—a process called *triangulation*. Seems natural enough, eh?

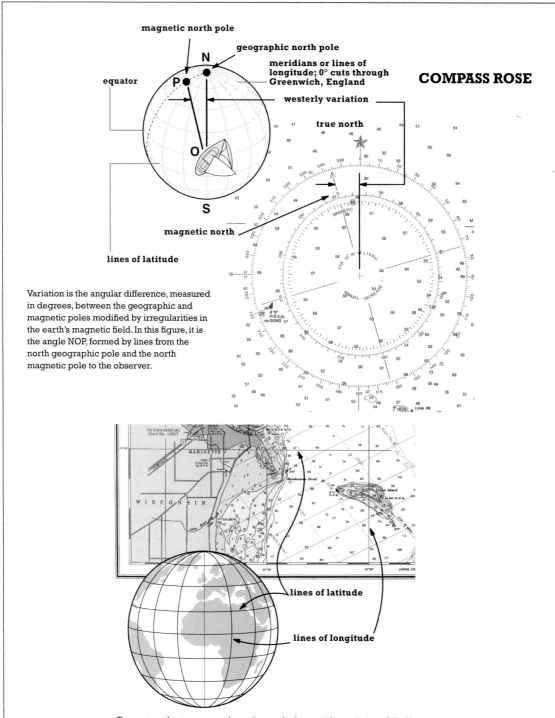

magnetic north pole

geographic north pole

meridians or lines of
longitude; 0° cuts through
Greenwich, England

equator

COMPASS ROSE

westerly variation

true north

magnetic north

lines of latitude

Variation is the angular difference, measured in degrees, between the geographic and magnetic poles modified by irregularities in the earth's magnetic field. In this figure, it is the angle NOP, formed by lines from the north geographic pole and the north magnetic pole to the observer.

lines of latitude

lines of longitude

To create a chart, cartographers choose the best grid, consisting of the lines of latitude and longitude, with just enough interval between the lines to be useful without being too "busy" to the eye.

Here's how:

- Aim your compass at the first landmark, say a water tower (see illustration on page 126). The compass reads 305°. Remember this number or (better yet) write it down.
- Aim the compass at two more landmarks, say a bluff and a bridge. (Any well-defined objects will do, as long as they appear on the chart.) Write down these two numbers. You have just taken three bearings.
- Using the parallel rules, lay one edge down on the compass rose, bisecting both its center and the number 305 on the rose's inner circle. Then "walk" the rules

over until one edge bisects the water tower.

- Using this edge as a straightedge, draw a line (called a *line of position*, or LOP) from the water tower out over the water an indefinite distance toward your assumed position.
- Do the same for the bluff and the bridge.
- You are somewhere inside the triangle where the three lines cross. The more careful you are, and the bigger the angles between the three landmarks you choose, the smaller the resulting triangle, and the more precisely you know your position.

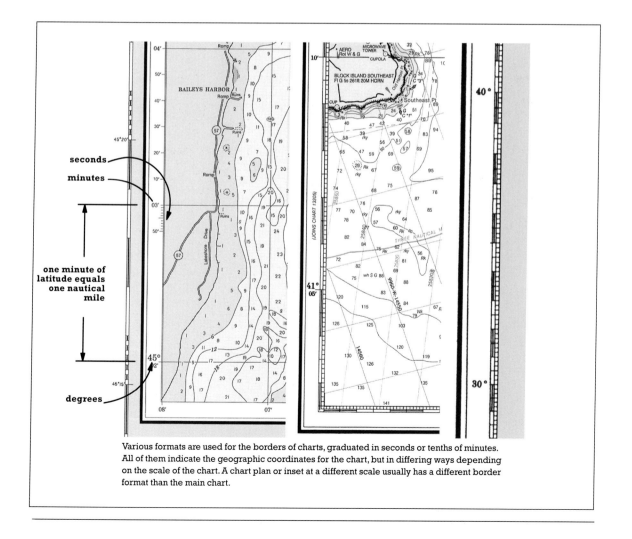

Various formats are used for the borders of charts, graduated in seconds or tenths of minutes. All of them indicate the geographic coordinates for the chart, but in differing ways depending on the scale of the chart. A chart plan or inset at a different scale usually has a different border format than the main chart.

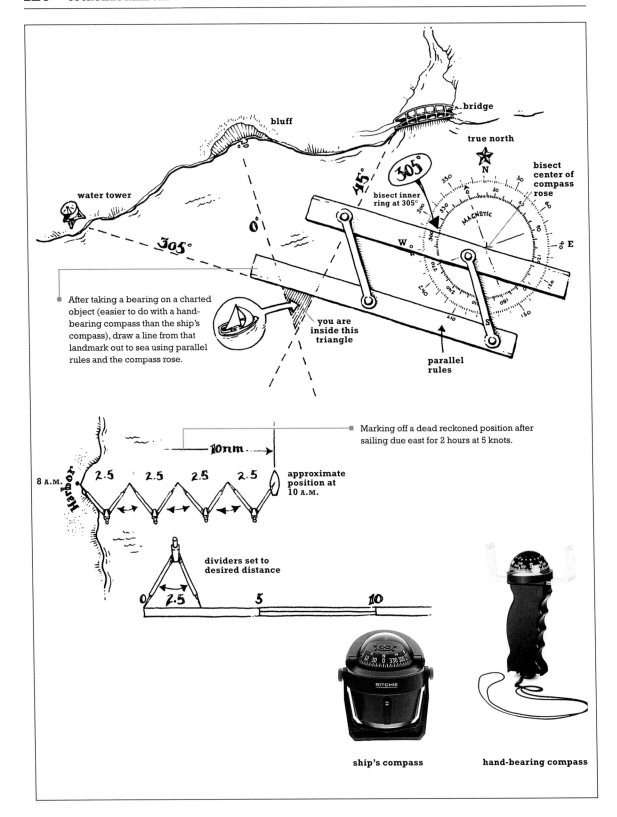

bridge

bluff

true north

bisect center of compass rose

305°

bisect inner ring at 305°

45°

MAGNETIC

N

W

E

S

0°

water tower

305°

After taking a bearing on a charted object (easier to do with a hand-bearing compass than the ship's compass), draw a line from that landmark out to sea using parallel rules and the compass rose.

you are inside this triangle

parallel rules

Marking off a dead reckoned position after sailing due east for 2 hours at 5 knots.

10 nm

8 A.M.

Harbor

2.5   2.5   2.5   2.5

approximate position at 10 A.M.

dividers set to desired distance

0   2.5   5   10

RITCHIE

ship's compass

hand-bearing compass

Celestial navigation using a sextant works sort of the same way, but is much more complicated and beyond the scope of this book. Although fun for the mathematically inclined, it has largely been supplanted by electronic satellite navigation systems. Before the advent of satnav and now GPS satellites, *radio direction finders* (RDFs) were used to triangulate positions, just as described above. The only difference was the use of radio towers for land reference, rather than any old visual landmark. The big advantage of an RDF was that it could be used at night, though it was not very precise compared with newer methods based on satellites, which of course can likewise be used at night.

Lastly, the most rudimentary form of position finding is called *dead reckoning*, or DR (see also chapter 27). This consists simply of recording estimated speeds, times, and distances. If you remember that speed × time = distance and have an idea of your direction of travel, you can estimate your position.

Suppose you left the harbor at 8 A.M. and sailed at about 5 knots for 2 hours. At 10 A.M., you've traveled a distance of about 10 nautical miles. Now, if you know from the compass heading that your course was, say, due east (90°), you can use the parallel rules to draw a line from the harbor out over the water at 90° magnetic; then use the dividers to measure 10 miles, using either the mileage legend printed on the chart, or the latitude hash marks on its left and right borders. (Note that 1 minute of latitude always equals 1 nautical mile, whereas 1 minute of longitude is a nautical mile only at the equator, diminishing to nothing at the poles.)

How Do I Know Where I'm Going?

Now that you know where you are, you can worry about where you're going.

For starters, you need to know where you want to go. Then you can plot a course to your destination.

Here's how. You'll need a chart (or charts) that shows where you are, where you want to go, and everything in between; a set of parallel rules; and a pencil to determine a course between, say, Harbor A and Island B, or a series of intermediate courses from one safe place to another that, when followed sequentially, take you from Harbor A to Island B. For starters, let's assume that you can lay a direct course from A to B that won't take you over or into any intervening hazards:

- Locate your beginning location on the chart. Let's say it is your marina at Harbor A.
- Next, locate your destination. Let's say it is Island B.
- Lay one edge of the parallel rules across both points.
- Now, "walk" the rules across the chart until either edge of one rule bisects the center of the compass rose (see chapter 25).

- Read the number where the rule crosses the inner circle of the rose. In our example it's 45°. That is your course to steer on the boat's compass . . . assuming that you're going in the right direction; more than one navigator has been 180° off!

Speaking of being turned around 180°, that brings back to mind the Who Bird, whose technique of flying backward to see where he's been so he knows where to go actually can work . . . to an extent. One of the first things you should learn about navigation is *reciprocal courses*. In our example above, the course you steered out is 45°, so the course you'll take to get home should be 180° opposite, or 225°. Reciprocal courses are handy for retracing steps. You leave Harbor A and sail to Island B for lunch. When it's time to return to Harbor A, simply calculate the reciprocal course. It's especially helpful if the fog has rolled in and you can no longer see the entrance to Harbor A!

Now, to inject just a bit more realism, let's assume that a single straight course from your marina to Island B will take you through an island in your harbor entrance and over a rock

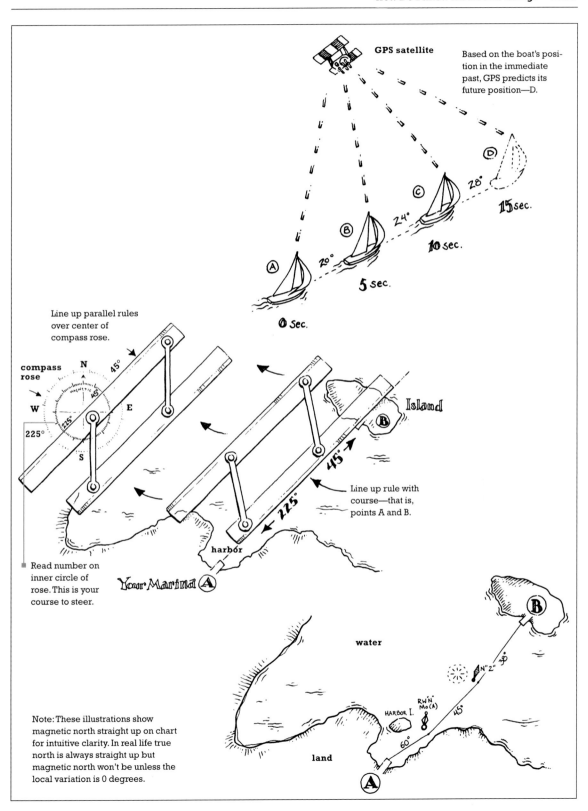

GPS satellite

Based on the boat's position in the immediate past, GPS predicts its future position—D.

Ⓓ

28°

15 sec.

Ⓒ

24°

10 sec.

Ⓑ

20°

5 sec.

Ⓐ

0 sec.

Line up parallel rules over center of compass rose.

compass rose

N

45°

45°

MAGNETIC

225°

W   E

225°

S

45°

225°

Line up rule with course—that is, points A and B.

Island

Ⓑ

harbor

Your Marina Ⓐ

■ Read number on inner circle of rose. This is your course to steer.

water

Ⓑ

N"2" 30°

RW"N" Mo(A)

45°

HARBOR I.

60°

land

Ⓐ

Note: These illustrations show magnetic north straight up on chart for intuitive clarity. In real life true north is always straight up but magnetic north won't be unless the local variation is 0 degrees.

that is exposed only at very low tides, but is clearly marked on your chart. Clearly that course isn't going to work. So you wend your way out of the harbor, giving its protective island a good berth, and sidle up to the harbor entrance navigation buoy (let's say it's a bell buoy) that was placed there by the Coast Guard for your convenience. Your tax dollars at work. The buoy is surrounded by navigable water, so it makes a great point for departure or arrival. From the buoy, you lay a course to another buoy (let's say it's one of those red, conical nun buoys) that marks that rock you want to be sure to miss. You can see from the chart that leaving that nun buoy to port will keep your boat safe. Then you lay another course from the nun to Island B. Voilà! And so it goes, through as many iterations as necessary to get from A to B, in the process we call piloting.

Just one other thing to mention before you steer by your compass. You know by now that a compass responds to the earth's magnetic field and therefore reads in degrees magnetic, which is not a problem in practice because you can read degrees magnetic from your chart's compass rose and thereby pilot your boat through a magnetic world. But compasses also respond to more local magnetic influences, which we call *deviation*. Your ship's compass has adjustable internal magnets, and when these are properly adjusted (and there are professional compass adjustors who do just that!), you should be able to ignore deviation. But when you leave a steel winch handle next to the compass or run some electric wires past it to carry power to a new toy (your cockpit music speakers?), you may dramatically disturb the local magnetic field in which the compass operates; the result will be spurious readings.

How can you be sure? On a clear, calm day, park your boat next to a known spot on the chart (perhaps your harbor entrance buoy or even your marina) and point your bow at various landmarks all around you whose bearings you can read from the chart. If the chart tells you that the lighthouse across the bay should bear 170° from your location, and your hand bearing compass tells you the same thing, does your steering compass read 170° when your bow is pointed there? Good. Now turn to another landmark and test again. All OK? Sounds like you don't need to worry about compass deviation.

If on the other hand the compass is consistently off on certain headings, it may be that the engine or something else on the boat is interfering. Make a note of these errors on a compass card and whenever you're on those headings, apply the noted amount of deviation to your course calculations.

Using GPS to Plot a Course

GPS works much the same way as the Who Bird. A GPS receiver picks up signals from satellites orbiting the earth, and from the data indicating your movement, it calculates all sorts of helpful information, such as where you are, how fast you're going, and in what direction you're heading. But the GPS bases its information on where you've been in the last 3 seconds, 10 seconds, or 1 minute (on some units, the averaging time is programmable, on others it's fixed). It thinks: If you were here (A), here (B), and here (C) at these times, a good educated guess is that in 10 more seconds, you'll be here (D). And the course between C and D is such and such degrees. Any change in speed or direction, even a brief one, alters the computer's predictions.

Such predictions are possible only because the GPS knows where it is, and that's what's really important. Punch a button, and it displays your position in terms of latitude and longitude, which may not mean much unless you have a chart on which to plot those coordinates. So you get out your parallel rules and dividers to extrapolate your position from the lat/lon lines on the chart. I say extrapolate because chances are your actual position will be somewhere between the printed lines on the chart.

Plotting a course with a GPS requires that you enter the coordinates of your destination, which you can lift from the chart by using your dividers again. These latitude and longitude coordinates, once you know them, define a *waypoint*. It might be an intermediate waypoint (such as the nun buoy in our earlier example) or a destination waypoint (Island B). Just give the GPS the coordinates of each waypoint in sequence. After the GPS knows where you are and where you want to go, it calculates the bearing between the two and displays that as a *course to steer* (CTS). It's your job to be sure that there are no hazards between here and there.

There you are, right on course . . . heading toward a reef!

Hard alee!

How Do I Steer a Course?

After you know the course that points to your island paradise, all you gotta do is hop in, turn the key (or raise the sails), and aim, right?

Well, sometimes it is that easy, but not often. Things happen: the boat doesn't necessarily follow the exact course over the sea bottom that you're steering on the compass; you may have to tack if the wind is coming from the general direction of the island; or there may be obstacles in the way that force you to change direction, like a rock (as we saw in chapter 26), another boat, or more land.

Let's look more closely at the first of these circumstances (the others are dealt with elsewhere in this book). We began chapter 26 by plotting a simple course from Harbor A to Island B, making a starting assumption of no intervening obstacles. That course is 45°. To steer it accurately, that number must be lined up with the lubber line on your steering compass. In a simplified world, steering 45° would take you right to the island, but in the real world it often doesn't work that way.

There are two reasons why your boat's actual course over the sea bottom might differ from what you're steering by the compass. One is that you're being carried sideways by a current (we'll look at that in chapter 28). The other is that, when close-hauled or reaching, the boat is pushed sideways by the wind even as it progresses forward. This is called *leeway*. The amount of leeway depends on the boat and strength of the wind. A boat with a lot of surface area in its keel (that is, the keel is deep or long or both) will make less leeway than a boat with a shallow, stubby keel.

The only time you can steer directly to your destination without compensating for leeway is when the wind is directly behind the boat.

To compensate for leeway, steer a number of degrees upwind of the destination. Robert Lindy, an old friend who taught me a lot about sailing, used to say, "Distance to windward is like money in the bank." The benefit of being to windward of your destination is that when you get near you can *fall off*; that is, turn away more from the wind, easing the sails accordingly, and reach in comfortably. Or, if the wind heads you, it might still be possible to make your target close-hauled without having to tack. When you're sailing close-hauled but still pointing to leeward of your destination, a tack is inevitable unless you get a big wind shift in your favor in the immediate future. And a tack adds time. Much as we love sailing, it's always nice to get to harbor, tidy the boat, and relax, especially if it's getting dark.

Over time, you'll learn how much leeway your boat makes. How much you compensate for it also depends on how far away your destination is. You can calculate the exact amount of correction by drawing a *vector diagram* (see chapter 28). But as you practice in close familiar waters, start by aiming 5° upwind of your destination. So, if your desired course between Point A and Point B is 45°, and the wind is coming from 355°, try steering 40° to compensate for leeway.

An ocean current also can cause your *course made good* (also known as "course over ground") to diverge from the course you're steering and must be similarly compensated (see chapter 28). Usually you can't see currents, but the directions and speeds of tidal currents are noted for many locations along the U.S. and Canadian coasts in books such as *Eldridge Tide and Pilot Book* (East Coast only) and *Reed's Nautical Almanac* (see the resources section).

Electronic Navigation

Most owners of larger boats have a GPS on board. Handheld models can be bought for as little as $100. To navigate with GPS, you'll need an understanding of latitude and longitude (see chapter 25).

As discussed in chapter 26, electronic navigation makes use of waypoints, which are simply positions identified by their latitude and longitude. Again, if your marina is in Harbor A and you want to get to Island B, you need to enter the latitude and longitude of Island B as a waypoint in your GPS. Then, when you're ready to

leave, punch GO TO (or a similar function key) on the GPS, and it will calculate the course to steer. And, if you fail to compensate for leeway or current, it will calculate *cross-track error*— that is, the difference in bearing (your course is a bearing) in degrees, and distance in miles, between what you are steering and what you need to steer to arrive at Island B.

When Your Course Isn't Straight

If Point B is upwind of Point A, you cannot steer a direct course from A to B. You'll have to tack back and forth, meaning you will never steer the exact course determined by your pretrip chart work. But you want to try to steer as close to that number as you can on each tack.

Drawing a series of vector diagrams would tell you fairly closely how much progress you're making, but that's a cumbersome thing to do while under way, and usually unnecessary. A GPS will tell you precisely. But it's also a good idea to make general calculations in your head. As noted in chapter 25, such mental bookkeeping is called dead reckoning, and it is important in case your electronic means of navigation fails or starts giving you funny numbers.

The foundations of dead reckoning are the simple speed-distance-time formulas that race through your mind when your kid asks, "Mommy, how long 'til we get there?"

Let's see. Twenty nautical miles to go. We're traveling 5 knots. The correct answer is either, "Four hours, sweetie!" or the vaguer (and more politic), "Just a little longer, sweetie," depending on a host of intangible factors best known only to you.

But it gets a little more complicated when you are tacking constantly. You may want to write down the time spent on each tack, your average speed on each tack, and the average course steered. From the illustration on this

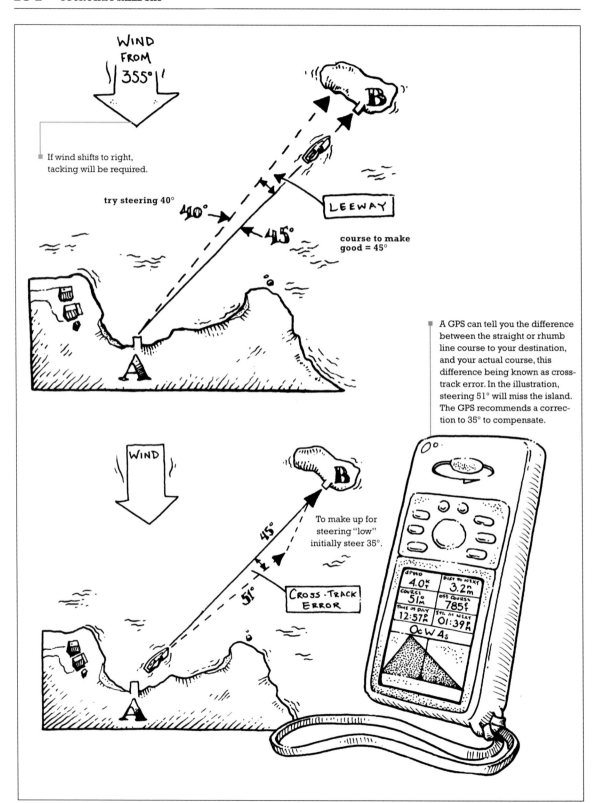

WIND FROM 355°

If wind shifts to right, tacking will be required.

try steering 40° 40°

LEEWAY

course to make good = 45°

45°

A

B

A GPS can tell you the difference between the straight or rhumb line course to your destination, and your actual course, this difference being known as cross-track error. In the illustration, steering 51° will miss the island. The GPS recommends a correction to 35° to compensate.

WIND

45°

To make up for steering "low" initially steer 35°.

51°

CROSS-TRACK ERROR

A

B

SPEED 4.0^Kᴛ DIST TO NEXT 3.2m

COURSE 51m OFF COURSE 785f

TIME OF DAY 12:57ₚ ETA AT NEXT 01:39ₚ

OcW 4s

page, for example: 45 minutes, 4 knots, 315°. If you have to, you can plot a new position on the chart, using as a starting point your last known position, which would be (if you're keeping track!) the beginning of the new tack. The illustration shows that you traveled 3 nautical miles, which can be measured with dividers along a course line drawn with parallel rules, walked over from the compass rose (see chapters 25 and 26 for the technique).

Rescued after more than a month at sea in a life raft, shipwreck survivor Dougal Robertson told his rescuers where he thought he was to within a few miles! The entire time he and his family were adrift, he kept mental track of their courses and drift rates, with only the stars and his intelligence as guides. His fascinating story is recounted in the classic book, *Survive the Savage Sea* (see the resources section).

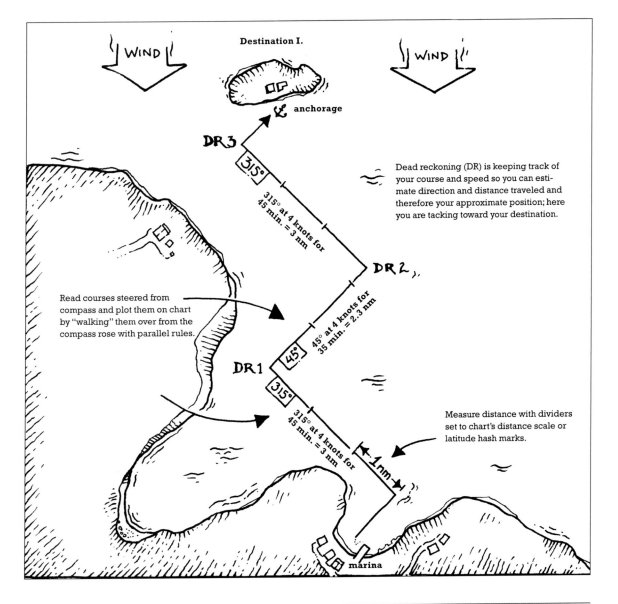

Destination I.

WIND

WIND

anchorage

DR 3

315°

315° at 4 knots for 45 min. = 3 nm

Dead reckoning (DR) is keeping track of your course and speed so you can estimate direction and distance traveled and therefore your approximate position; here you are tacking toward your destination.

DR 2

45° at 4 knots for 35 min. = 2.3 nm

Read courses steered from compass and plot them on chart by "walking" them over from the compass rose with parallel rules.

45°

DR 1

315°

315° at 4 knots for 45 min. = 3 nm

1nm

Measure distance with dividers set to chart's distance scale or latitude hash marks.

marina

Currents Keep Screwing Me Up

28

Once I was helping friends deliver a boat from the Hudson River to Newport, Rhode Island. Our last night aboard was spent at Shelter Island on Long Island Sound. In the morning we departed for The Race, where the Sound opens to the ocean. Currents run very quickly there, as they do elsewhere in the Sound. As we motored away from Shelter Island in thick fog, we could see only a few hundred feet around us. The current diagrams in our copy of the annual *Eldridge Tide and Pilot Book* indicated that at that hour of the day we would be set sideways at an oblique angle due to a current that would begin imperceptibly and gain speed until it reached more than 2 knots. Accurate calculations were critical because the boat would be set toward a line of rocks that were either just above or just below the surface. As it turned out, our dead reckoning estimates didn't compensate quite enough, because suddenly two rocks appeared out of the fog, and we were swept between them! Fortunately, they were at the end of the rock line, and after this fortuitous miss we were in the clear. But the ending could have been ugly.

Vector Diagrams

As noted in previous chapters, solutions to leeway and current problems can be solved with vector diagrams. A *vector* is a straight line with an arrow at its outer end pointing in the direction of the motion it represents (boat or current), and with its length scaled to the speed of that motion. Solutions using vectors include (1) determining a corrected course to steer so that you arrive at your intended destination; (2) determining the effect of a known current on your intended course and speed; (3) determining the nature (direction and speed, otherwise known as *set* and *drift*) of an unknown current based on your actual course and speed from a known previous position to a known current position; and (4) determining the necessary course and speed to arrive at your destination at a specific time (as you would in a rendezvous or rally contest). We'll look at the first three; the fourth is not often needed unless you want to time your arrival at, say, a cut between two islands for slack water, or to make landfall at a certain time of day.

Although vector diagrams can be solved using trigonometry and a calculator, the simpler solution is to draw them on graph paper. The illustrations on pages 138 and 139 show how. In Example A, the boat is traveling at 5 knots on an easterly course from West Palm Beach toward West End on Grand Bahama Island, and the Gulf Stream is setting the boat north (360°) at 3 knots (this is the drift). Open a pair of dividers to 3 nautical miles using the chart mileage scale or the latitude hash marks, then mark off the 3 miles on line ON and label that point "W." Next, set the dividers to your speed through the water—5 knots—and place one point of the dividers on point W and then swing an arc through your desired track. Label the point where the arc intersects the desired track as "P." Last, using a protractor, determine the angle of WP to WN—130°. (If you're plotting this directly on the appropriate navigation chart, you won't need to use a protractor. Instead, align your parallel rules to line WP, then "walk" them over to the compass rose to find out what course that is.) This is the course you should steer to achieve your desired course made good of 90°, and the length of OP is your speed of advance—about 3.75 knots. If West End is 50 miles from West Palm Beach, it will take about 13.3 hours to get there. In effect, the boat crabs along at an angle to its desired course. This feels strange when you can see West End because your instincts tell you to steer straight for it. But if you steer 90°, you'll be swept north by the current and miss West End by many miles.

If you use true directions for your vectors, as here, remember that the course to steer must be converted to a compass course by adding or subtracting degrees of *variation* (magnetic anomalies in your area) and *deviation* (the aggregate effect of nearby metals on your compass). As discussed before, if you play your cards right, you won't have to worry about deviation. And as mentioned earlier, you may find it easier to work through these solutions in degrees magnetic, but you must be consistent. Because most tidal current tables give predicted current sets in degrees true, you'll have to do some corrections for variation no matter which approach you follow.

What would have happened if you hadn't made a course correction for the set and drift of the current? Example B shows you. Suppose that you're leaving Miami and heading a bit farther south, say to Nassau. Your intended track is 110°, and your speed through the water is 6 knots. Let's pretend that current set and drift is different from that in our previous example—say, 20° at 4 knots. (Note that current set is given in the direction the current is traveling to, whereas wind is characterized according to the direction it is blowing from. Go figure.) Using a pair of dividers, measure six units (for boat speed) along your intended track and label that point "DR." This is your dead reckoned position. Now, use your protractor (or parallel rules, if working on the chart) to set up a 20° vector from DR and measure four units along this vector from DR with the dividers. Label this point "P." Connect O and P. Using the protractor, you'll find that your course over ground will be about 76°, and your speed of advance will be a little over 7 knots. Maybe you'll end up in West End after all!

But what if you've been sailing for a while and determine that you are not where you thought you'd be, which happens all the time! Look at Example C. Suppose that you left West Palm Beach hugging the coast and steering 150°. Then, by using GPS or taking bearings on coastal landmarks, you determine your actual position is P. Whoa! The land is getting hard to see! You know you need to make a course correction to get back closer to the coast, but don't know how much to allow for current set and drift. The difference between where you intended to be at this time (DR) and where you actually are (P) is the answer. Use the protractor to measure the direction of

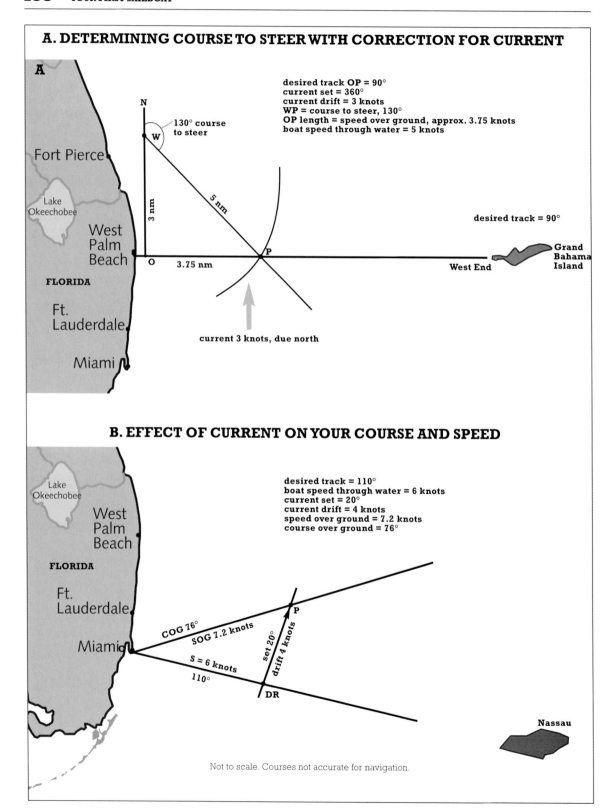

A. DETERMINING COURSE TO STEER WITH CORRECTION FOR CURRENT

A

Fort Pierce

Lake Okeechobee

West Palm Beach

FLORIDA

Ft. Lauderdale

Miami

N

W 130° course to steer

3 nm

5 nm

O   3.75 nm   P

desired track OP = 90°
current set = 360°
current drift = 3 knots
WP = course to steer, 130°
OP length = speed over ground, approx. 3.75 knots
boat speed through water = 5 knots

desired track = 90°

West End   Grand Bahama Island

current 3 knots, due north

B. EFFECT OF CURRENT ON YOUR COURSE AND SPEED

Lake Okeechobee

West Palm Beach

FLORIDA

Ft. Lauderdale

Miami

desired track = 110°
boat speed through water = 6 knots
current set = 20°
current drift = 4 knots
speed over ground = 7.2 knots
course over ground = 76°

COG 76°
SOG 7.2 knots
P
set 20°
drift 4 knots
S = 6 knots
110°
DR

Nassau

Not to scale. Courses not accurate for navigation.

DR-P, and the dividers to measure the length of DR-P. You'll find that the current has been setting you 90° eastward at a rate of 3.5 knots. This is the average of all influences over the course of your trip so far, and not necessarily the instantaneous effect at point P, but adjusting your course according to the principles in Example A is better than making no adjustments at all.

Life can be simple when there are no currents to be reckoned with or devilishly challenging in places like The Race, where the coast, islands, and underwater features conspire to swirl the currents in constantly differing directions.

C. FIGURING THE SET AND DRIFT OF CURRENT

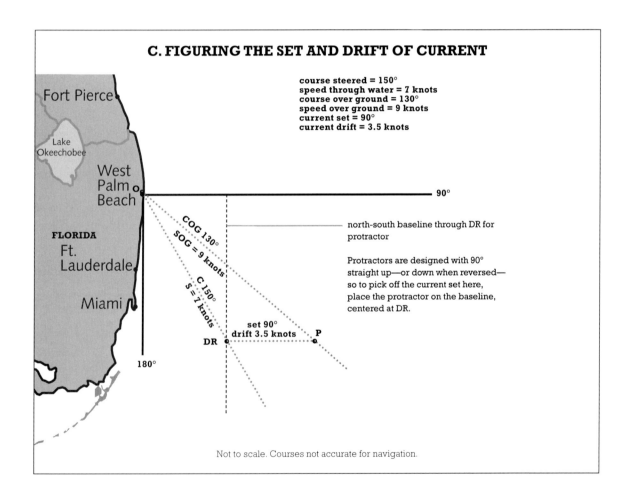

course steered = 150°
speed through water = 7 knots
course over ground = 130°
speed over ground = 9 knots
current set = 90°
current drift = 3.5 knots

90°

north-south baseline through DR for protractor

Protractors are designed with 90° straight up—or down when reversed—so to pick off the current set here, place the protractor on the baseline, centered at DR.

Fort Pierce
Lake Okeechobee
West Palm Beach
FLORIDA
Ft. Lauderdale
Miami
180°

COG 130°
SOG = 9 knots
C 150°
S = 7 knots
set 90°
drift 3.5 knots
DR
P

Not to scale. Courses not accurate for navigation.

How Fast Can I Go?

29

Speed. It intoxicates some and scares others. But everyone itches for velocity at one time or another, if only to bring an end to a long trip. Among sailors there are two distinct groups—loafers (cruisers and daysailors) and racers. That's an oversimplification, but the dichotomy is grounded in at least some degree of truth; there are those who like to compete and those who like to lounge. Me? I've done both, but given my druthers, I prefer the latter. That doesn't mean, however, that I don't like speed. Quite the contrary.

Sailors, like fishermen, tend to exaggerate: "I was doing 8 knots in my O'Day 27. Passed a J/35!"

Not likely.

So how fast can a sailboat really go?

It depends on the kind of boat and its size.

Displacement Boats

Big boats are measured by the weight of water displaced by the hull at rest. The number is expressed in pounds or long tons (1 long ton = 2,240 pounds, or 35 cubic feet of seawater at 64 pounds per cubic foot).

So-called *displacement boats* are essentially those that sit in the water rather than on top of it. A displacement boat therefore has to push water out of its way in order to move. A lightweight, *nondisplacement sailboat*, such as the Open Class 60 that is raced single-handed around the world, is much like a surfboard in that it skims over the surface. Because such boats displace very little, their top speeds are not subject to the same physical limitations.

Maximum hull speed of a displacement boat is roughly 1.34 times the square root of its waterline length in feet. For example, a boat with a 30-foot waterline has a maximum hull speed of $5.47 \times 1.34 = 7.3$ knots. The limiting factor has to do with the waves created by the hull; the faster the boat goes, the farther aft its stern wave moves, until the distance between the crest of the bow wave and the crest of the stern wave equals the length of the boat at its waterline. At that point, the boat begins to squat in the wave trough it has created, and it cannot go any faster without climbing out of that hole—in essence, climbing its own bow wave.

And why does this happen at 1.34 times the square root of waterline length? Because waves in deep water—when they're not slowed by friction with the sea bottom—travel at 1.34 times the square root of their length as measured from crest to crest. Put yet another way, a displacement boat can't outrun the wave it creates. Of course, if you put a huge engine in a boat, you can force it to go a little faster. The secret to gaining more speed, however, is not a bigger engine or a larger sail plan, but lies in redesigning the hull with either a longer waterline or a much lower displacement/length ratio, which essentially means making the boat flatter on the bottom with a skinny fin keel, so that it is more easily driven.

Nondisplacement Boats

Daysailers and modern ultralight displacement boats (ULDBs) are so flat on the bottom that they can plane, or at least surf.

Planing is when the hull lifts out of the water ever so slightly, like a hydrofoil. The speed increase is rapid and dramatic, as is the change in motion. No longer does the boat seem to roll laconically with the waves, but feels jet driven, more like a speedboat.

Surfing is essentially the same as planing, but it occurs when the boat is sliding down the face of a wave. Boats that are too heavy to plane may still be able to surf, because they have gravity working for them as well as wind power.

Boat speed while planing or surfing is a function of hull resistance, hull length, and sail area. World speed records under sail are held by long, skinny multihulls that reduce resistance by using hydrofoils to get the hulls completely out of the water. They can reach 50 knots and more.

Typical Cruising Speeds

Regardless of the boat you own, you'll spend most of your time traveling between 3 and 8 knots. As wind strength rises and falls, averaging 5 knots over a lengthy period of time is fairly typical of boats under 40 feet. This speed will seem a lot faster on a small daysailer, in which you sit much closer to the water, than on a 38-foot heavy-displacement cruiser.

If 5 knots seems slow, maybe you'd be happier with a powerboat. But remember this distinction: on a powerboat, you wonder how long until you get there; on a sailboat, you're already there.

To get the D/L ratio, multiply the waterline length in feet by 0.01, raise the result to the third power, and divide that number into the displacement in long tons (2,240 lb.).

$$D/L = \frac{\text{Displacement (long tons)}}{(\text{Length (ft)} \times 0.01)^3}$$

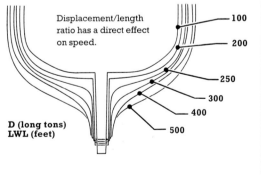

Displacement/length ratio has a direct effect on speed.

D (long tons)
LWL (feet)

You can tell a lot about a sailboat's purpose and performance from its D/L ratio. Here's a guide, repeated from chapter 1 for convenience:

100: Strictly racing, thrill sailing, and overnighting.
200: Racing, weekending, and light cruising.
250: All-around good sailing, motoring, long and short cruising with moderate liveability.
300: Fair sailing for long cruises but excellent motoring with good liveability.
400: Poor sailing but excellent motoring, seakindliness, and liveability.
500: Terrible sailing, but superb liveabilty. Motoring is good with lots of power.

BOAT SPEED* AND HANDLING AS A FUNCTION OF WIND SPEED

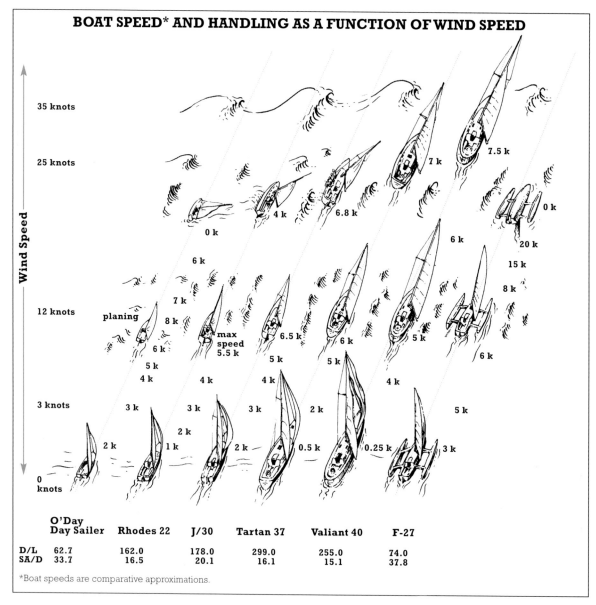

	O'Day Day Sailer	Rhodes 22	J/30	Tartan 37	Valiant 40	F-27
D/L	62.7	162.0	178.0	299.0	255.0	74.0
SA/D	33.7	16.5	20.1	16.1	15.1	37.8

*Boat speeds are comparative approximations.

The table above shows representative boats from the six types we've discussed. For each, the displacement/length (D/L) and sail area/displacement (SA/D) ratios are given. These numbers give a fair idea of how well a conventional displacement sailboat will perform, but they are not as relevant to daysailer and multihull planing hull forms. Nevertheless, their low D/L ratios and high SA/D ratios

(see chapter 1) make for interesting comparisons.

Let's examine the fortunes of each boat as wind and wave increase.

The 16-foot 9-inch O'Day Day Sailer will ghost along nicely in the faintest breeze, easily picking up speed with a freshening wind. Depending on crew weight and point of sail, the hull will begin to lift out of the water and plane

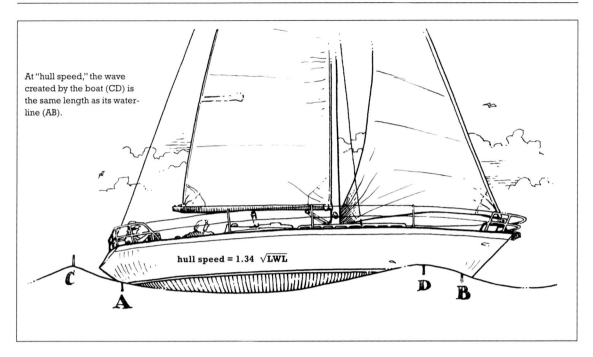

At "hull speed," the wave created by the boat (CD) is the same length as its waterline (AB).

hull speed = 1.34 $\sqrt{\mathrm{LWL}}$

once the wind reaches the teens. As the wind continues to increase, it's a good idea to put a reef in the mainsail; that is, lower the mainsail and secure the unused foot portion. Unfortunately, many small boats are not equipped with reefing systems. Another option is to drop the mainsail altogether and sail with just the jib. As waves increase in height and the wind blows in the mid-20s, the Day Sailer is definitely threatened by knockdown and capsize. In these conditions, the boat is best left at the dock, or better yet, on its trailer.

The Rhodes 22 trailer sailer has a modest D/L and generous SA/D, so it should sail briskly in low to moderate winds. Its top speed is about 6 knots and it will achieve this when winds begin to exceed double digits. Because it cannot plane, it is not as fast as the Day Sailer in 12 to 14 knots of wind. When the wind strength increases, the Rhodes 22 cannot go any faster due to the limitations of its hull, as described in the Sailboat Guide in the back of this book. In fact, as the waves increase in size, the Rhodes 22 will begin to slow down, and in 25-knot winds, it will be overpowered and will heel severely unless well reefed. Time to head back to the harbor!

The J/30 is a slippery raceboat and will perform nicely in light-air conditions. It will certainly be faster than the smaller Rhodes 22 and probably similar to the Day Sailer. Owing to its longer waterline, the J/30 will hit its top speed of nearly 7 knots when the wind strength reaches the high teens or low 20s, but will require crew sitting on the rail as human ballast to keep her from heeling excessively. Many modern raceboats are designed to carry on even in severe weather, but they usually require large, experienced crews oblivious to hardship. Due to their flat bottoms, they pound when sailing upwind in waves.

The Tartan 37 is a performance-oriented cruiser and club racer. In most conditions, it is faster than a heavy, all-out cruiser, increasing speed commensurate with the wind. A reef in 25-knot winds will not slow the boat because it makes more efficient use of the remaining sail area.

The Valiant 40 was heralded as a performance cruiser when it was introduced in the 1970s. Its fin keel was considered fairly radical for a nonracer. Note that its D/L ratio is lower than the Tartan 37's, but so is its SA/D, with the result being that it won't be a great light-air boat. In 10 to 12 knots of wind the Valiant 40 moves at around 5 knots but as the wind strengthens, its speed steadily accelerates. When wind speeds top 25 to 35 knots, the Valiant 40 is likely the only boat of our six left standing.

The F-27 trimaran is exceedingly fast in all conditions. When it reaches double-digit speeds it often is moving at the same speed as the wind. But when wave crests start blowing off, great care must be taken to safely sail the F-27. Reefed and properly handled, it can survive radical conditions, though it will be moving much more slowly with little if any sail up. If something goes wrong, it can capsize.

Note: Boat speeds are approximate and given only for comparative purposes. Different boats in different conditions perform—you guessed it—differently. In addition, as the discussion of the F-27 above suggests, seamanship of the crew also plays a significant role in a boat's performance.

What If It Gets Dark?

30

Sooner rather than later, you're likely to find yourself staying out later than you should. Maybe you will underestimate the time to return to harbor, or maybe you just don't want the day to end. Maybe the wind and your engine both quit at the same time. In any case, darkness will fall, and you will still have a mile or more to go.

This happened to me once while returning to Newport Harbor from Block Island, Rhode Island, a distance of 22 miles. Fog had set in early on the passage, and because there were high-speed powerboats about, not to mention ferries and commercial fishing boats, I elected to sail rather than run the engine. Under sail, we made just 2 knots, but at least we could hear other traffic and sound our bell and foghorn—for whatever they were worth!

To cap things off, darkness fell while my friend and I were still several miles from the Castle Hill lighthouse at the entrance to Narragansett Bay. Newport Harbor lay 2 more miles up the bay. Fortunately, I recalled the advice of a fisherman who told me that if I ever got in this fix, I should find the lighthouse and then follow the shore in because there is deep water right up to the rocks.

Thanks to doing our DR all the way from Block Island, we managed to find the Brenton Reef tower outside the bay entrance and we plotted a chart course from there to the Castle Hill lighthouse. Seeing the revolving light pierce the gloom was reassuring, to put it mildly. Remembering the fisherman's advice, we sailed slowly along the shore. When I heard water on the rocks, I steered away 5 or 10 degrees, and when I could no longer hear water on the rocks, I steered back.

At one point, we heard the loud engine of a motorboat, and while I conned my head trying to figure out where it was coming from and going to, I lost my bearings. Before I knew it, our boat had done a 180 and the sails were backwinded. Like an airplane pilot flying on instruments alone, the sailor at night must trust his compass over his easily tricked senses. Fortunately, there was no collision, we got back on course, and in due time rounded the light at Fort Adams and entered Newport Harbor.

Nerve-racking as this experience was, it

LIGHTS FOR POWER-DRIVEN VESSELS UNDER WAY

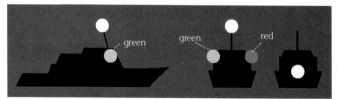

Under 164 ft. (50 m), masthead light, sidelights, and sternlight.

Over 164 ft. (50 m).

Lights When Towing

Under 164 ft. (50 m), two white steaming lights and towing light aft (yellow over white).

Vessel being towed shows sidelights and sternlight.

If tow is over 657 ft. (200 m), three steaming lights.

Lights When Pushing

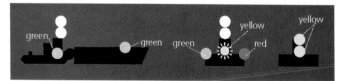

In inland waters only, the lights are as shown, with the yellow bow light flashing. In international waters, there is no yellow bow light, and the two yellow stern lights are replaced by a white stern light.

DECIPHERING LIGHTS AT NIGHT

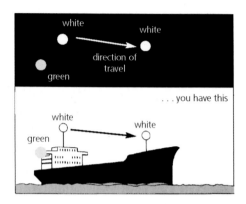

. . . you have this

If you see this at night . . .

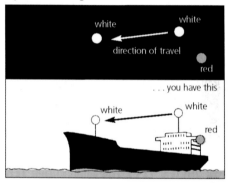

. . . you have this

If the two white lights are aligned . . .

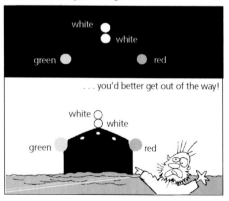

. . . you'd better get out of the way!

SOME SPECIAL LIGHTS

Fishing Vessels. Note: A fishing vessel whose gear extends more than 492.5 ft. (150 m) may show a white light in the direction of the gear.

starboard side view   bow   stern

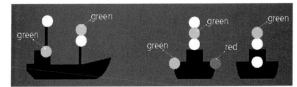

Trawling vessel under 164 ft. (50 m) shows all-round green over white lights (not shown); vessels over 164 ft. show additional white steaming light over green (as shown).

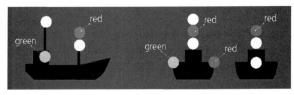

Other fishing vessels (not trawling) under 164 ft. (50 m) show all-round red over white lights (not shown); vessels over 164 ft. show additional white steaming light (as shown).

Pilot Vessels on Duty and Underway

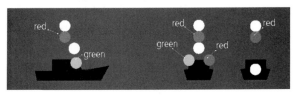

Show all-round white over red vertical lights plus normal anchor or navigation lights.

Vessels over 164 ft. (50 m) Constrained by Draft

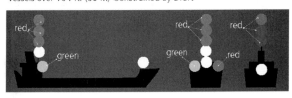

Vessels constrained by draft (eg. a vessel confined to the center of a channel) show three vertical all-round red lights as well as normal navigation lights.

Vessels Not Under Command (eg. with mechanical or steering breakdown) and Not Underway

Two clearly visible all-round red lights. Note: although it is unlikely that a vessel not under command would be using her engines, she would, if making way, show navigation lights as well as NUC lights.

ended safely because we'd done certain things, and those things apply to every outing:

- Note the time you leave the dock or marina. Knowing how long you have been sailing away from the dock gives you at least a rough idea of how long it will take to get back.
- Know when the sun sets. And remember that the wind often dies at dusk, so if you have no motor, your speed will drop, delaying your ETA (estimated time of arrival).
- Note your course at all times. Returning to your point of origin can be as simple as turning around and sailing the reciprocal course; that is, your original course plus 180°. For example, if you left sailing 23°, the reciprocal is 203°.
- When you have to tack, keep a mental picture of your course from a bird's-eye view: time and speed on each course (see chapter 25). If you anticipate ANY problem, draw your DR on a piece of paper, or better yet, on a chart. That way, you always have a rough idea of where you are.
- As darkness falls, make yourself visible. On a small sailboat, you might do no more than shine a flashlight on your sail. Flashlights with the lens divided red/green can be affixed to the bow with a suction cup. Same for the white stern light. On a boat with an electrical system, turn on your permanent navigation lights. If motoring, turn on the steaming light on the mast.

- Identify the lights you see, especially those that are moving. After you familiarize yourself with the lights required under the nautical rules of the road, you can determine the kind of boat and which way it is heading. For example, when you see a red light, you know you're looking at the left side of the boat. If you can see both a red and green light close together, the boat is coming straight at you!

Other lights you might see could be on bridges, highways, radio towers, and navigation aids. Locating them on the chart will help you determine your position. A more precise method is to take bearings on known lights or landmarks with a hand bearing compass and then draw the bearing lines on the chart. Two or three crossing lines indicate your position (see chapter 25). To get even more precise, whip out your handheld GPS, acquire several satellites, read your latitude and longitude, and then find that intersection on the chart. There you be! Punch in the lat/lon of your next waypoint and steer the course indicated.

■ ■ ■

Night sailing is a special treat. In the summer, the air is soft and cool. If you're lucky, you may see phosphorescence in the bow wave. In the sky, the stars seem bigger and brighter than on land. And should the moon come up, its reflection will form a dancing line on the surface that looks like a trail of silver leading to the edge of the world.

What If It Gets Foggy?

It might seem that the skills needed for navigating and boat handling in fog are the same as for darkness. But there are differences. In darkness there are usually lights—either from shore, the moon, or the stars—to help you find your way. In dense fog, you see nothing. Your world is suddenly reduced to a small circle of water with you at its center. It is a world of altered states in which disorientation is the rule.

Here's what you can do:

- Keep a DR log of your assumed position. Do this even if you have a GPS, in case it craps out, which has been known to happen. And even when the circuits hang together, batteries run down.
- When you're navigating in the fog, break your journey into short legs from one waypoint to the next. Try to avoid long legs and choose the safest waypoints available, even if they take you a little out of your way. A midchannel gong buoy surrounded by deep water makes a wonderful waypoint; you'll hear it before you see it. A can or nun buoy marking a ledge is not a great waypoint: miscalculate on one side and you might never see it; err the other way and you might run aground.

- A GPS is wonderfully reassuring in the fog, but it can't tell you where the other boats are. (For that, you need radar.) If you're under power, stop the engine every now and then to listen for foghorns, bells, and engines. Remember that the navigation buoys you're using for waypoints are being used by other boaters as well. Traffic is busier around them.
- If your boat is less than 36 feet long, the nautical rules of the road require you to sound a horn or whistle at 2-minute intervals. Don't put too much faith in this measure, however; anyone aboard a powerboat has little chance of hearing it. In practice, you can fire a blast from an air-powered foghorn, but you might be best advised to save it for when you actually hear another vessel.
- If your boat is longer than 36 feet, you're supposed to give two prolonged blasts every 2 minutes when the engine is running, or one long blast followed by two

short ones when you're under sail alone. Again, most skippers temper the rule with common sense.

- When sailing near the shore, a depth-sounder can provide important navigational information. I once found safe harbor in a thick fog by tacking along the coast of Martha's Vineyard, relying on the depth-sounder to tell me when to tack. Note the depth contours on the chart. They won't pinpoint your position but can tell you how near you are to land. In this case, I tacked away from the coast whenever the depth-sounder showed us on the 20-foot contour. When depths dropped to 60, I tacked back toward land. Eventually, we stumbled across the lighted marker at the entrance to Menemsha harbor.

- Remember that rocks may rise up above the bottom. Another time while sailing in the fog, cutting margins too close, I punched a hole in the keel by hitting a rock. (Fortunately, the boat didn't sink because the ballast cavity of that full-keeled boat was sealed from the interior.) At times like this, all you can do is repeat the adage, "If you haven't run aground, you haven't gone anywhere."

- Sometimes, fog comes upon you so quickly that there is nothing you can do but deal with it. This, however, is rare. Fog is often predicted in NOAA weather forecasts. And you can often see it forming in the distance. Rather than take chances when there is a risk of fog, stay home and sail another day. But if you're already out on the bay when fog comes rolling in, take some bearings on landmarks while you can still see them and make a note of any nearby boats.

- Sometimes, it is safer to stop than to proceed blindly. On a number of occasions, I have dropped anchor and waited for the fog to clear, often overnight. Better to miss a day of work than wreck the boat and endanger yourself and crew. Heaving-to (see chapter 19) is another strategy worth considering.

IN RESTRICTED VISIBILITY

Power vessel making way —
Power vessel underway but stopped — —
Manned tow — • •
Pilot vessel—optional signal • • •
Not under command, restricted in ability to maneuver, constrained by draft, sailing, fishing, towing or pushing, fishing at anchor, or restricted at anchor — • •
Anchored:
    <100 m—ring bell rapidly for 5 sec. once per min.
    ≥100 m—ring bell 5 sec. forward, then gong 5 sec. aft
Aground: 3 bell claps + rapid 5-sec. bell + 3 claps; repeat all 1/min.
    ≥100 m—add gong 5 sec. aft
    <12 m Inland option—horn, bell, or gong once per 2 min.

What to Do in Fog *(Rule 19)*

Fog Situation	What You Should Do
Regardless of traffic	Maintain safe speed; power-driven vessels sound one 5-sec. blast every 2 minutes. Most other vessels sound one 5-sec. and two 1-sec. blasts every 2 minutes.
Hear sound signal forward	Slow to bare steerageway or stop.
Radar target forward	Slow; do NOT turn to port unless you are overtaking the target vessel.
Radar target aft or abeam	Maintain speed; do NOT turn toward the target vessel.

PART FIVE

Worst-Case Scenarios

Despite What You Say, What If I Still Get Lost?

Anyone can get lost. Even those with a superior sense of direction. But what is a "sense of direction"? It sounds like some mysterious instinct, when in fact it may be nothing more than a heightened awareness of one's surroundings. If it appears more acutely in some than in others, perhaps it is just a matter of making it a priority. With attention and practice, a sense of direction can constitute the following:

- **Remembering your route.** As noted earlier, steering a reciprocal course is the simplest way to return home. A Maine lobsterman's sister married a man from the city. On his first visit, the brother-in-law asked to accompany the lobsterman on his rounds. They stocked the boat with bait and left the dock and harbor, motoring into a pea-soup fog. The lobsterman steered to port for awhile, then steered to starboard, made a few more turns, and after an hour the first pot marker appeared through the fog. The brother-in-law was totally confounded. While the lobsterman hauled the pot aboard, his brother-in-law scratched his head and said, "How on earth did you find this pot?" The lobsterman thought for a moment and then answered, "Waaall, I put it there."

- **Mentally calculating DR (see chapter 25), beginning with your point of origin.** If you know what direction you were heading when you left the marina, you have a basis for orientation. Each subsequent turn must be remembered. For example, you might say to yourself, "I left the harbor heading south. After about an hour, I turned hard to port, which is east. After another half hour, the wind direction changed, so I turned to port again, but only 30° or so. What direction am I heading now?" Answer: east by northeast, or about 60°.

- **Mentally noting your orientation to the sun.** In the Northern Hemisphere, the sun tracks to the south. It rises in the east and sets in the west. From these simple observations, the four cardinal points can be roughly estimated. When trying to find a major body of land, such as the East or West Coast (any port in a storm!), sailing

WAYS TO STAY ORIENTED

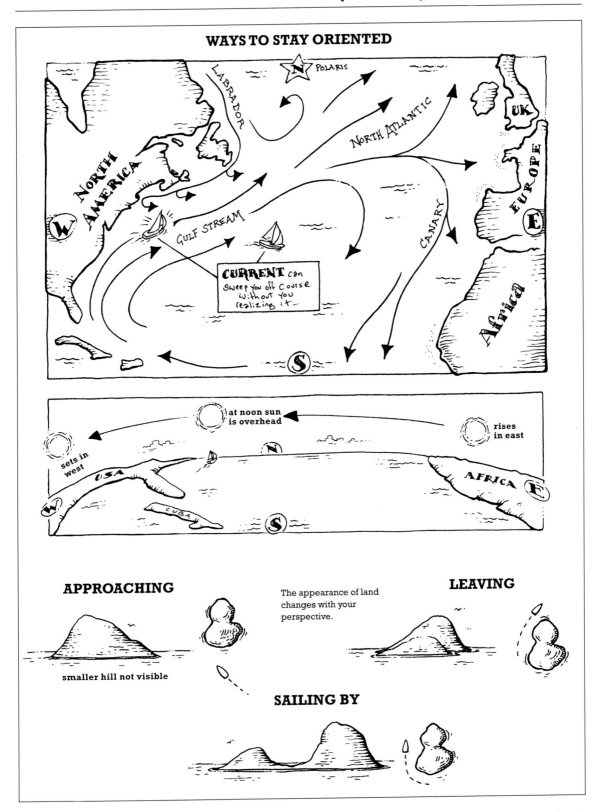

The appearance of land changes with your perspective.

APPROACHING

smaller hill not visible

LEAVING

SAILING BY

west or east will eventually bring you to a landfall.

- **Finding the North Star (Polaris) when sailing at night.** If you can determine north, when facing it you know that east is always 90° to the right and west is 90° to the left.
- **Visualizing topographic features from different angles.** As you move about a headland, for example, its appearance may change dramatically, so that when you turn back it looks different. It may take awhile to realize that it is the same land feature you passed earlier. This talent also is useful when looking at the elevation contours on a chart and trying to imagine what that feature looks like when viewed from the deck of your boat, not from above.

Survival guides offer many additional tricks, such as the smell of land, presence of shorebirds, and directions of currents. Although they make for fascinating study, there is little reason today for anyone to get so lost that they have to call up the primal wilderness skills of their distant ancestors. Instead, never leave the dock without a compass, even if it's a Junior Woodchuck model in your pocket. A handheld GPS isn't a bad idea either. Throw in a knotmeter, depth-sounder, chart, and parallel rules, and you have all the tools you need to navigate safely and accurately most anywhere in the world.

What If the Mast Falls Down?

A dismasting is a strange experience. I've lost one stick, and the thing that surprised me was the sudden silence. One minute we were racing along, the boat crashing through the waves and the wind whistling in the rigging. The next. . . nothing. The boat stopped quickly and sat bobbing. Aside from the wreckage, the effect was actually calming.

Some boats, large and small, have unstayed masts. They can be made of aluminum, wood, fiberglass, or carbon fiber wound on a mandrel to make a hollow tube. Other than periodically examining the mast for cracks, there's not much you can do in the way of preventive maintenance.

Most masts are kept upright by wires, or stays, as they are called in the marine world: forestays, backstays, and shrouds. The stays must be connected to the mast and to the boat; though this can be accomplished in a variety of ways, it usually involves a terminal fitting that squeezes the stay so firmly that its breaking strength is more than 90 percent of the wire itself. Terminal fittings are in turn connected to the mast and boat by clevis pins, and these in

their turn are kept from slipping out by cotter pins or rings. As you can see, a rig is comprised of a lot of little parts; should any one fail, the mast could come down. Annual inspection is prudent, and heavy use of the boat requires more frequent checks.

How long wire and other fittings last depends on many variables, including whether the boat is sailed year-round or seasonally; whether parts get dirty or damaged when the rig is out of the boat; and where the boat is kept (stainless steel corrodes faster in tropical climates). Wire rigging can last 20 years or longer, but replacement before then is recommended.

Despite your best precautions, however, the dread event still may happen (though it's rare). If your mast falls down, do this:

- Make sure that no crew are injured.
- Do not immediately start the engine. There may be lines or stays in the water that will foul the propeller.
- Assess the damage. Likely areas of secondary damage are the deck and (with a keel-stepped mast) interior furniture. Make sure that the boat isn't leaking.

WHEN THE RIG GOES DOWN

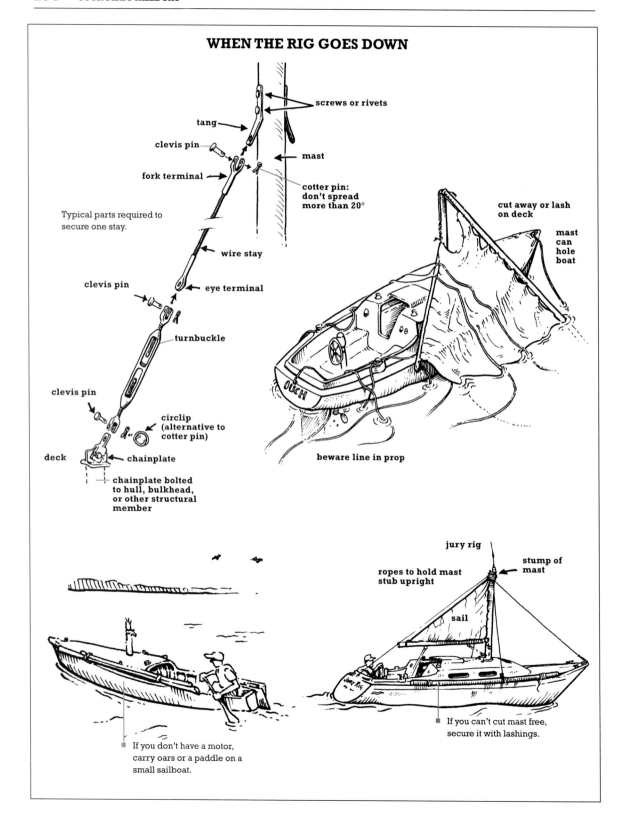

screws or rivets

tang

clevis pin

fork terminal

mast

cotter pin:
don't spread
more than 20°

Typical parts required to
secure one stay.

wire stay

eye terminal

clevis pin

turnbuckle

clevis pin

circlip
(alternative to
cotter pin)

deck

chainplate

chainplate bolted
to hull, bulkhead,
or other structural
member

cut away or lash
on deck

mast
can
hole
boat

beware line in prop

jury rig

stump of
mast

ropes to hold mast
stub upright

sail

If you don't have a motor,
carry oars or a paddle on a
small sailboat.

If you can't cut mast free,
secure it with lashings.

- Assuming that the mast has fallen overboard, secure it to keep it from causing additional damage. Try rope lashings.
- Determine whether you should bring the mast aboard and try to save it, or cut it loose and let it sink. The mast cannot be allowed to hit the hull repeatedly as the boat rolls in the waves.
- An important consideration in this decision is whether you need part of the mast to make a jury rig. Mast stumps, or the shorter of the two broken sections, can be useful. I say the shorter section because you probably won't be able to raise a long, heavy section. But the longer the piece you can raise, the more sail you can set, and the faster your passage home will be.
- If your decision is to cut everything loose, hopefully you have foreseen this possibility and are carrying heavy-duty wire cutters or a heavy hammer and punch to drive out clevis pins. The cotter pins restraining the clevis pins should not have been spread more than 20 degrees, or they will be hard to remove.
- Without the inertia of the mast, the boat will roll more quickly, perhaps violently. Take seasickness remedies as soon as you can catch your breath.
- After you are sure all lines are out of the water or gone, start the engine and head toward shore. If you are a long way from land, use the engine to orient the boat in the most comfortable attitude possible. Now you will have to use your ingenuity to figure out how to propel the boat home. There are books illustrating ways to do this (see the resources section as well as the illustration opposite); if you are heading offshore, read one before you go.

What If the Boat Starts to Sink?

34

We're really into worst-case scenario paranoia now! It's everyone's nightmare: the boat is sinking and there's no help in sight. Maybe you're trapped in the cabin with your lips planted on the overhead, sucking air like a guppy.

Forget it! Ain't gonna happen.

But once in a blue moon, a boat does sink. So suppose that you're at the helm, and someone down below calls up, "Hey, there's water over the floorboards. You'd better come have a look." Although not an everyday occurrence, thankfully, it's not uncommon to discover a leak in the boat.

A friend related a typical story. He and his sailing partner had dismantled the manual bilge pump for cleaning, and they forgot to retighten the hoses. The outlet hose on their boat exited through a transom fitting. A few days later, they went sailing and spent a glorious day off the Maine coast. Returning to their mooring required motoring up a river a few miles. Motoring into an ebb tide made the stern squat, submerging the transom bilge pump fitting and thereby letting water into the boat. The boys were enjoying a beer or two and reveling in their day, oblivious to the mounting threat. Only when one went below to grab some sail ties did he notice that the boat was half-full of water. Fortunately, they diagnosed the source quickly, and no real harm was done. (Except to their pride . . .)

If this happens to you, here's what to do:

- Put the boat on autopilot or give the helm to someone else.
- Pull up the floorboards to see if you can identify the source of the incoming water.
- Taste the water. If it's fresh (and you're in salt water), suspect a leak in the water tank. Whew!
- Check the propeller shaft stuffing box for leakage. This is a common source of water ingress. In fact, conventional stuffing boxes intentionally leak water as part of the lubricating process. As the packing flax wears, the gland must be tightened; if not, the rate of water incursion increases.
- Check the rudder stock stuffing box for leakage. This is probably under the cock-

pit and may be difficult to access. Think about that when you stow stuff back there.

- If none of the above applies, stop and think about the location of all your through-hulls. Many skippers keep a record of their locations in the ship's log. These bronze or reinforced plastic flanged pipe fittings in the hull, to which hoses are connected either to drain water from sinks and showers or to admit seawater, can include the following:

    sink drain
    engine raw-water intake
    cockpit scuppers
    toilet flush water source
    toilet discharge

    Check each of these fittings. There should be a positive-action valve, called a *seacock*, mounted on each through-hull. Turn it to the "off" position while you hunt. A hose may have slipped off the end of a seacock. A hose may have split. Hoses are the most likely culprit.

- Raw-water-cooled engines have seawater circulating throughout their insides. Remove the engine compartment cover and look for signs of water weeping from areas such as the water pump.
- Check the exhaust manifold and water-cooled muffler.

These are the most logical sources of leakage because they are places where water has intentionally been brought into the boat. If none yields the answer, begin to suspect other sources, such as a crack in the hull or, in a wooden boat, a bad seam. To search for hull failures, you may need to remove bunk boards and backrests.

If the boat has been taking green water over the deck, the source could be an opening in the deck or cabin: a hatch, a portlight, or loose hardware.

Once the source has been verified, be prepared to:

- Caulk the opening with a tube of something, such as silicone or polysulfide sealant. Adhesion on a wet surface may be a problem.
- Smear a two-part epoxy putty that can cure underwater into the crack.
- Tack the boat if the source of the leak can be raised out of the water by doing so.
- Shut the seacock on a leaking through-hull. If it is the raw-water intake for cooling the engine, you won't be able to run the engine until the problem is fixed.
- Replace the hose if there is no seacock or other valve on the through-hull to stop water (this would be a serious no-no, however; all underwater through-hulls MUST have seacocks).
- If the seacock itself is leaking, remove the hose and pound a tapered wooden plug into the opening.
- Cover a crack in the hull from the outside with canvas or other fabric. Commercial "collision mats" are sold for this purpose.

Oh, and did I say to turn on the electric bilge pump? If this pump can't keep up with water coming in, start working the manual pump, too. If pumping requires the entire crew, searching for the leak may have to be done at intervals when a pump can be left for a few minutes. It is said that the best bilge pump is a scared crew with a bucket.

As a last resort, close the raw-water intake for the engine cooling, remove its hose, and run the engine, which now will use bilge water for cooling, expelling it through the exhaust.

And if all else fails, send a Mayday via single-sideband (SSB) or VHF radio, activate your EPIRB (emergency position-indicating radio beacon), and get the life raft ready.

TYPICAL BOAT PLUMBING AND SOME COMMON SOURCES OF LEAKS

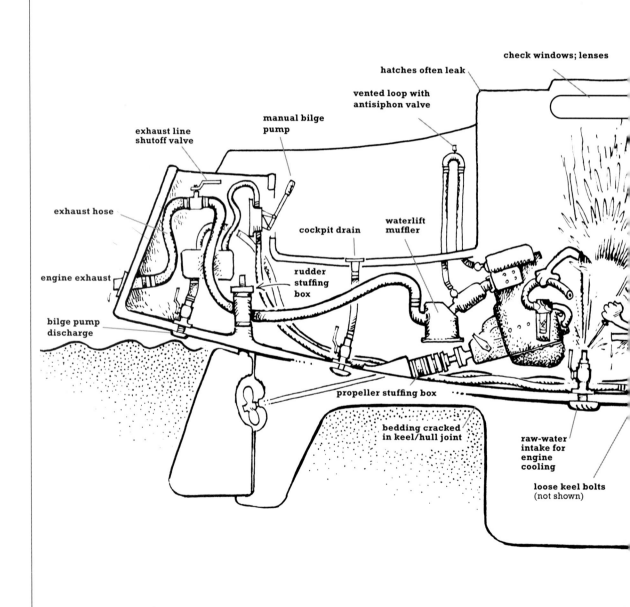

check windows; lenses

hatches often leak

vented loop with
antisiphon valve

exhaust line
shutoff valve

manual bilge
pump

exhaust hose

waterlift
muffler

cockpit drain

engine exhaust

rudder
stuffing
box

bilge pump
discharge

propeller stuffing box

bedding cracked
in keel/hull joint

raw-water
intake for
engine
cooling

loose keel bolts
(not shown)

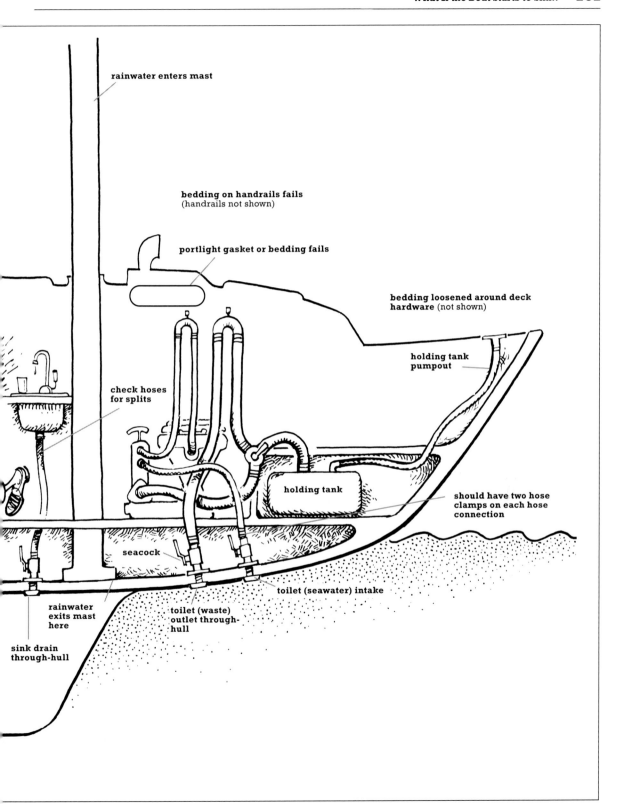

rainwater enters mast

bedding on handrails fails
(handrails not shown)

portlight gasket or bedding fails

bedding loosened around deck
hardware (not shown)

holding tank
pumpout

check hoses
for splits

holding tank

should have two hose
clamps on each hose
connection

seacock

toilet (seawater) intake

rainwater
exits mast
here

toilet (waste)
outlet through-
hull

sink drain
through-hull

TYPICAL STUFFING BOX

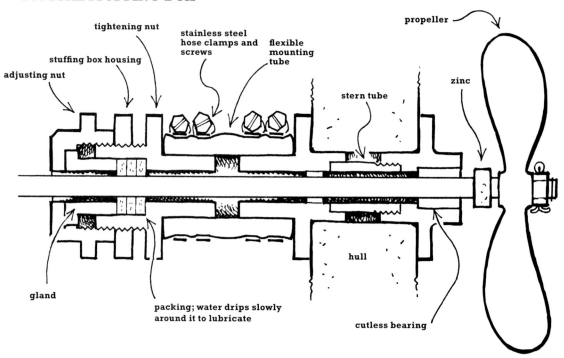

adjusting nut

stuffing box housing

tightening nut

stainless steel
hose clamps and
screws

flexible
mounting
tube

stern tube

propeller

zinc

hull

gland

packing; water drips slowly
around it to lubricate

cutless bearing

DESPERATE MEASURES

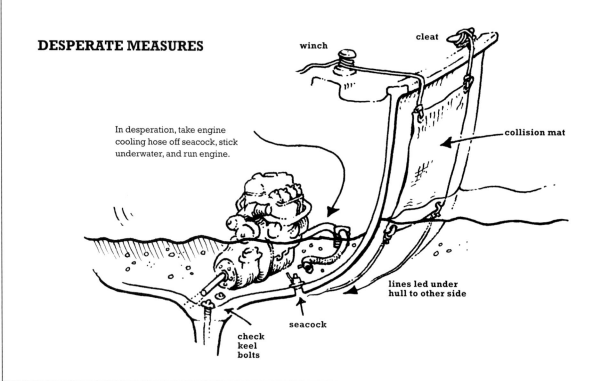

winch

cleat

In desperation, take engine
cooling hose off seacock, stick
underwater, and run engine.

collision mat

lines led under
hull to other side

seacock

check
keel
bolts

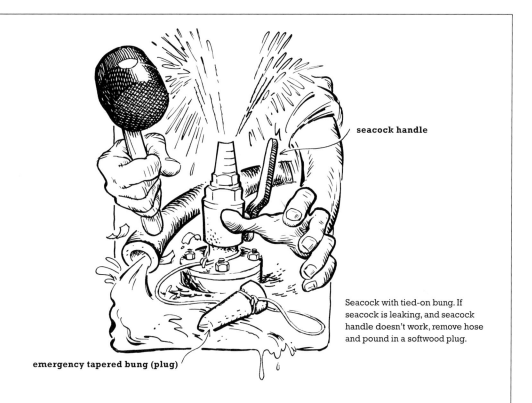

seacock handle

Seacock with tied-on bung. If seacock is leaking, and seacock handle doesn't work, remove hose and pound in a softwood plug.

emergency tapered bung (plug)

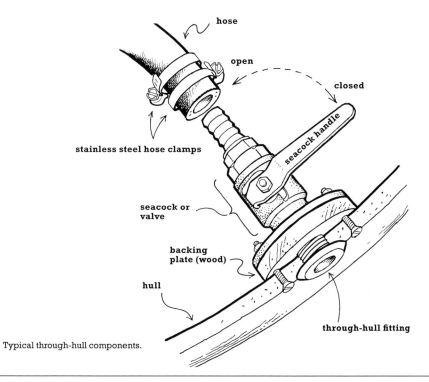

hose

open

closed

seacock handle

stainless steel hose clamps

seacock or valve

backing plate (wood)

hull

through-hull fitting

Typical through-hull components.

What If the Boat Does Sink?

35

The general rule is to stay with the boat . . . as long as it floats. Obviously, you don't want to stay with your vessel if it's heading toward the bottom.

Daysailers

Most small, open boats have sufficient flotation (usually foam packed into the bow and stern, and under the seats) to keep the boat afloat even when full of water or upside down.

- If you are not already wearing a life jacket, put one on now.
- Stay with the boat. Hang onto any part of the boat that is convenient and easy.
- Staying dry will be difficult. Water saps more body heat than air, so if you can perch yourself on the overturned hull, so much the better.
- If possible, right the boat according to the instructions given in chapter 21.
- Do not try to swim to shore unless it is very close or you have waited a long time

and believe that survival dictates taking this risk.

Keelboats

Most keelboats do not have sufficient flotation to keep them afloat when full of water. There are a few exceptions, such as the Etap line of small cruising sailboats built in Belgium, which are packed with foam. The trade-off is loss of stowage space.

If the boat is upside down with sufficient air trapped inside, it may float for a period of time. In rough weather, portlights, hatches, and companionways must be kept closed and positively latched.

A boat that has lost its keel may float indefinitely owing to the buoyancy of the interior wood work, hull core, other parts, and trapped air.

Nevertheless, you should be prepared for the fact that a swamped keelboat will eventually sink, perhaps quickly.

Therefore:
- Activate your EPIRB.
- Make Mayday calls on all radios and com-

munication devices available—VHF, SSB, satellite phone, cell phone, and so on. Identify yourself and your boat, and give your location.

- Make a Mayday call by any digital means available, such as by computer via satellite service (mini M, and so on). Identify yourself and your boat, and give your location.
- Launch your life raft and tether it to the boat.
- Get in the life raft, even if the boat hasn't sunk yet, because the tether may snap and allow the raft to blow away.

- Sever the tether when it is apparent that the boat is sinking.
- Survival experts say the best thing you can do now is to retain confidence in yourself. Remember that Steve Callahan, author of *Adrift* (see the resources section), spent 76 days in a raft, essentially subsisting on raw fish. If you've planned well, you have an abandon-ship bag aboard the raft that contains water, watermaker, signal mirror, flares, fishhooks, space blanket, and other essentials.

What If Someone Gets Hurt or Falls Overboard?

36

Treating injuries suffered on a boat is not much different from the first-aid procedures that could be required when camping or at any locale removed from nearby medical facilities. Probably the most common injuries are burns (say, from a galley stove), concussions (perhaps suffered when hit by the boom during a jibe), and cuts (bare feet striking cotter pins in the rigging, knife accidents, and so on). First-aid training is certainly an advantage when you're called upon to deliver effective treatment, and everyone can profit from a course in CPR (cardiopulmonary resuscitation). Lacking formal training, reading or at least carrying a basic first-aid handbook is smart. There are a number of good medical books written by sailing doctors especially for sailors (see the resources section). Buy one.

Crew Overboard

I've never had a crew member fall overboard, but once I did encounter a dicey situation with a crew member in the water unattached to the boat. It was a hot, calm day, and we were taking turns towing each other behind the boat. Our

speed was about 2 knots. When it was Dave's turn, he jumped in and treaded water while looking for the long line we were trailing behind the boat.

As the line started passing him by, I yelled, "Grab the line!"

He called back, "I can't see it!"

"Just to your left!" I said. "Just reach out and you'll feel it."

He didn't move. I couldn't figure out why.

Then the bitter end of the line was past him.

"I'll come back around," I called.

"Better hurry!" Dave yelled. "I can't swim!"

Can't swim?! He had no life jacket! I couldn't believe it. How could he do such a stupid thing?!

Dave's sister jumped in with a flotation cushion and swam to him while I brought the boat around, which took a few minutes. Back on board, we asked Dave what on earth he was thinking, jumping in without a life jacket when he couldn't swim.

"Grabbing the line seemed so easy," he said. "I watched everyone else do it and figured I could, too. Once I was in the water, though, I panicked."

QUICK STOP

1. Regardless of the point of sail, the boat is brought hard on the wind.

2. The boat is tacked, leaving the headsail sheeted to windward.

3, 4, 5. Sail back to the person, aiming for a point just to windward.

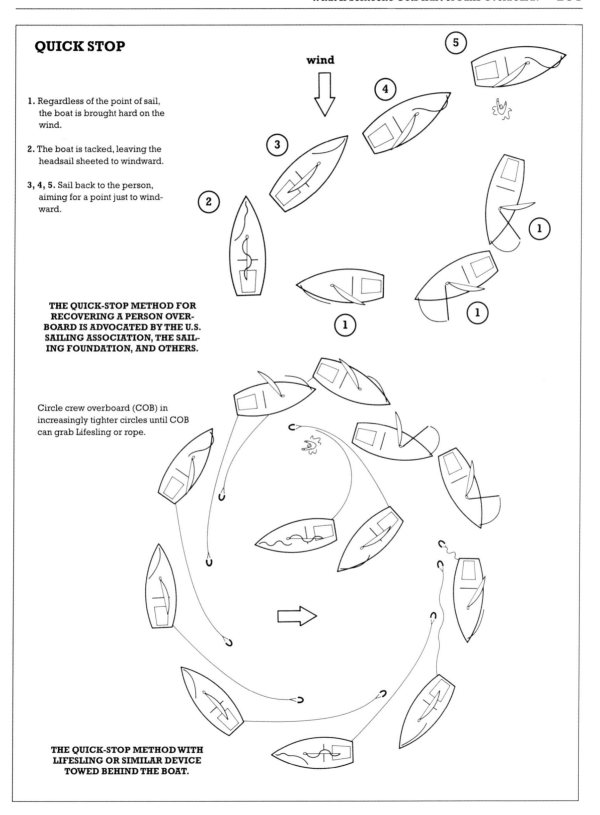

THE QUICK-STOP METHOD FOR RECOVERING A PERSON OVERBOARD IS ADVOCATED BY THE U.S. SAILING ASSOCIATION, THE SAILING FOUNDATION, AND OTHERS.

Circle crew overboard (COB) in increasingly tighter circles until COB can grab Lifesling or rope.

THE QUICK-STOP METHOD WITH LIFESLING OR SIMILAR DEVICE TOWED BEHIND THE BOAT.

TWO WAYS TO HOIST SOMEONE ABOARD

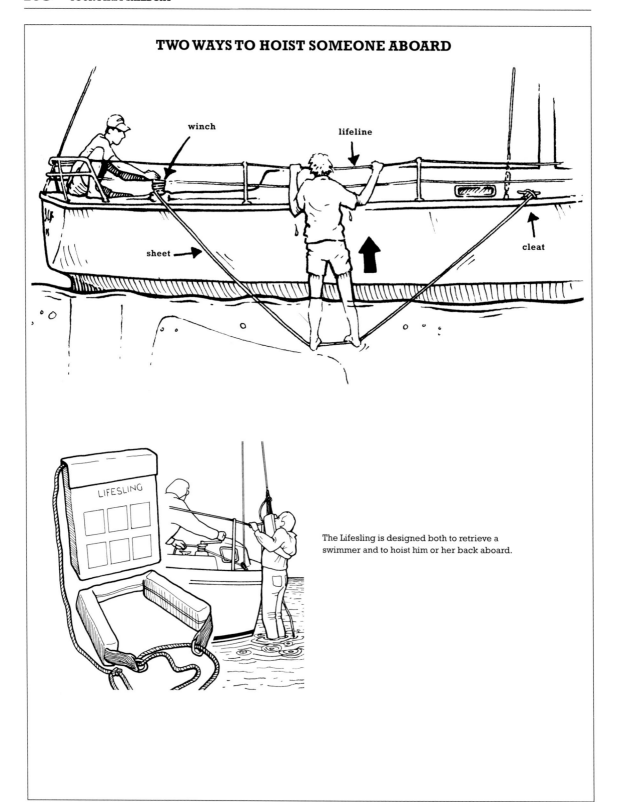

winch

lifeline

sheet

cleat

The Lifesling is designed both to retrieve a swimmer and to hoist him or her back aboard.

LIFESLING

Fortunately, this story had a happy ending.

Whether in a lake or the ocean, there's a fairly standard tactic for dealing with crew-overboard (COB) situations. Here are the essentials:

- As soon as you know that a person is in the water, call out, "Crew overboard!" (Or yell "Man overboard!" or "Woman overboard!" This is no time for gender correctness.)
- As skipper, direct another crew member (if there is one) to point at the COB and keep pointing. It is easy to lose sight of a person, especially in waves or darkness.
- If there is a GPS handy, hit the COB (more likely MOB) button. This freezes the location, enabling you to return to it with some degree of precision.
- Throw anything that floats in the direction of the COB: cushion, horseshoe flotation aid, MOM (Man Overboard Module—an automatically inflating module with air-filled horseshoe and flag)—anything.
- Tack the boat to return to the COB. Approach from downwind, just as you would a dock or mooring. If necessary, drop your sails and start the motor.
- Alternatively, execute a specific maneuver known as the *Quick Stop*: throw the helm over (tiller away from you) as in a tack, but do not unsheet the jib. As the boat passes through the eye of the wind, the jib will backwind, pulling the boat around onto the new tack. Aim for the COB.
- If there is crew available, drop the jib. If there is no crew to help, leave it backed for the moment unless it tries to force your course away from the COB; in that case, cast off the jibsheet and let it flap.
- Deploy a Lifesling or a floating (polypropylene) line with a float at its end (a fender works).

- Continue to circle the COB until the Lifesling is within his or her reach. The COB should pull the flotation harness over his head and fit it under his arms.
- Pull the COB to the boat and help him aboard. A block and tackle may be necessary if the COB is too weak to help or if the freeboard is too high for onboard crew lifting without aid. Secure the COB to the boat with his head supported above water by any means available while you rig other means to hoist the person aboard. This is a critical maneuver that must be planned and practiced in advance. I know of several people who drowned right by the boat because they could not be brought aboard in time.

Hindsight is, of course, 20/20. The odds of successfully retrieving a COB are increased if the weather is calm (often it's bad weather that causes the accident), if the accident occurs in bright daylight, if a marker is quickly deployed, and if the COB is a good swimmer wearing a life jacket. Remove any one of these factors and the odds diminish rapidly.

Life jackets should be equipped with whistles and (if sailing at night) with small, personal, waterproof lights.

Several skippers with whom I've made offshore passages begin each trip by tossing a floating object into the water and yelling, "Someone has just fallen overboard! We're losing him at the rate of 10 feet per second. Let's get him!"

And they're not kidding. The rest of us know it's a drill, but we react as if there's a life in danger. No one rests until the plastic milk bottle is safely back on board. We all know that next time it could be one of us.

What If the Engine Won't Start?

I f you don't have an engine, you won't have to worry about this vexing but predictable eventuality.

If your boat does have an engine, you expect it to work. And when it doesn't, it's an aggravation, to say the least.

Entire books deal with the principles of internal combustion (or "infernal combustion," as it's often called), the parts such as cylinders and valves that make it happen, and the complicated tests that must be performed to troubleshoot failures. This brief treatment of the subject describes only the most obvious causes and solutions.

Gasoline Engines

Combustion requires three things: fuel, air, and a spark to ignite the combination of the two. Troubleshooting should verify that all three of these things are present:

- Is there fuel in the tank? If not, fill the tank.
- Is there fuel in the carburetor? If not, check, clean, and possibly replace fuel filter(s).

- If you answer yes to both of the preceding questions, there probably is fuel in the cylinder (combustion chamber).
- Is the air filter clogged? If yes, clean or replace.
- Do the spark plugs emit sparks? To be sure, remove a spark plug, reattach the wire, and lay the plug on the engine so that the metal part of the plug that your socket fits over is touching engine metal (to ground it). Do not touch the wire or plug because they may give you a small shock. Have someone turn the engine over with the ignition key. Any spark emitted should be evident unless viewed in direct sunlight.
- If in doubt about the condition of the spark plugs, replace them. Dirt and carbon may have fouled the electrode, or the gap may be incorrect.
- If the engine still fails to start, you'll have to investigate the previous three areas more deeply: fuel quality, ignition timing, and so on.

ENGINE MAINTENANCE TASKS

TASK	FREQUENCY
Check oil level; add oil if necessary. Check to be sure oil has no gooey white substance; change if necessary.	Before starting engine.
Check (listen and look) for presence of water in exhaust as it exits through-hull. If you don't hear/see it, shut off engine.	When starting engine, and periodically when engine is running.
Check and clean seawater strainer.	Before starting engine first time each day.
Check engine cooling water level. Add distilled water as necessary.	Once a week; more frequently if leak is suspected.
Check vented loop antisiphon valve.	Once a month.
Add antibacterial substance to fuel.	When adding fuel as directed on additive bottle.
Change oil and filter.	As recommended by engine manufacturer, or about every 100 hours.
Change fuel filters.	As recommended by engine manufacturer, or about every 150 hours.
Replace heat exchanger zinc.	Depends on boat and environment, or between once a month and once every two years.
Adjust valves.	As recommended by engine manufacturer, or about every 600 hours.
Check tightness of hose clamps and engine hoses for wear. Replace as necessary.	Once a year.
Check seawater through-hull and seacock, and exhaust through-hull and seacock. Replace as necessary.	During haulout; close and inspect once a month.
Replace spark plugs (gasoline only).	As recommended by engine manufacturer, or about every two years.
Replace impeller in impeller pump.	As needed, or once every 2,000 hours.
Replace injectors.	As recommended by engine manufacturer, or about every 2,000 to 4,000 hours.
Change engine cooling water and antifreeze.	When you buy boat and then every two years.

Diesel Engines

Diesel engines require the same three ingredients for combustion as gasoline, but the spark is derived not from a spark plug but from super-heating the fuel-air mixture inside the cylinder. Therefore, there is no spark plug or electric ignition system, which greatly simplifies the diesel engine.

- Most diesel problems have to do with fuel, which must be clean.
- Drain fuel filters of any collected sludge. There should be two filters: a primary and a secondary. Be careful not to let air enter the fuel line while cleaning.
- Air in the fuel lines will prevent the engine from starting. Consult your engine manual for instructions on how to bleed the system. This process involves slightly unscrewing bolts at several locations on the engine to let air escape. To force the air out, the fuel pump must be operated. On some engines, this can be done manually or possibly electrically. If neither is available, the engine will have to be turned over with the start key. Most manuals advise that you turn the compression levers on each cylinder so that the engine doesn't accidentally start. After solid fuel is coming out of all the checkpoints, turn the compression levers back and start the engine.
- In cold weather, diesel engines are more difficult to start because the fuel is colder. Many diesels are fitted with preheat devices that use an electrical charge to warm the fuel before actually trying to start the engine. Press the preheat button the recommended length of time, then try to start the engine.

If you are out sailing and trying to return to a dock or mooring when the engine won't start, you may have to execute the maneuver under sail (see chapter 22). Think through your plan carefully. Make sure that your crew knows what to do. Go slowly. Everything will be fine.

When the boat is secure, find a good mechanic to diagnose and fix the problem. If at all possible, be present to watch him work. Next time, maybe you can make the repair yourself.

Performing recommended maintenance dramatically reduces problems. Be nice to your engine and it will be nice to you.

What If the Wind Stops Blowing?

The short answer is this: that's why even sailboats have engines.

But not all sailboats do, of course; and besides, engines, although not as fickle as the wind, are known to quit, too (see chapter 37).

Daysailers

This class of small, open boats, which might range from 7 feet to, say, 20-plus feet, can be subdivided, with each category having its own possibilities for auxiliary power as well as its inherent limitations.

Very small boats, such as sailing dinghies, can be rowed when the wind fails. Furl the sail, maybe even break down the two-part mast to reduce windage, stow as best you can, and put your back to it, laddie!

Boats without oarlocks can be propelled with a paddle, though they probably won't track like a canoe because they require constant shifting from side to side.

Even an 8-foot sailing dinghy, however, can be propelled by an electric or gasoline motor. One and 2 hp outboard motors that weigh just 30 pounds will fit on the flat transom. A motor probably isn't something you want to take with you every time you go out, but if you're cruising on a larger boat, a small outboard for the dinghy is a good option for when you might be traveling a long distance from the mother boat and want to guarantee a timely return. An electric trolling motor will work, too, though the weight and space of a sufficiently large battery must be factored in. An advantage of an electric motor is that it will prove more reliable than microgasoline motors. I once built a $1\frac{1}{2}$ hp motor from a kit and although it ran, albeit sporadically, it was the devil to live with.

Larger daysailers, such as the Rhodes 19 or O'Day Day Sailer, are easily fitted with a 2 to 4 hp outboard motor. Though there is always a performance penalty for added weight, the security of knowing that you can power home when the afternoon sea breeze fails may make it a worthwhile trade-off.

Even on these boats, do not dismiss the alternative of oars. They can be stowed under the side deck and are much lighter, quieter, less smelly, and less expensive than an outboard. Good exercise, too.

Three other options when the sails go perfectly slack: use the rudder to move the boat by pushing the tiller from side to side, with judicious pauses in between; push and pull on a single sculling oar fitted to the transom, like a Venetian gondolier—romantic and effective; or swim the boat to shore. The latter isn't always practical or sensible, but sailors are frequently neither.

Keelboats

Not everyone believes that auxiliary engines are necessary on larger keelboats. World cruisers (and authors—see the resources section) Lin and Larry Pardey, for example, eschew engines due to their smell, cost, and space hogging. Of course, their largest boat is less than 30 feet long. A pair of sweeps (long oars) can propel a moderately heavy boat in calm conditions. With any kind of breeze, the Pardeys sail. In calm air, a foul tide might easily overpower oar power, so you have to be careful not to get into sketchy situations. And you have to believe that the Pardeys have spent more than one unwanted night at sea.

Inventive cruisers also have been known to lash their dinghies to their big boats, then maneuver both by means of the dinghy outboard, which is much smaller, lighter, and less expensive than a big gasoline or diesel auxiliary for the big boat.

If the wind and auxiliary die together, there's little choice but to sit and wait.

Here are a few things you might do:
■ Call a tow service. Agree on the fee beforehand and beware of any form that mentions salvage rights.
■ Set an anchor if there is any chance that waves or current might push you toward shoal water.
■ Use the boat's lights or a flashlight to alert other vessels to your presence.

Getting stuck out on the water with no means of propulsion isn't much fun. After it happens a few times, you'll figure out how to avoid it in the future. In the meantime, as you sit roasting in the summer sun with the sails slatting and the flies buzzing, put a positive spin on it, for your crew's sake, if not your own:

"Hey, you're always whining about the world turning too fast!"

"I thought you said you wanted to slow down!"

"You said I never stop to smell the roses . . . well, sorry about the roses, but how about that sea air?"

"What a great time to meditate. Ommmmm . . ."

How Do I Know When It's Time for My Next Boat?

Believe me, you'll know! And don't feel guilty. Most people keep their first boat just a few years. The more you sail, the more you learn. And learning clarifies your interests and predilections. At the suggestion of a friend, you may have started out racing Hobie catamarans, only to discover that competition makes you nervous. Or quite the opposite could occur: your first boat may have been a pokey family boat, which you find frankly boring.

For most of you, however, the feeling inside for a new boat will be as strong, clear, and undeniable as falling in love.

One or more of the following symptoms may manifest itself:

- Your boat feels small and slow.
- You bought an old wooden boat cheap and have no idea how to caulk seams, remove dry rot, or sand and varnish brightwork to a fare-thee-well . . . and you have no desire to learn.
- There is an active fleet of Sonars on the lake and you want to join—except that you own an O'Day Javelin, and no one has ever heard of it.
- Another boat catches your eye. It seems to you as lovely and perfect as the Venus de Milo. Her sheer! Her bow! Surely they were sculpted by da Vinci!
- You find yourself studying boat brochures at the dinner table, at bedtime, or in the bathroom, and carrying them to work concealed in your briefcase.
- Your spouse says she won't spend another night on a boat unless it has a private head (bathroom).
- Your spouse hits his head on the companionway hatch for the third time in one day and says he won't go cruising again until you buy a boat with standing headroom.
- You find yourself wondering if there's enough equity in your house to finance a Princess 36.
- You begin to nitpick your current boat and start rationalizing: "Well, it needs new sails and settee cushions. Then there's the scratch in the hull. She's 12 years old, after all . . . why throw good money after bad?"

- You haven't won a race in three years, and it's getting harder to pull a crew together, even though you're buying better beer than you used to.
- Whenever possible, you wander through boatyards and down docks admiring other people's boats. Especially that Pearson Triton—she's a classic!
- Your son and daughter refuse to share the same cabin.
- Your wife announces that the family size will again be expanding.
- You feel like quitting work and going cruising.

The Sailboat Guide

One of the best things about buying a boat is the search. I like to look at boats. Nautical tire kicking as it were. There are so many types of boats to consider, so many fantasies to feed. Even with the boat stuck on dry land ("on the hard") you can hike out with your back over the "water," pretending you're about to get the gun at your first regatta. Stand at the helm seeing yourself piloting through coral reefs into the lagoon of Bora Bora. Walk forward and lean against the mast, imagining yourself barreling along on a flat, blue sea with dolphins in the bow wave and no land in sight. Go below and lie in the bunks, listening to the thrum of the rigging.

Then the questions arise:

Like, how much time—and money—do I want to spend on this boat? A major appeal of the daysailer is its simplicity—likely there are no electrical, mechanical, or plumbing systems to break down, and the rig is straightforward. They are far less expensive to own than larger boats, and most can be trailered and stowed in the backyard. Daysailers are quick, too, though part of it is just feel, because you sit closer to the water than on larger boats. But their speed is real, too, and those daysailers that plane are faster than almost any keelboat. Quick to get under way and quick to tidy up at the end of a sail, the daysailer is the recommended type of boat on which to learn to sail.

Whenever I'm looking at boats to buy I remember times like when I was sailing across Lake Michigan in an Aquarius 23 trailer sailer, when it was so cold that I shivered even though fully dressed inside my sleeping bag. In the early morning hours we were passed by a gentleman in a Fisher 30 motor sailer who saluted us through the pilothouse window with his cup of coffee. Envy has fixed that image with me for nearly 30 years. But whenever I've confided to friends my secret love of motor sailers, they've always chided me. "You're not old enough for a motor sailer!" I guess the general attitude is that motor sailers are retirement boats. Bah.

Then I recall the versatility of the trailer sailer that allowed me to be on that crossing that morning, and how those I've owned have enabled me to explore areas of the country so far apart that one could never hope to visit them all in a big boat. Some of my Montana friends regularly trailer their Montgomery 15 and MacGregor 26 all over the place: to the San Juan Islands in Washington State one year, down to the Sea of Cortez in Mexico the next, then to the Chesapeake Bay and Florida Keys. For them, and most of us, it would be prohibitively expensive to truck a large, fixed keelboat to those destinations.

The third category of boats we've discussed is the catch-all general-purpose. These are the mainstream designs conceived with the needs of the average owner in mind; most aren't intended to cross oceans or make maximum speed across a lake. Rather, they are comfortable, safe boats, usually designed with the family in mind. They are stable, roomy, and sail well enough to keep you satisfied. Compared to full-blown cruisers, all-out racers, and multihulls, the general-purpose boat (cruiser/racer or racer/cruiser, whatever you want to call it) is moderately priced. In the United States, Catalina and Hunter sell more boats than anyone else, and that's largely because they are positioned at the low end of the moderate price point.

When I think about exotic ports of call, I begin to think outside of the United States—the West Indies, the Mediterranean Sea, and the South Pacific. Though small, open boats and lightly built trailerable boats have made impressive ocean passages, they are risky. Give me a stout cruising boat with refrigeration, an autopilot, and a versatile rig that can handle everything from calms to gales. These boats are becoming increasingly complex, however, and you must be prepared to educate yourself in their modes of operation, maintenance, and repair. There is a lot to learn to successfully manage the modern cruising boat; for gearheads, that's half the fun, and the challenge.

But cruising boats can be sluggish. They're solid, but generally slow. (Recent lighter-weight performance cruisers come at a price—reduced stowage.) Maybe I'd prefer a lightweight racer that keeps moving in light air when other boats are dead in the water. I could dig that. As designer Bill Lee says, "Fast is fun." And as long as I'm quoting famous people, multihull designer Dick Newick says, "People sail for fun and no one has yet convinced me that it's more fun to go slow than it is to go fast." And if you get off on competition, round-the-buoys racing is a sport of great skill and intelligence that can bewitch and confound you for the rest of your years.

You can cruise or race a multihull as well. They are more expensive, but they also have more room and a much different motion that is faster and jerkier. Handling a multihull requires a bit of relearning of sailing skills, such as knowing when the boat is overpowered and maintaining way through a tack. Ah, but their speed and lack of heel are so appealing! And the lightest catamarans and trimarans can sail at the speed of the wind. While it is true of any boat that longer is generally better (faster, more comfortable, and more stable), it is especially true of multihulls.

I've chosen 75 boats representative of the six categories we've discussed. All have virtues, all have vices. Some are faster than others, some more comfortable, some of higher construction quality. Both new and used models are included, as are as their prices and builder contacts, if available. A great service of the Internet is the burgeoning of owner groups and forums, where you can ask questions, share experiences, and enjoy the camaraderie of other owners who, like you, were drawn to a particular boat.

Make looking fun. Collect brochures. Talk to other sailors. Read magazines and books. Look at pictures. Test-sail when and what you can. And when you find your boat, make an offer. If it's more money than you can afford to lose, make the deal contingent on the boat passing a survey. Never fool yourself into thinking you can detect all its problems yourself. Even if you have the skill and experience, you lack the impartiality necessary to look coldly at the flaws.

OPTIMIST INTERNATIONAL

With more than 100,000 of these sailing worldwide, the International Optimist is perhaps the most popular sail trainer ever designed. (*International* here and elsewhere means the class is sanctioned by the International Sailing Federation—ISAF.) Sometimes called a Florida orange crate, this boxy little pram dinghy is especially popular with yacht clubs for their junior sailing programs. Kids begin sailing the Opti at around age 6 and progress through the Green, White, and Blue fleets as they grow older. By 14, they're ready for a bigger boat and more excitement. As the class association says, this is the boat the youth of the world learn to sail in. Single- or double-handed, it's hard to find a simpler, less-expensive boat on which to learn to sail. Builders licensed by the class association include H & H, Russell, McLaughlin, Winner, Johnson, Camet, Lange, and Vanguard.

LOA	7'8"
BEAM	3'10"
DRAFT	6"–2'6" (CB UP, CB DOWN)
WEIGHT	65 LB.
SAIL AREA	35 SQ. FT.
DESIGNER	CLARK MILLS
PRICE NEW	$2,550 (VANGUARD)
PRICE USED	$1,000–$1,300
CONTACT	VANGUARD SAILBOATS
	300 HIGHPOINT AVE.
	PORTSMOUTH RI 02871
	800-966-SAIL (800-966-7245)
	WWW.TEAMVANGUARD.COM
	INTERNATIONAL OPTIMIST
	DINGHY ASSOC.
	BALSCADDEN VIEW, ABBEY ST.
	HOWTH
	DUBLIN
	IRELAND
	FAX: 353-1-839-4528
	E-MAIL: 100540.2646@
	COMPUSERVE.COM
	WWW.OPTIWORLD.ORG
SIMILAR BOATS	AMERICAN SAIL DINK
	CATALINA U.S. SABOT
	HUNTER CLUB TRAINER

ESCAPE RHUMBA

Designed by Garry Hoyt, founder of Freedom Yachts, who has made it his mission in life to simplify sailing, the rotomolded polyethylene Escape line of small sailboats features the AutoSail Self-Teaching Sailing System and SmartRig rigging scheme that allows you to instantly adjust sail size. The aft cockpit features sculptured bucket seats with good lower back support. Other features include self-draining cockpits, drink holders, mast steps, mast and boom that securely lock into the boat during use, high-visibility safety yellow hull, and two-piece mast. Sailing doesn't get much easier than with an Escape. It's a great boat to learn on, and it's hard to hurt.

LOA	12'9"
BEAM	5'0"
DRAFT	3'3" (CB DOWN)
WEIGHT	150 LB.
SAIL AREA	N/A
DESIGNER	GARRY HOYT
PRICE NEW	$2,599
PRICE USED	$1,700–$2,050 (1999 MODEL) $2,250–$2,650 (2001 MODEL)
CONTACT	ESCAPE SAILBOATS JOHNSON OUTDOOR WATERCRAFT SPORTS AND LEISURE GROUP 4855 BROADMOOR SE GRAND RAPIDS MI 49512 800-552-6287 WWW.JOWATERCRAFT.COM
SIMILAR BOATS	WINDRIDER 10 HOBIE BRAVO 12 CATALINA EXPO 12.5

SUPER SNARK

The Snark has been around since the 1960s, and its low, low price has encouraged many people to learn to sail on their own boat. During the 1970s, a cigarette company sold the boats for $100 with its logo on the sail. Now the white-and-yellow-striped hull carries the logo of a sunflower. One reason the Snark is priced so low is that its hull is not fiberglass; instead, it is foam that is covered with a tough ABS plastic. The foam makes the hull unsinkable—a reassuring safety feature—but beware of damaged areas in which the covering has exposed the foam. The rig is called *lateen*, an ancient type used centuries ago by both Polynesian and Arabian sailors.

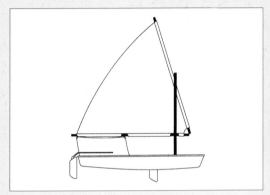

LOA	11'0"
BEAM	3'2"
DRAFT	6"–2'6" (CB UP, CB DOWN)
WEIGHT	50 LB.
SAIL AREA	45 SQ. FT.
DESIGNER	N/A
PRICE NEW	$699 (CASTLECRAFT)
PRICE USED	$100–$300
CONTACT	CASTLECRAFT P.O. BOX 3 BRAIDWOOD IL 60408 888-274-8490; 815-458-3590 WWW.CASTLECRAFT.US MEYERS BOAT CO. 343 LAWRENCE ST. ADRIAN MI 49221 800-247-6275; 517-265-9821 WWW.MEYERSBOAT.COM
SIMILAR BOATS	SUNFLOWER 3.3 (MEYERS BOAT CO.) SEA SKIMMER (MEYERS BOAT CO.) AQUA FINN (AMERICAN SAIL) SUNFISH (VANGUARD)

SUNFISH

Another 50-something sail trainer, the International Sunfish is probably the most popular sailboat ever produced. Originally developed as a paddleboard for lifesaving, Heyniger and Bryan stuck a sail on it and began building its predecessor, the Sailfish, for friends. A 1948 article in *Life* magazine brought fame and fortune to the two high school buddies. First built of mahogany plywood (many were completed from kits), the boats were converted to fiberglass in 1959. The Sunfish, which arrived in 1962, featured a small footwell that the Sailfish lacked. Both boats are a wet ride in any kind of chop and are best sailed in a bathing suit or shorts. The wooden boats are prone to leaking, and the centerboard trunk is difficult to seal. The fiberglass Sunfish is a durable, simple boat that's fun for persons of all ages, although bending to duck under the boom during tacks might dissuade some older sailors.

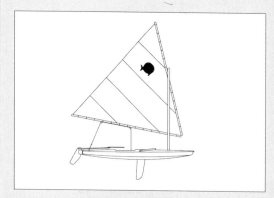

LOA	13'9"
BEAM	4'1"
DRAFT	2'1" (CB DOWN)
WEIGHT	120 LB.
SAIL AREA	75 SQ. FT.
DESIGNER	CORTLAND HEYNIGER AND ALEX BRYAN
PRICE NEW	$3,095
PRICE USED	$815–$980 (1992 MODEL)
	$2,300–$2,650 (1999 MODEL)
CONTACT	VANGUARD SAILBOATS 300 HIGHPOINT AVE. PORTSMOUTH RI 02871 800-966-SAIL (800-966-7245) WWW.TEAMVANGUARD.COM
	U.S. SUNFISH CLASS ASSOC. P.O. BOX 300128 WATERFORD MI 48330-0128 248-673-2750 WWW.SUNFISHCLASS.ORG
	INTERNATIONAL SUNFISH CLASS ASSOC. WWW.SUNFISHCLASS.ORG
SIMILAR BOATS	SUNFLOWER 3.3 (MEYERS BOAT CO.) SEA SKIMMER (MEYERS BOAT CO.) AQUA FINN (AMERICAN SAIL) SUPER SNARK (MEYERS BOAT CO.)

LASER (INTERNATIONAL)

The Laser was developed as an improvement on the lateen-rigged and somewhat sluggish Sunfish; upon its introduction in 1970, it was hailed as a "second generation, off-the-beach" fun boat. Many yacht clubs maintain a fleet of Lasers as a step up from the introductory Optimist. It's much faster than either the Optimist or Sunfish, but does require hiking out. The reward is the rush of getting the boat up on plane, "free" of the water, and accelerating rapidly. Children and adults enjoy sailing the Laser. While raced by one person, two can enjoy a leisurely sail. It's a great beachable boat to keep at the family cabin on the lake. Lasers compete in the Olympic Games.

LOA	13'10"
BEAM	4'6"
DRAFT	4" (CB UP)
WEIGHT	130 LB.
SAIL AREA	76 SQ. FT.
DESIGNER	BRUCE KIRBY
PRICE NEW	$4,790
PRICE USED	$920–$1,100 (1992 MODEL) $2,550–$2,950 (1999 MODEL)
CONTACT	VANGUARD SAILBOATS 300 HIGHPOINT AVE. PORTSMOUTH RI 02871 800-966-SAIL (800-966-7245) WWW.TEAMVANGUARD.COM INTERNATIONAL LASER CLASS ASSOC. OF NORTH AMERICA P.O. BOX 6120 ANNAPOLIS MD 21401 410-991-3719 WWW.LASER.ORG/ INTERNATIONAL LASER CLASS ASSOC. P.O. BOX 26 FALMOUTH TR11 3TN UNITED KINGDOM 44-1326-315064 WWW.LASERINTERNATIONAL.ORG
SIMILAR BOATS	TERN CATALINA WAVE BARNETT 1400 FORCE 5 ZUMA (VANGUARD)

AMERICAN 14.6

American Sail, founded in 1976, has built more than 20,000 boats. It specializes in boats for beginners. Its model line includes daysailers, board boats, catamarans, and sailing dinghies. The American 14.6 is made of hand-laid fiberglass and has foam flotation. The cockpit is self-bailing. It has a kick-up rudder and centerboard. The mast is stepped on a tabernacle (pivot pin), so that raising and lowering is made easier. A roller-furling jib, motor mount, and trailer are optional.

LOA	14'6"
LWL	13'5"
BEAM	6'2"
DRAFT	4"–3'6" (CB UP, CB DOWN)
WEIGHT	340 LB.
SAIL AREA	112 SQ. FT.
DESIGNER	AMERICAN SAIL INC.
PRICE NEW	$4,695
PRICE USED	$4,350–$5,000 (1999 MODEL) $5,100–$5,900 (2002 MODEL)
CONTACT	AMERICAN SAIL INC. 7350 PEPPERDAM AVE. CHARLESTON SC 29418 800-844-2399; 843-552-8548 WWW.AMERICANSAIL.COM
SIMILAR BOATS	CATALINA 14.2 HUNTER 140 LIDO 14 AMERICAN 14.6 PRECISION 15

SNIPE (INTERNATIONAL)

The Snipe was designed during the Great Depression (in 1931) for economical plywood construction, which is why it has a hard chine (a near-right angle between the sides of the boat and the bottom). Today, it is available in fiberglass. One of the most popular one-design classes, more than 20,000 are sailed worldwide. Spars can be wood or aluminum. In favorable conditions, the boat will plane. Because these boats have been around for a long, long time, used boats may be found at prices much lower than those for the boats listed above.

LOA	15'6"
BEAM	5'0"
DRAFT	6"–3'3" (CB UP, CB DOWN)
WEIGHT	400 LB.
SAIL AREA	116 SQ. FT.
DESIGNER	WILLIAM F. CROSBY
PRICE NEW	$8,000
PRICE USED	$3,750–$4,350 (1993 MODEL)
CONTACT	NICKELS BOAT WORKS
	2426 SOUTH LONG LAKE RD.
	FENTON MI 48430
	810-750-1855
	WWW.NICKELSBOATS.COM
	SNIPE CLASS INTERNATIONAL
	RACING ASSOC. (SCIRA) USA
	P.O. BOX 83866
	LINCOLN NE 68501
	WWW.SNIPEUS.ORG
	SNIPE CLASS INTERNATIONAL
	RACING ASSOC. (SCIRA)
	1833 TUSTIN ST.
	SAN DIEGO CA 92106
	619-224-6998
	WWW.SNIPE.ORG
SIMILAR BOATS	MUTINEER
	RHODES BANTAM
	WINDMILL

DAY SAILER

In 1958, Olympic gold medalist George O'Day commissioned the revered English designer Uffa Fox to design a good all-around family boat. The Day Sailer is just that—roomy, safe, and comfortable, with deep seats and good backrests. The O'Day Corporation built many good small boats because George O'Day believed that they are the best way to learn to sail, and are more fun to boot. Improvements to the original boat resulted in the Day Sailer II. When O'Day Corporation went out of business, the molds for the original Day Sailer changed hands several times. Today, the boat is built by Cape Cod Shipbuilders, under license from the Day Sailer Association, which owns the molds. The Day Sailer is eminently trailerable, easy to sail, and just big enough to keep you out of the water.

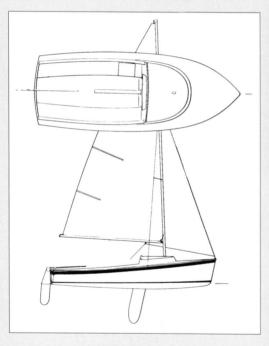

LOA	16'9"
LWL	16'0"
BEAM	6'3"
DRAFT	7"–3'9" (CB UP, CB DOWN)
WEIGHT	575 LB.
SAIL AREA	145 SQ. FT.
DESIGNER	UFFA FOX
PRICE NEW	$8,400–$11,330
PRICE USED	$1,500–$1,750 (1982 MODEL) $4,400–$5,050 (1991 MODEL)
CONTACT	CAPE COD SHIPBUILDING CO. P.O. BOX 152 7 NARROWS RD. WAREHAM MA 02571 508-295-3550 WWW.CAPECODSHIPBUILDING. COM THE DAY SAILER ASSOC. WWW.DAYSAILER.ORG
SIMILAR BOATS	CATALINA 16.5 HUNTER 170 PRECISION 185 REBEL TOWN CLASS

FLYING SCOT

Designer Gordon Douglass was a partner in Douglass & McLeod of Grand River, Ohio—builders of several popular one-designs, including the Thistle and Highlander. This firm later joined with Charlie Britton to form Tartan Marine. The Flying Scot is a big, heavy daysailer. Designed in 1957, her hull form is more rounded and modern than the Snipe or Lightning. Its substantial beam gives it a lot of stability. You can stand on the edge of the deck (rail), hold onto one of the shrouds (side stays), and not tip the boat very much. A powerful sailer, when up on plane she can pull a water-skier (or at least that's what an early brochure shows). She can be raced with a crew of two to four, but usually just two persons. If you don't mind sleeping under the stars (you could rig a boom tent and sleep on the floor), the Flying Scot is also suitable for camp cruising.

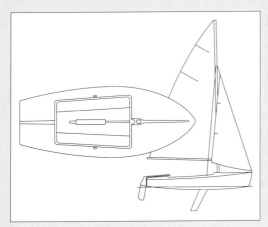

LOA	19'0"
BEAM	7'1"
DRAFT	8"–4'0" (CB UP, CB DOWN)
WEIGHT	835 LB.
SAIL AREA	190 SQ. FT.
DESIGNER	GORDON K. DOUGLASS
PRICE NEW	$12,000
PRICE USED	$1,100–$1,300 (1967 MODEL)
	$2,500–$2,950 (1982 MODEL)
	$5,300–$6,100 (1992 MODEL)
CONTACT	FLYING SCOT INC.
	157 CEMETERY ST.
	DEER PARK MD 21550
	800-864-7208; 301-334-4848
	WWW.FLYINGSCOT.COM
	FLYING SCOT SAILING ASSOC.
	1 WINDSOR COVE, SUITE 305
	COLUMBIA SC 29223
	803-252-5646; 800-445-8629
	WWW.FSSA.COM
SIMILAR BOATS	BUCCANEER
	CYGNUS
	RAVEN

LIGHTNING (INTERNATIONAL)

Another Depression-era one-design, the Lightning was drawn by the prestigious New York firm of Sparkman & Stephens in 1938, and she's still one of America's top daysailer and club racers. When raced, she carries a 300-square-foot spinnaker and can get up on plane. At 19 feet, she exhibits the stability and performance of bigger boats. Like the Snipe, the Lightning has hard chines; first built in wood, construction in recent decades has been in fiberglass. Even if yacht clubs are beginning to drop the Lightning as a somewhat dated design, she's still an excellent family boat.

LOA	19'0"
BEAM	6'6"
DRAFT	1'5"–4 11
WEIGHT	700 LB.
SAIL AREA	177 SQ. FT.
DESIGNER	SPARKMAN & STEPHENS
PRICE NEW	$13,884 (NICKELS BOAT WORKS)
PRICE USED	$1,150–$1,400 (1967 MODEL) $4,250–$4,950 (1993 MODEL)
CONTACT	ALLEN BOAT CO. 655 FUHRMAN BLVD. BUFFALO NY 14203 716-842-0800
	NICKELS BOAT WORKS 2426 SOUTH LONG LAKE RD. FENTON MI 48430 810-750-1855 WWW.NICKELSBOATS.COM
	INTERNATIONAL LIGHTNING CLASS ASSOC. P.O. BOX 10747 MURFREESBORO TN 37129 615-89-FLASH (615-893-5274) WWW.LIGHTNINGCLASS.ORG
SIMILAR BOATS	BUCCANEER INTERLAKE RHODES 18

RHODES 19

The Rhodes 19 evolved from the 1950s-era Hurricane class designed by the distinguished American yacht designer Philip Rhodes. A keel version known as the Smyra (after the Southern Massachusetts Yacht Racing Association) was used as a plug by Marscot Plastics to make a fiberglass model. When George O'Day bought Marscot, he changed the name of the Smyra to Rhodes 19. When O'Day Corporation ceased operations in the 1980s, Stuart Marine picked up construction. Like the Flying Scot, the Rhodes 19 is a powerful daysailer and club racer that can seat a crowd and stand up to a breeze. The small cuddy makes camp cruising possible. Built as a keel and keel-centerboard boat, the same hull is used for the four-berth Mariner, built by both O'Day and Stuart Marine.

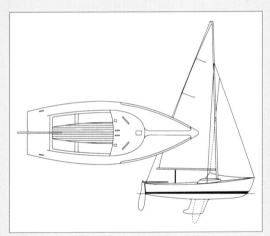

LOA	19'2"
LWL	17'9"
BEAM	7'0"
DRAFT	10"–4'11" (CB UP, CB DOWN) 3'3" (KEEL)
WEIGHT	1,325 LB.
SAIL AREA	175 SQ. FT.
DESIGNER	PHILIP RHODES
PRICE NEW	$15,399
PRICE USED	$3,700–$4,850 (1985 MODEL) $15,700–$20,100 (2002 MODEL)
CONTACT	STUART MARINE CORP. P.O. BOX 469 38 GORDON DR. ROCKLAND ME 04841 207-594-5515
	RHODES 19 CLASS ASSOC. C/O DOUG TREES P.O. BOX 489 557 BAY RD. HAMILTON MA 01936 WWW.RHODES19.ORG
SIMILAR BOATS	MARINER FLYING SCOT SONAR 23

ENSIGN

Designed in 1962 by Carl Alberg (who did all the Cape Dory cruisers built during the 1970s and 1980s), the Ensign was built by Pearson Yachts for many years and is still actively raced in New England yacht club fleets. Though there have been fleets on the West and Gulf Coasts, today they are most popular in the Northeast. Classified as a one-design keelboat, it races with a crew of two to three. The small cuddy makes camp cruising possible. The cockpit is not self-bailing, so it's not suitable for offshore sailing because it can swamp. But for lake, bay, and inshore sailing, it's a comfortable boat with deep seats. Its heavy displacement and long keel give the feel of a larger boat. Pearson built a cruising version with cabin and berths called the Electra, but few were built. The Ensign is now constructed by Ensign Spars and called the Ensign Classic.

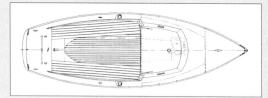

LOA	22'6"
BEAM	7'0"
DRAFT	3'0"
DISPLACEMENT	3,000 LB.
SAIL AREA	201 SQ. FT.
DESIGNER	CARL ALBERG
PRICE NEW	$29,500
PRICE USED	$5,050–$5,800 (1982 MODEL)
CONTACT	ENSIGN SPARS INC.
	736 SCOTLAND ST.
	DUNEDIN FL 34698
	727-734-1837
	WWW.ENSIGNSPARS.COM
	ENSIGN CLASS ASSOC.
	P.O. BOX 3128
	POUGHKEEPSIE NY 12603-3128
	WWW.ENSIGNCLASS.COM
SIMILAR BOATS	RHODES 19 KEEL
	MERCURY
	RAINBOW
	SHIELDS
	TEMPEST

SONAR 23 (INTERNATIONAL)

Designed by Bruce Kirby, who also designed the Laser, the Sonar 23 is a keelboat suitable for daysailing, but is a spirited racer as well. Recently granted international status, it was chosen for the Woman's 2000 Match Racing Worlds and the 2004 Paralympic Games. The 11-foot 6-inch cockpit has plenty of room for eight people, and the lockable cuddy provides stowage and shelter. There's room for a portable toilet. The rig is uncomplicated, making it a good boat to learn on.

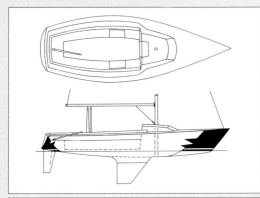

LOA	23'0"
BEAM	7'10"
DRAFT	3'11"
DISPLACEMENT	2,100 LB.
BALLAST	900 LB.
SAIL AREA	250 SQ. FT.
DESIGNER	BRUCE KIRBY
PRICE NEW	$27,900
PRICE USED	$4,500–$5,150 (1982 MODEL) $7,800–$8,950 (1992 MODEL)
CONTACT	SHUMWAY MARINE 70 PATTONWOOD DR. ROCHESTER NY 14617 800-433-2518, 585-342-3030 WWW.SHUMWAYMARINE.COM THE SONAR CLASS ASSOC. 43 COTTAGE FARM RD. BROOKLINE MA 02446 617-738-1021 WWW.SONAR.ORG
SIMILAR BOATS	RHODES 19 KEEL MERCURY RAINBOW SHIELDS TEMPEST

SHIELDS 30

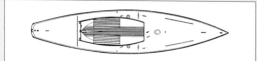

In the early 1960s, yachtsman Cornelius Shields was a major stockholder in Chris-Craft, and it was he who instigated the famous powerboat company's brief foray into sail. One, designed in 1962, was the Shields one-design keelboat. Long, narrow, and very beautiful, she looks a bit like an America's Cup Twelve Meter. The boat's size enables her to handle heavy weather, and the small jib makes headsail trimming easy. Note the very high ballast/displacement ratio—67 percent! Forty years later, there are still active fleets in parts of the country, principally New England.

LOA	30'2"
LWL	20'0"
BEAM	6'5"
DRAFT	4'9"
DISPLACEMENT	4,600 LB.
BALLAST	3,080 LB.
SAIL AREA	360 SQ. FT.
DESIGNER	SPARKMAN & STEPHENS
PRICE NEW	$43,400
PRICE USED	$19,400–$21,600 (1982 MODEL)
CONTACT	CAPE COD SHIPBUILDING CO. P.O. BOX 152 7 NARROWS RD. WAREHAM MA 02571 508-295-3550 WWW.CAPECODSHIPBUILDING. COM SHIELDS CLASS SAILING ASSOC. P.O. BOX 236 NEWPORT RI 02840 WWW.SHIELDSCLASS.COM
SIMILAR BOATS	ATLANTIC COLUMBIA 5.5 ETCHELS INTERNATIONAL 210

WEST WIGHT POTTER 15

With more than 2,000 built since 1969, the lovable West Wight Potter has introduced many people to the joys of cruising. The cabin sleeps two in 6-foot 6-inch berths. The cockpit also can be converted to a berth. Though the boat does not have ballast, one intrepid young man sailed his West Wight Potter from California to Hawaii. Auxiliary power is a 2 hp outboard motor. The hull has hard chines, which give it good initial stability. The simple three-stay rig is easy to step and unstep. This saucy little sloop is about as small as cruising sailboats go. All the similar boats listed below are larger; there's really nothing quite like the West Wight Potter.

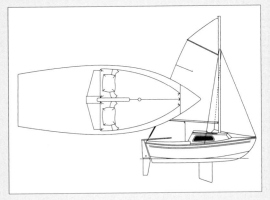

LOA	15'0"
LWL	12'0"
BEAM	7'0"
DRAFT	6"–3'0" (CB UP, CB DOWN)
WEIGHT	495 LB.
SAIL AREA	87 SQ. FT.
DESIGNER	STANLEY T. SMITH
PRICE NEW	$8,495
PRICE USED	$2,750–$3,200 (1993 MODEL) $6,500–$7,450 (2002 MODEL)
CONTACT	INTERNATIONAL MARINE 922 WEST HYDE PARK INGLEWOOD CA 90302-3308 800-433-4080; 310-674-5959 WWW.WWPOTTER.COM
SIMILAR BOATS	PRECISION 165 PRECISION 18 CAPRI 18 CATALINA 18 MARINER 19 WEST WIGHT POTTER 19

VENTURE 21

Roger MacGregor started his boatbuilding company as a graduate thesis at Stanford University. Determined to prove the viability of his ideas, he started MacGregor Yacht Corporation. One of his first creations was the Venture 21, a swing-keel trailer sailer that helped define the genre—and created a market for it. Like others of its kind, the centerboard is replaced with a ballasted keel, though it pivots on a single pin in the same manner. This reduces draft for trailering yet provides stability for higher winds and bigger waves. The line of Ventures eventually included models from 17 to 25 feet, including the stylized Venture of Newport, replete with trail boards like the nineteenth-century clipper ships. Overall quality is low, but so are the prices. Today, MacGregor builds only the hugely popular MacGregor 26 "power sailer."

LOA	21'0"
LWL	18'6"
BEAM	6'10"
DRAFT	1'–3'6" (KEEL UP, KEEL DOWN)
DISPLACEMENT	1,200 LB.
BALLAST	400 LB.
SAIL AREA	175 SQ. FT.
DESIGNER	ROGER MACGREGOR
PRICE NEW	NOT IN PRODUCTION
PRICE USED	$1,150–$1,350 (1968 MODEL)
	$1,700–$2,000 (1981 MODEL)
	$2,350–$2,750 (1986 MODEL)
SIMILAR BOATS	BALBOA 20
	ENSENADA 20
	GULF COAST 20
	CAL 21
	AQUARIUS 21
	SAN JUAN 21
	GULF COAST 21
	NEWPORT 21
	SANTANA 21

CATALINA 22

SAIL magazine's tenth-anniversary issue in 1980 listed the Catalina 22 as the boat that best represented the "breakthrough" in trailer cruising. Though there are many other similar designs, none has equaled the success of the Catalina 22. More than 15,000 have been sold (one to yours truly) since 1969. It's hard to figure, given the boat's shortcomings (wasted storage space, some dubious construction practices, uncomfortable bunks, need for a trailer tongue extension at some ramps, etc.). But it looks more shippy than some other boats, and the double lower shrouds suggest a certain readiness for sea. A fixed-keel version was offered but the percentage sold was very low. A few years ago, an updated MKII design was offered, and is still in production.

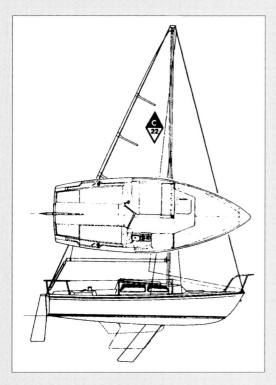

LOA	21'6"
LWL	19'4"
BEAM	7'8"
DRAFT	1'8" (KEEL UP)
DISPLACEMENT	1,850 LB.
BALLAST	550 LB.
SAIL AREA	212 SQ. FT.
DESIGNER	FRANK BUTLER
PRICE NEW	$14,326
PRICE USED	$2,350–$2,750 (1970 MODEL) $3,750–4,350 (1982 MODEL) $4,800–$5,200 (1986 MODEL)
CONTACT	CATALINA YACHTS 21200 VICTORY BLVD. WOODLAND HILLS CA 91367 818-884-7700 WWW.CATALINAYACHTS.COM CATALINA 22 NATIONAL SAILING ASSOC. C/O TED MCGEE 3790 POST GATE DR. CUMMING GA 30040 WWW.CATALINA22.ORG
SIMILAR BOATS	O'DAY 22 CHRYSLER 22 RHODES 22 SOUTH COAST 22 KELLS 22 VENTURE 222 TANZER 22

RHODES 22

It's not easy to think of Philip Rhodes, one of America's great yacht designers, drawing the lines to a plain vanilla trailer sailer, but apparently he did just that in 1960, about the same time he was working on the Twelve-Meter *Weatherly*, which defended the America's Cup in 1962. Like the O'Day 23, the Rhodes 22 has a stub keel, which a centerboard drops from. The hull has considerable flare at the gunwales, which looks a bit odd, but strengthens the hull, deflects spray, and widens the side decks. Enclosed foam flotation makes the boat unsinkable. The hull is laid up of chopped strand mat, woven roving, and Coremat. The deck is foam-cored. The cockpit is long at 7 feet 4 inches. The interior incorporates many clever ideas of manufacturer Stan Spitzer, such as the dinette table that can be moved to the cockpit and the enclosed head with a multipaneled door that opens up the area when not in use. In many respects, the Rhodes 22 is very similar to other trailer sailers, like those listed below. There is one big difference, however; production of most of those boats ceased in the 1970s, whereas the Rhodes 22 continues to be built, evolving slowly for the benefit of those who like to tow their boat to new destinations.

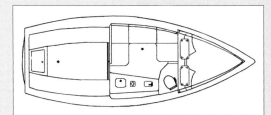

LOA	22'0"
LWL	20'0"
BEAM	8'0"
DRAFT	1'8"–4'0" (CB UP, CB DOWN)
DISPLACEMENT	2,900 LB.
BALLAST	700 LB.
SAIL AREA	210 SQ. FT.
DESIGNER	PHILIP RHODES
PRICE NEW	$27,995
PRICE USED	$4,550–$5,250 (1982 MODEL)
	$6,850–$7,850 (1988 MODEL)
CONTACT	GENERAL BOATS
	144 MIDWAY DR.
	EDENTON NC 27932
	252-482-4372
	WWW.RHODES22.COM
SIMILAR BOATS	CATALINA 22
	O'DAY 22
	CHRYSLER 22
	SOUTH COAST 22
	KELLS 22
	TANZER 22
	VENTURE 222

TANZER 22

Johann Tanzer, designer and builder of the Tanzer line of sailboats, was born in Austria and later emigrated to Canada, where he founded his business. The Tanzer 22 flush deck is a bit unusual, though it provides additional space below. The flip side is that there's no cabin to brace against when going forward on deck. Note how much heavier it is than the Catalina 22. The advantage of this is that it is stiff, with a big boat feel. The disadvantage is that there is more weight to lug around on a trailer. And the 2-foot draft makes launching on some ramps difficult. The cabin is smallish, but the cockpit is large. Construction quality is above average. Interestingly, the keel versions are not that much slower than a J/24; PHRF (Performance Handicap Rating Formula) ratings are between 92 and 98 (seconds per mile). Production started in 1970 and ended with 2,270 of them being built, making it one of the more popular trailer sailers of that decade.

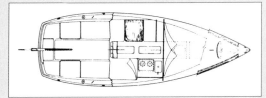

LOA	22'6"
LWL	19'9"
BEAM	7'10"
DRAFT	2'–4'(CB UP, CB DOWN) 3'5" (FIXED KEEL)
DISPLACEMENT	3,100 LB. (CENTERBOARD WITH STUB KEEL)
BALLAST	1,500 LB.
SAIL AREA	227 SQ. FT.
DESIGNER	JOHANN TANZER
PRICE NEW	NOT IN PRODUCTION
PRICE USED	$2,650–$3,250 (1970 MODEL) $3,950–$4,800 (1981 MODEL) $5,450–$6,600 (1986 MODEL)
CONTACT	TANZER 22 CLASS ASSOC. P.O. BOX 11122 STN. H NEPEAN ON K2H 7T9 CANADA WWW.TANZER22.COM
SIMILAR BOATS	CATALINA 22 O'DAY 22 CHRYSLER 22 RHODES 22 SOUTH COAST 22 KELLS 22 VENTURE 222

TRAILER SAILERS

TRAILER SAILERS

O'DAY 23

George O'Day, founder of the O'Day Corporation, was no longer involved with the company when the O'Day 23 was introduced around 1972. And C. Raymond Hunt, in the years prior to his death in 1978, had turned over much of the design duties to his partner John Deknatel. Nonetheless, the two companies produced one of the better trailer sailers in the O'Day 23. Like the Tanzer 22, and unlike most trailer sailers, the O'Day 23 does not have a swing keel; rather, it has a modestly weighted centerboard that pivots up and into a stub keel, which contains the ballast. The advantage is that there is not so much weight on the pivot pin; the disadvantage is that the center of gravity is higher (this means that you need more ballast to achieve the same righting moment—stability). As for quality, think of O'Day as a Ford or Chevrolet—nice, but nothing fancy or extraordinary. Draft and displacement make the O'Day 23 marginally trailerable, but eminently storable in the driveway or backyard on its trailer, thereby saving yard fees.

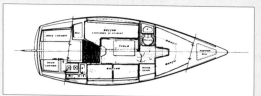

LOA	22'9"
LWL	19'6"
BEAM	7'11"
DRAFT	2'3"–5'4" (CB UP, CB DOWN)
DISPLACEMENT	3,085 LB.
BALLAST	1,200 LB.
SAIL AREA	246 SQ. FT.
DESIGNER	C. RAYMOND HUNT ASSOCIATES
PRICE NEW	NOT IN PRODUCTION
PRICE USED	$3,100–$3,600 (1977 MODEL) $4,200–$4,900 (1982 MODEL) $5,150–$5,900 (1985 MODEL)
SIMILAR BOATS	AQUARIUS 23 COLUMBIA 23 GRAMPIAN 23 GULF COAST 23 PACESHIP 23 SEAFARER 23

COM-PAC 23

The Com-Pac line of small sailboats was developed by businessman Les Hutchins and boatbuilder Buc Thomas in 1974. After a successful debut with the Com-Pac 16, Clark Mills, designer of the Optimist and Windmill, was commissioned to draw something bigger. Aimed at the Florida market, it has a long, shallow fixed keel. This hurts windward performance, but avoids the potential trouble of a centerboard or swing keel. Heavy, slow, and barely trailerable, the boat nevertheless has a loyal following, owing in large part to its traditional looks. And traditional somehow suggests safe and seaworthy, even if the specs say otherwise. That's not necessarily the case here, however. For cruising in the protected waters of lakes and bays, this is a safe and comfortable family boat. Simply rigged, it's an easy boat to sail, too.

LOA	23'11"
LWL	20'2"
BEAM	7'10"
DRAFT	2'3"
DISPLACEMENT	3,000 LB.
BALLAST	1,340 LB.
SAIL AREA	250 SQ. FT.
DESIGNER	**CLARK MILLS**
PRICE NEW	**$24,995 FOR 23/3 MODEL**
PRICE USED	**$6,000–$6,900 (1984 MODEL)** **$11,100–$15,500 (1992 MODEL)** **$23,100–$25,700 (2000 MODEL)**
CONTACT	**COM-PAC YACHTS** **THE HUTCHINS CO.** **1195 KAPP DR.** **CLEARWATER FL 33765** **727-443-4408** **WWW.COM-PACYACHTS.COM**
SIMILAR BOATS	**CATALINA 22** **O'DAY 22** **CHRYSLER 22** **RHODES 22** **SOUTH COAST 22** **KELLS 22** **VENTURE 222**

CATALINA 250

Trying to design the largest possible trailerable cruising sailboat poses a variety of challenges and dilemmas. For starters, the maximum beam allowed on most U.S. highways is 8 feet 6 inches, and the maximum towing weight for most standard automobiles is under 2 tons. Because nearly half of a boat's weight is in its ballast, great weight savings are possible by using water instead of lead to give the boat stability. That is, if you can dump the water for trailering, which is what the Catalina 250 does.

The downside is that water isn't nearly as dense as lead, so it doesn't provide equivalent righting moment. The Catalina 250 features a large double berth under the cockpit, as well as a V-berth forward. The boat sails surprisingly well for a water-ballasted boat and comes standard with sails, mast-raising system, pulpits, and lifelines.

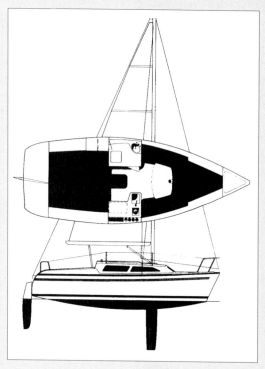

LOA	25'0"
LWL	21'3"
BEAM	8'6"
DRAFT	1'8"–5'9" (CB UP, CB DOWN)
DISPLACEMENT	3,600 LB.
BALLAST	1,200 LB. (WATER)
SAIL AREA	268 SQ. FT.
DESIGNER	CATALINA YACHTS
PRICE NEW	$19,783
PRICE USED	$10,000–$11,400 (1994 MODEL) $17,200–$19,500 (2000 MODEL)
CONTACT	CATALINA YACHTS 21200 VICTORY BLVD. WOODLAND HILLS CA 91367 818-884-7700 WWW.CATALINAYACHTS.COM
SIMILAR BOATS (BOTH WATER-BALLASTED)	HUNTER 260 MACGREGOR 26

MACGREGOR 26

If you read the description of the Venture 21 (see page 194), you know that Roger MacGregor was at the forefront of the trailer sailer revolution. Over the years, he's also built a 36-foot catamaran and a 65-foot ULDB (ultralight displacement boat). But the MacGregor 26 has been so phenomenally successful that he has built no other model for many years. One of the reasons for its popularity is its low price. Another is the option of mounting a 50 hp outboard that enables speeds of 24 mph. When the wind dies, you don't have to chug home at 5 knots. The interior features three double berths, if you can believe that—well, if you're an average-size adult, don't. MacGregor has built nearly 40,000 boats in his career; the 26 alone numbers more than 5,000. Innovation, flexibility, and price are his watchwords.

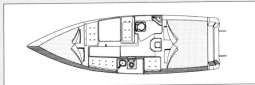

LOA	25'10"
LWL	23'0"
BEAM	7'10"
DRAFT	9"–5'6" (CB UP, CB DOWN)
DISPLACEMENT	2,350 LB.
BALLAST	1,400 LB. (WATER)
SAIL AREA	275 SQ. FT.
DESIGNER	ROGER MACGREGOR
PRICE NEW	$17,990 WITH SAILS AND TRAILER
PRICE USED	$7,000–$8,050 (1990 MODEL) $14,000–$15,900 (2000 MODEL)
CONTACT	MACGREGOR YACHT CORP. 1631 PLACENTIA COSTA MESA CA 92627 949-642-6830 WWW.MACGREGOR26.COM MACGREGOR OWNERS GROUP TREVOR MACLACHLAN 206-WEB-SAIL (206-932-7245), x45 WWW.MACGREGOROWNERS.COM MACGREGOR OWNERS ASSOC. 69 GREEN RIVER RD. GREENFIELD MA 01301 413-773-7525
SIMILAR BOATS (BOTH WATER-BALLASTED)	CATALINA 250 HUNTER 260

SEAWARD 25

Like the Com-Pac 23, Hake yachts eschew centerboards, preferring long, fixed, shoal keels instead. Not surprisingly, they are also built in Florida, whose prime cruising grounds in Florida Bay and along the Keys are quite shallow, often less than 4 or 5 feet. The same advantages and disadvantages that apply to the Com-Pacs also apply to the Seaward 25. The Seawards (19, 23, 25, and 32) have a reputation for above-average quality; also like the Com-Pacs, their popularity stems from their traditional looks. Incidentally, the Seaward 25 really is 25 feet on deck; the short bowsprit accounts for the LOA of 26 feet 9 inches.

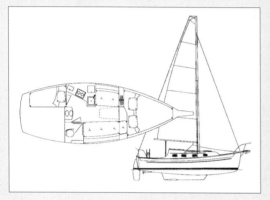

LOA	26'9"
LWL	22'2"
BEAM	8'4"
DRAFT	2'1"
DISPLACEMENT	3,600 LB.
BALLAST	1,200 LB.
SAIL AREA	265 SQ. FT.
DESIGNER	NICK HAKE
PRICE NEW	$34,000 FOR SEAWARD 26 RK, SAME HULL AS 25, BUT WITH REVISIONS
PRICE USED	$22,900–$25,400 (1997 MODEL) $27,500–$30,500 (1999 MODEL)
CONTACT	HAKE YACHTS 4550 SE HAMPTON COURT STUART FL 34997 772-287-3200 WWW.SEAWARDYACHTS.COM
SIMILAR BOATS	COM-PAC 25

MARSHALL SANDERLING 18

No representative list of sailboats would be complete without at least one catboat. This indigenous American watercraft was developed in the 1800s for pleasant sailing in the many shallow bays of the East Coast. The hulls are wide and flat, and the so-called "barn door" rudders are also shallow (to avoid hitting bottom), but are long to provide the necessary surface area for control. Breck Marshall founded Marshall Marine after leaving American Boatbuilding, where he was involved in the construction of the Block Island 40 and other early fiberglass boats. He took Pop Arnold's drawings and modified them to suit his own concepts, giving the Sanderling a prettier sheer, a crowned cabin, and a tapered house. The stem is slightly angled. He built the first in 1962 and the company still sells about 20 a year. Although they are raced in some East Coast fleets, most are for afternoon outings on the bay. The large cockpit can seat a nice group of friends. (Unlike a lot of modern boats, you sit *in* the Sanderling, not *on* it.) And if you want to overnight at some favorite anchorage, there are two 6-foot 6-inch berths, stowage, and a built-in head.

LOA	19'2"
LWL	20'0"
BEAM	8'6"
DRAFT	4'0"
DISPLACEMENT	1,750 LB.
BALLAST	300 LB.
SAIL AREA	268 SQ. FT.
DESIGNER	POP ARNOLD/BRECK MARSHALL
PRICE NEW	$27,500
PRICE USED	$6,700–$7,700 (1982 MODEL) $14,100–$16,000 (1992 MODEL) $31,100–$34,500 (2001 MODEL)
CONTACT	MARSHALL MARINE CORP. P.O. BOX P-266 SHIPYARD LANE SOUTH DARTMOUTH MA 02748 508-994-0414 WWW.MARSHALLCAT.COM
SIMILAR BOATS	MARSHALL SANDPIPER 15 COM-PAC SUN CAT 17 MENGER CAT 19 COM-PAC HORIZON CAT 20 MARSHALL 22 MENGER CAT 23

GENERAL-PURPOSE

MORGAN 24

In the early 1960s, Charlie Morgan was a hotshot sailmaker, yacht racer, and designer in St. Petersburg, Florida. Success in all three fields prompted him to start his own boatbuilding company. The Morgan 24, launched in 1965, was his fourth model. It proved to be a popular racer/cruiser, though by today's standards it looks a bit frumpy. Like many Florida designers-builders, many of Morgan's boats have shoal draft; Morgan favored the keel-centerboard configuration. It sails very well, with good balance and tracking. There are berths for four. Two accommodation plans were offered: one with opposing settees in the main cabin; the other with a convertible dinette. These boats are getting long in the tooth and should be surveyed carefully, but if you find one that passes muster, it will be a good value. When Morgan Yachts was sold to Beatrice Foods in 1968, the 24 was renamed the Morgan 25, but except for some minor changes, such as replacing the teak toe rail with one of molded fiberglass, they are the same.

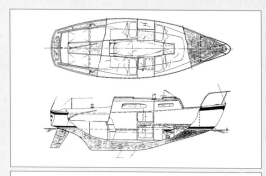

LOA	24'11"
LWL	21'6"
BEAM	8'0"
DRAFT	2'9"–6'6" (CB UP, CB DOWN)
DISPLACEMENT	5,000 LB.
BALLAST	1,900 LB.
SAIL AREA	310 SQ. FT.
DESIGNER	CHARLIE MORGAN
PRICE NEW	NOT IN PRODUCTION
PRICE USED	$4,750–$5,400 (1966 MODEL) $5,450–$6,550 (1972 MODEL) $6,200–$7,100 (1976 MODEL)
SIMILAR BOATS	C&C 25 CORONADO 25 IRWIN 25 COLUMBIA 26 GRAMPIAN 26

CAL 25

Cal boats were built by Jack Jensen in Costa Mesa, California—the mecca of fiberglass boatbuilding during the 1960s and 1970s. The Cal 40 was a breakthrough design (one of the first to separate the keel and rudder) that won many races. For his smaller designs, Bill Lapworth favored the flush deck, as seen on the Cal 20 and Cal 25. Although it opens up space below, moving about the deck takes some getting used to. Construction quality is very similar to the other southern California mass producers of the day—Columbia, Islander, Yankee, and Ericson—but maybe a tad more solid; it's certainly no fancier. The Cal 25 sleeps five in two cabins, with an enclosed toilet. She is a well-behaved boat.

LOA	25'0"
LWL	20'0"
BEAM	8'0"
DRAFT	4'0"
DISPLACEMENT	4,000 LB.
BALLAST	1,700 LB.
SAIL AREA	286 SQ. FT.
DESIGNER	C. WILLIAM LAPWORTH
PRICE NEW	NOT IN PRODUCTION
PRICE USED	$4,700–$5,400 (1968 MODEL) $5,950–$6,850 (1977 MODEL)
CONTACT	CAL 25 SAILBOAT CLASS ASSOC. WWW.CAL25.COM
SIMILAR BOATS	C&C 25 CORONADO 25 IRWIN 25 NORTHSTAR 500 NORTHERN 25 MORGAN 25

GENERAL-PURPOSE

PEARSON 26

Pearson Yachts was a pioneer in the building of fiberglass auxiliary sailboats; its 28-foot 6-inch Triton (1959) was one of the early success stories. The founding cousins, Clint and Everett, sold out to Grumman Industries in 1964. Two years later, Bill Shaw, fresh from the prestigious New York design firm of Sparkman & Stephens, was hired as chief in-house designer. His conservative approach to design and construction earned Pearson Yachts the reputation of above-average quality, but hardly scintillating looks. The Pearson 26 (1970) was an overnight success, forcing the company to start a second production line. To achieve standing headroom (only 5 feet 9 inches), the tall cabin seems slightly out of proportion to the hull. She makes a decent cruiser for a small family, and many mom-and-pop teams also had fun participating in club races. The boat sails well to weather, balances nicely, and is dry. No wonder 1,777 were sold, plus 262 of the 26 One Design—the same boat with a longer cockpit and lower cabin.

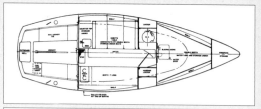

LOA	26'1"
LWL	21'8"
BEAM	8'8"
DRAFT	4'0"
DISPLACEMENT	5,400 LB.
BALLAST	2,200 LB.
SAIL AREA	321 SQ. FT.
DESIGNER	WILLIAM SHAW
PRICE NEW	NOT IN PRODUCTION
PRICE USED	$6,800–$7,850 (1971 MODEL) $7,400–$8,500 (1974 MODEL) $9,600–$10,900 (1980 MODEL)
CONTACT	NATIONAL PEARSON YACHT OWNERS ASSOC. C/O WILLIAM J. LAWRENCE 28 VESEY ST., SUITE 2172 NEW YORK NY 10007 WWW.PEARSONCURRENT.COM
SIMILAR BOATS	COLUMBIA 26 GRAMPIAN 26 RANGER 26 SANTANA 26 YANKEE 26

ERICSON 27

Ericson Yachts was another West Coast builder spawned in southern California, this time in Santa Ana. Designed back when production builders commissioned "name" designers, her lines come from Bruce King, now better known for big custom yachts like *Whitehawk*, the 92-foot replica of *Ticonderoga*. The first Ericsons sold mostly on the West Coast, but later boats like the 27, launched in 1971, sold well across the country. Billed as an IOR competitor, the 27 proved to be more popular as a small cruiser. About 80 percent of the boats had inboard power, usually the Atomic 4 gasoline engine, and the other 20 percent had outboards mounted in a cockpit well. Most were delivered with tillers, but many have been retrofitted with wheel steering. Handling under sail or power isn't the best, and with her heavy displacement and short rig, performance is sluggish. On the plus side, construction quality is certainly adequate for her intended purpose—coastal cruising.

LOA	26'9"
LWL	20'6"
BEAM	9'0"
DRAFT	3'11"
DISPLACEMENT	7,000 LB.
BALLAST	2,900 LB.
SAIL AREA	323 SQ. FT.
DESIGNER	BRUCE KING
PRICE NEW	NOT IN PRODUCTION
PRICE USED	$7,300–$8,400 (1971 OUTBOARD MODEL)
	$9,200–$10,400 (1971 INBOARD MODEL)
	$13,000–$14,800 (1979 OUTBOARD MODEL)
	$13,200–$15,000 (1979 INBOARD MODEL)
SIMILAR BOATS	CAL 27
	C&C 27
	DUFOUR 27
	MORGAN 27
	NEWPORT 27
	SANTANA 27

GENERAL-PURPOSE

C&C 27

Once upon a time, in the late 1960s and 1970s, the Canadian builder C&C Yachts ruled. George Cuthbertson and George Cassian's hot designs won the SORC (the Southern Ocean Racing Circuit, a major yachting event in southern Florida), and generally dominated the North American racer/cruiser market. The first C&C 27 rolled off the Niagara-on-the-Lake, Ontario, assembly line in 1971; it's a good example of what made the company successful—contemporary good looks with sharp, crisp lines that still appeal today. In 1974, the swept-back keel and scimitar-shaped rudder were redesigned. Over the years, the design was updated with MKII and MKIII versions that were progressively faster. The hulls and decks are balsa sandwich construction. Like most modern fiberglass boats, it has a molded pan interior that comprises the sole and berth foundations. A C&C trademark is the slotted aluminum toe rail that allows for infinite placement of snatch blocks. The boat is a smart, quick sailer. Nearly 1,000 were built before production ceased in 1987.

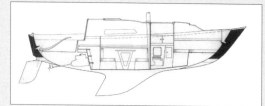

LOA	27'4"
LWL	22'2"
BEAM	9'2"
DRAFT	4'3"
DISPLACEMENT	5,500 LB.
BALLAST	2,512 LB.
SAIL AREA	348 SQ. FT.
DESIGNER	C&C DESIGN TEAM
PRICE NEW	NOT IN PRODUCTION
PRICE USED	$9,900–$11,200 (1974 MODEL)
CONTACT	C&C 27 ASSOC. C/O BOB WILSON 883 WALTON COURT WHITBY ON L1N 7R5 CANADA WWW.CC27ASSOCIATION.COM
SIMILAR BOATS	CAL 27 DUFOUR 27 ERICSON 27 MORGAN 27 NEWPORT 27 SANTANA 27

S2 8.5 METER

Leon Slikkers, founder of Slickcraft powerboats, turned his talents to sailboats in 1973, first with cruising boats and later with the so-called Grand Slam line of performance racer/cruisers. The line included the S2 7.9, 10.3, and 11.2. The hulls are solid fiberglass, and the workmanship is good. The glasswork is neat and properly done. Seacocks are bronze ball valves. Many of the boats came with rigs from Hall Spars, with airfoil spreaders and internal tangs. The T-shaped cockpit was designed for the optional wheel steering. The windows mimicked the European style at the time of its production run, 1981 to 1983. The boat is reasonably fast; its PHRF rating of around 175 is lower than many similar boats, including the Pearson 28, which rates around 195 and the O'Day at about 198. S2 fans were disappointed when Slikkers ceased building sailboats in 1986.

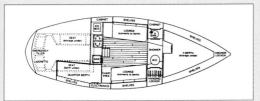

LOA	28'0"
LWL	22'6"
BEAM	9'6"
DRAFT	4'6" OR 3'11"
DISPLACEMENT	7,600 LB.
BALLAST	3,000 LB.
SAIL AREA	400 SQ. FT.
DESIGNER	SCOTT GRAHAM AND ERIC SCHLAGETER
PRICE NEW	NOT IN PRODUCTION
PRICE USED	$19,600–$22,100 (1982 MODEL)
SIMILAR BOATS	TANZER 28
	NEWPORT 28
	O'DAY 28
	PEARSON 28

GENERAL-PURPOSE

ALERION EXPRESS 28

The original Alerion sloop was designed and built about 1912 by Nathanael Herreshoff, perhaps America's greatest yacht designer. Beginning in the 1970s, a number of spin-offs began to appear—one by grandson Halsey Herreshoff, and another by Alfred Sanford of Nantucket. In the late 1980s, Carl Schumacher was asked by Connecticut sailor Ralph Schacter to design a similar boat—traditional above the waterline and modern below. The result is the Alerion Express 28, first built by Holby Marine of Bristol, Rhode Island. Today it is sold by Garry Hoyt's Newport R&D company. If automobile analogies work for you, think of the Alerion as a gentleman's sports car—a Porsche or Jaguar. The emphasis is on speed, comfort, and simplicity. Although equipped with berths and a small galley for overnighting, its forte is the afternoon sail on the bay. It's quick to get under way, and with Hoyt's patented Jib Boom, the entire rig (mainsail and jib) is self-tending (which means that you don't have to trim the sails when

tacking). The boats are built by TPI using balsa core sandwich and the SCRIMP process, in which the fiberglass cloths are laid up dry inside a plastic envelope in the mold; vacuum draws in the resin through a system of tiny hoses. It yields a higher glass-to-resin ratio and minimizes environmental hazards. The Alerion is a very classy (and pricey) small yacht. Many owners buy them on their way down in size, not up. There are very few similar boats.

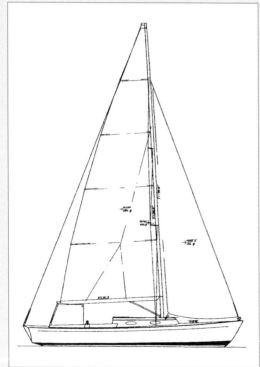

LOA	28'3"
LWL	22'10"
BEAM	8'2"
DRAFT	4'6"
DISPLACEMENT	4,400 LB.
BALLAST	2,000 LB.
SAIL AREA	352 SQ. FT.
DESIGNER	CARL SCHUMACHER
PRICE NEW	$55,724
PRICE USED	$46,800–$51,400 (1997 MODEL) $72,700–$79,800 (2002 MODEL)
CONTACT	NEWPORT R&D INC. ONE MARITIME DRIVE PORTSMOUTH RI 02871 401-683-9450 WWW.ALERIONEXPRESS28.COM
SIMILAR BOATS	ANTRIM 27

SABRE 28

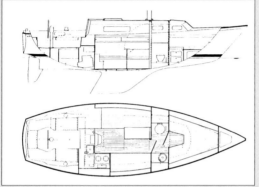

Roger Hewson, designer of the Sabre 28 and founder of Sabre Yachts, was a Canadian building contractor who was fascinated with sailboats. This, his first creation, is a near classic. Production lasted from 1972 to 1986. From the outset, Hewson decided to aim at the high end of the market; that is, with above-average quality and above-average price. Today, Sabre and Tartan Yachts are arguably the two best builders of production sailboats in the United States. The 28 has good clean lines that aren't easily dated. It's a bit heavier than comparable boats, so it's solidly built, but not particularly fast. The interior is all wood, tabbed (fiberglass strips of mat) to the hull and deck. This is a much more expensive way to build interior furniture and cabinets than plopping in a molded fiberglass pan; plus it makes for a quieter, drier, and more easily modified interior.

LOA	28'5"
LWL	22'10"
BEAM	9'2"
DRAFT	4'8" OR 3'10"
DISPLACEMENT	7,900 LB.
BALLAST	3,100 LB.
SAIL AREA	403 SQ. FT.
DESIGNER	ROGER HEWSON
PRICE NEW	NOT IN PRODUCTION
PRICE USED	$12,700–$14,600 (1970 MODEL)
	$25,100–$27,800 (1981 MODEL)
	$33,600–$37,400 (1986 MODEL)
CONTACT	SABRE CORP.
	P.O. BOX 134
	HAWTHORNE RD.
	SOUTH CASCO ME 04077
	207-655-3831
	WWW.SABREYACHTS.COM
SIMILAR BOATS	CAPE DORY 28
	COLUMBIA 8.7
	S2 8.5 METER
	YANKEE 28

GENERAL-PURPOSE

CATALINA 30

Since its inception in 1974, nearly 7,000 Catalina 30s have been sold, although the current 30 MKIII isn't quite the same boat as the original. Any way you read it, this boat is one of the most successful 30-footers ever built. Displacement, which is a bit on the heavy side, is still the same, however. It has a spade rudder and swept-back keel, which are out of fashion nowadays. The rig is a simple masthead sloop with single spreaders (wooden on older boats) and double lower shrouds. A tall rig was offered for areas of light prevailing winds. An interior pan completely obscures the hull interior; this makes for a neat appearance and easy cleaning, but prevents examination of some key areas. The accommodation plan has been tweaked over the years, most notably by the recent addition of a double berth under the cockpit. Under sail, the boat is stiff. Speed is average. She has no discernible vices. Catalinas are priced slightly below their competition. Plain vanilla.

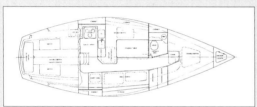

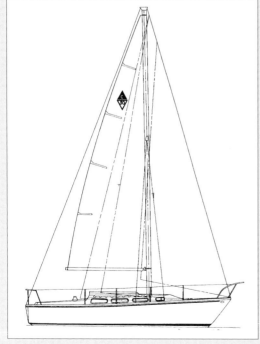

LOA	29'11"
LWL	25'0"
BEAM	10'10"
DRAFT	5'3" OR 4'4"
DISPLACEMENT	10,200 LB.
BALLAST	4,200 LB.
SAIL AREA	444 SQ. FT.
DESIGNER	CATALINA YACHTS
PRICE NEW	$73,563
PRICE USED	$14,600–$16,600 (1974 MODEL)
	$20,400–$23,700 (1981 MODEL)
	$42,600–$47,400 (1992 MODEL)
	$83,500–$93,200 (2002 MODEL)
CONTACT	CATALINA YACHTS
	21200 VICTORY BLVD.
	WOODLAND HILLS CA 91367
	818-884-7700
	WWW.CATALINAYACHTS.COM
	CATALINA 30 YACHT OWNERS ASSOC.
	P.O. BOX 9840
	FAYETTEVILLE AR 72703
	WWW.CATALINA30.COM
SIMILAR BOATS	NEWPORT 30
	O'DAY 30
	PEARSON 30
	PEARSON 303
	TARTAN 30

TARTAN 30

The racer/cruiser concept originated in the early 1970s as a result of the popular MORC (Midget Ocean Racing Class) rating rule that had a maximum length of 30 feet, and the public's desire for real cruising accommodations: full galley, standing headroom, enclosed head, and full-length berths for four to five people. The Tartan 30 is all these things. The boat was fast in its day and still offers a good turn of speed. The reverse transom still sports a modern look. Tartan Marine (now Tartan Yachts), located in Ohio on the shores of Lake Erie, is one of the highest-quality production builders in the United States. An unusual feature of the Tartan 30 is the placement of the engine in the middle of the boat, under the dinette. Locating this heavy object near the boat's center of gravity reduces hobby-horsing in choppy seas, but creates a bit of an obstacle. Production was from 1971 to 1980. If you're looking for a classic racer/cruiser of the 1970s era, this is one of the best.

LOA	29'11"
LWL	24'3"
BEAM	10'0"
DRAFT	4'11"
DISPLACEMENT	8,750 LB.
BALLAST	3,800 LB.
SAIL AREA	451 SQ. FT.
DESIGNER	SPARKMAN & STEPHENS
PRICE NEW	NOT IN PRODUCTION
PRICE USED	$16,200–$18,400 (1971 MODEL) $23,300–$25,900 (1980 MODEL)
CONTACT	CHESAPEAKE TARTAN 30 ASSOC. C/O ROBERT GLEESON 180 DIVIDING COURT ARNOLD MD 21012 301-865-1832 WWW.TARTAN30.ORG
SIMILAR BOATS	CAL 2-30 MORGAN 30/2 NEWPORT 30 O'DAY 30 PEARSON 30 PEARSON 303 SCAMPI YANKEE 30

NIAGARA 31

George Hinterhoeller, an Austrian who emigrated to Canada in the 1950s, was a partner in the formation of C&C Yachts. After leaving C&C, he founded Hinterhoeller Yachts, best known for the line of Mark Ellis–designed Nonsuch catboats with unstayed masts. He also built four boats called Niagaras—the 26, 31, 35, and 42. The 31 was designed by Argentinean German Frers, one of the world's most successful designers of racing yachts. The Niagara 31 has above-average construction quality and design, and is a good all-around boat for a couple or small family. And with a generous sail plan, it is reasonably quick, though it is not light by today's standards. Built between 1980 and 1984, the 31's hull is balsa cored, and the ballast is external lead bolted to the hull. Standard auxiliary power was a small Volvo diesel and Sail Drive (like the lower half of an outboard motor fitted into the bottom of the hull between the keel and rudder), and owners report poor motoring performance. Better to look for a 31 with a conventional drive system.

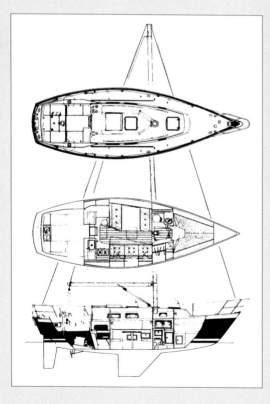

LOA	31'3"
LWL	24'3"
BEAM	10'3"
DRAFT	5'0"
DISPLACEMENT	8.500 LB.
BALLAST	3,550 LB.
SAIL AREA	492 SQ. FT.
DESIGNER	GERMAN FRERS
PRICE NEW	NOT IN PRODUCTION
PRICE USED	$25,400–$28,300 (1980 MODEL) $31,900–$35,500 (1984 MODEL)
SIMILAR BOATS	CAL 31 COLUMBIA 9.6 PEARSON 31 TARTAN 31

HUNTER 326

Hunter Marine was founded in 1972 by Warren Luhrs, a year after he and his brother John started the Silverton powerboat company in New Jersey. Hunter competes with Catalina Yachts for title of America's largest builder of sailboats. They are built on assembly lines and are priced lower than most comparable brands. Warren Luhrs participated in a number of single-handed ocean races during the 1980s and 1990s, and some of the innovations he and his team developed for these races were later incorporated into production models. Hunter boats differ from mainstream designs in several ways: a complicated rig-staying system that on many models eliminates the need for a backstay and makes a high roach mainsail possible, stainless steel arches over the cockpit, the use of many molded fiberglass components, and a modern Euro look. Few are raced, and most cruising is coastal. Hunter emphasizes innovation, ease of handling, and value. The Hunter 326 was introduced in 2002 and gone two years later; Hunter cranks out models like an auto maker.

LOA	31'11"
LWL	28'4"
BEAM	10'10"
DRAFT	4'4" OR 5'10"
DISPLACEMENT	8.300 LB.
BALLAST	3,200 LB.
SAIL AREA	540 SQ. FT.
DESIGNER	HUNTER MARINE CORP.
PRICE NEW	NOT IN PRODUCTION
PRICE USED	$75,200–$82,600 (2002 **MODEL**)
CONTACT	HUNTER MARINE CORP. ROUTE 441, P.O. BOX 1030 ALACHUA FL 32616 800-771-5556; 386-462-3077 WWW.HUNTERMARINE.COM
SIMILAR BOATS	BENETEAU 311 CATALINA 310

SABRE 34

Another late 1970s–early 1980s design, the Sabre 34 is a well-built boat that is an excellent value in today's market. It followed not long after the Sabre 28 in the growing company's line of elegant racer/cruisers. Keel and keel-centerboard models were offered. The masthead sloop rig is straightforward, with single spreaders and double lower shrouds. The interior layout is the usual for this size boat: V-berth forward; head and hanging locker; settees and table in the saloon; and galley, navigation station, and quarter berth aft. Sabre uses a small but tasteful amount of teak trim; on the 34, this consists of the toe rail, handrail, and eyebrow (the narrow wood strip above the portlights that accentuates the corner of the cabin sides and coachroof. A 1980 Sabre 34 sold new for a base price of $50,750 (less sails), and a 1984 sold for $69,900. Today, you can pick one up for under $40,000.

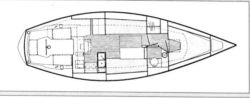

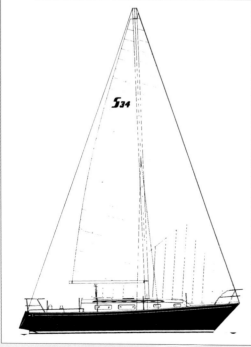

LOA	33'8"
LWL	26'3"
BEAM	10'6"
DRAFT	5'6" (KEEL)
	3'11"–7'9" (KEEL/CB)
DISPLACEMENT	11,400 LB.
BALLAST	4,600 LB.
SAIL AREA	507 SQ. FT.
DESIGNER	SABRE DESIGN TEAM
PRICE NEW	NOT IN PRODUCTION
PRICE USED	$30,400–$34,000 (1977 MODEL)
	$40,400–$46,500 (1981 MODEL)
	$47,300–$52,300 (1992 MODEL)
CONTACT	SABRE CORP.
	P.O. BOX 134
	SOUTH CASCO ME 04077
	207-655-3831
	WWW.SABREYACHTS.COM
SIMILAR BOATS	BENETEAU FIRST 345
	C&C 34+
	CS 34
	DUFOUR 35
	ERICSON 35
	O'DAY 34
	O'DAY 35
	PEARSON 34
	TARTAN 3500

BENETEAU OCEANIS 350

French boatbuilder Beneteau is the world's largest producer of sailboats. In the 1980s, it opened a manufacturing facility in Marion, South Carolina. Beneteau uses a number of outside designers for the basic shape. Beneteau has had a strong influence on other European and American sailboat styles. The Oceanis 350 was built between 1986 and 1993, with 144 built in the United States (more in France). The boat is quite beamy for its length, which makes for a roomy interior. Beamy boats like to be sailed flat, which means reefing sails early; otherwise, they might become difficult to handle. The hull is solid fiberglass with a complex pan or liner. Bulkheads, instead of being glassed to the hull and deck, fit into channels molded into the pan. The interior sleeps six, including two in the double berth under the cockpit. Inboard auxiliary power is a 28 hp Volvo diesel with 21 gallons of fuel. The overall design is somewhat conservative, so she makes a good family boat.

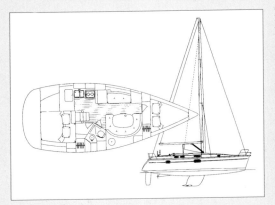

LOA	33'10"
LWL	29'10"
BEAM	11'3"
DRAFT	4'2" OR 5'2"
DISPLACEMENT	10,582 LB.
BALLAST	3,968 LB.
SAIL AREA	488 SQ. FT.
DESIGNER	**PHILIPPE BRIAND**
PRICE NEW	**NOT IN PRODUCTION**
PRICE USED	**$37,300–$41,400 (1989 MODEL)** **$47,300–$52,300 (1992 MODEL)**
CONTACT	**BENETEAU USA** **1313 WEST HWY 76** **MARION SC 29571** **843-629-5300** **WWW.BENETEAUUSA.COM** **BENETEAU OWNERS ASSOC.** **WWW.BENETEAUOWNERS.NET**
SIMILAR BOATS	**BENETEAU FIRST 345** **C&C 34+** **CS 34** **DUFOUR 35** **O'DAY 35** **PEARSON 34** **TARTAN 3500**

GENERAL-PURPOSE

TARTAN 37

Several hundred Tartan 37s were built during a long production run that ended in 1989. Two keel configurations were offered, but most sold were keel-centerboards; even with the board up, the keel is deep enough for sufficient stability. The rudder is hung on a skeg. The hull and deck are balsa cored. Tartan quality is above average. The largely wooden interiors are put together well, with bulkheads bonded to the hull and deck. The hull-to-deck joint is an internal hull flange bedded with butyl and polysulfide, and bolted to the deck and through the teak toe rail with stainless steel bolts. The 37 is a smart sailer, but not of grand prix caliber; although some are club-raced, most were purchased for family cruising . . . with a sparkle. Standard engine was a 41 hp Westerbeke diesel. One reviewer called the Tartan 37 a "gray flannel Buick," styled (and priced) for bankers, lawyers, and stockbrokers. Like most Sparkman & Stephens boats, the 37 is handsome, well mannered, and well engineered. If you can't find a 37 or its successor, the 372, there's always a brand new 3700!

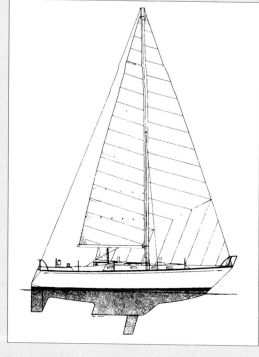

LOA	37'3"
LWL	28'6"
BEAM	11'9"
DRAFT	4'2"–7'9" (KEEL/CB) 6'7" (DEEP KEEL)
DISPLACEMENT	15,500 LB.
BALLAST	7,500 LB.
SAIL AREA	625 SQ. FT.
DESIGNER	SPARKMAN & STEPHENS
PRICE NEW	NOT IN PRODUCTION
PRICE USED	$40,600–$45,200 (1976 MODEL) $53,700–$59,000 (1981 MODEL) $81,300–$89,300 (1988 MODEL)
CONTACT	TARTAN YACHTS 1920 FAIRPORT NURSERY RD. FAIRPORT HARBOR OH 44077 440-357-7777 WWW.TARTANYACHTS.COM
	TARTAN 37 SAILING ASSOC. C/O ADE CHWASTYK 10212 EDGEWOOD AVE. SILVER SPRING MD 20901-1906 WWW.MINDSPRING.COM/~ SAILING_FOOL/INDEX.HTML
	TARTAN OWNERS ORGANIZATION WWW.TARTANOWNERS.ORG

SIMILAR BOATS: HOOD 38; SABRE 38; C&C LANDFALL 38

GENERAL-PURPOSE

BRISTOL 38.8

Bristol Yachts was founded by Clint Pearson after he left Pearson Yachts in 1964 (actually, he bought a small Rhode Island outfit called Sailstar, which evolved into Bristol Yachts). The first boats were small and simple, without many extras. But as has been the trend throughout the industry, the boats got bigger, fancier, and more expensive. When Bristol went belly-up for the last time in 1998, its boats were definitely at the high end of the market, competing with the likes of Alden and Hinckley.

The 38.8, introduced in 1982, fits somewhere between these two extremes; it's definitely a top-quality yacht. Like the Tartan 37, it has a keel-centerboard and skeg-mounted rudder, but is about 4 tons heavier! Part of this is due to the solid mahogany joinery down below. You pay extra for the details, and this boat has them. And despite being heavy, she has a lot of sail to drive her.

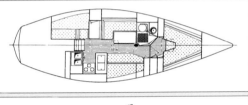

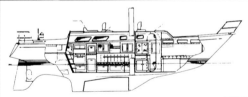

LOA	38'3"
LWL	28'6"
BEAM	12'1"
DRAFT	4'6"–6'7" (CB UP, CB DOWN)
DISPLACEMENT	19,150 LB.
BALLAST	9,000 LB.
SAIL AREA	766 SQ. FT.
DESIGNER	TED HOOD
PRICE NEW	NOT IN PRODUCTION
PRICE USED	$90,300–$99,300 (1984 MODEL) $152,000–$167,000 (1992 MODEL) $188,500–$207,000 (1995 MODEL)
SIMILAR BOATS	BRISTOL 35.5 ENDEAVOUR 38 SABRE 38 SWAN 371 SWEDEN 38 TARTAN 372

C&C 121

A devastating fire put C&C Yachts out of business for the last time. In 1998, its name was bought by Fairport Marine, also owner of Tartan Yachts. Not interested in C&C's old surviving molds, Tartan designer Tim Jackett drew three new designs, the largest of which is this 40-footer. Although Tartans have become heavier, finely finished cruising boats, C&C (as its ad says) has always been about "getting there first." The C&C 121 carries its beam well aft for power off the wind, and the deep fin keel provides a lot of lift to windward. And with a displacement of just 14,100 pounds, she's a mover. To save weight and money, the interior incorporates a fiberglass pan bonded to the hull. Modern materials such as Kevlar, Core-Cell foam, and vinylester resin (to help prevent hull blisters) are used in the construction of the hull and deck. Hardware is good quality. The generous beam makes for a roomy boat below. The galley is large, as is the owner's stateroom aft. If you want a fast, sexy boat for local racing or spirited cruising, it would be hard to go wrong with one of the new C&Cs.

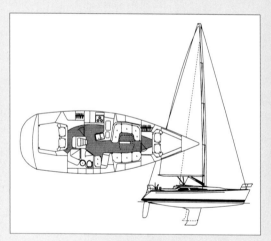

LOA	40'0"
LWL	35'6"
BEAM	13'1"
DRAFT	8'0" OR 6'6" OR 5'0"
DISPLACEMENT	14,100 LB.
BALLAST	5,500 LB.
SAIL AREA	846 SQ. FT.
DESIGNER	TIM JACKETT
PRICE NEW	$234,000
PRICE USED	$217,000–$238,000 (1999 MODEL) $246,500–$270,500 (2002 MODEL)
CONTACT	C&C YACHTS 1920 FAIRPORT NURSERY RD. FAIRPORT HARBOR OH 44077 440-357-7223 WWW.C-CYACHTS.COM
SIMILAR BOATS	SWEDEN 390 BAVARIA 40 BENETEAU FIRST 40.7 IMX-40 X-412 JEANNEAU 40 SABRE 402

FLICKA

Illustrator Bruce Bingham designed the Flicka as a pint-sized, go-anywhere cruising sailboat. Pacific Seacraft acquired the molds in 1978 from the original builder and has built 435 to date. It is out of production . . . unless the company receives five orders, which it will then fill. The last boat came out the builder's door in 2001. With headroom of 5 feet 11 inches and 6,000 pounds displacement, she seems larger than her 20-foot LOA would suggest. Pacific Seacraft's reputation for quality is very good, which makes it a little surprising that a one-piece fiberglass pan is used for the Flicka's interior furniture foundations. The hull is solid fiberglass, and the deck is cored with plywood. She is not particularly fast, and prefers stronger winds because of her displacement. The Flicka has been sold with both inboard and outboard engines, though the former is to be preferred. If you could get on the new boat list as number 5, the price will be somewhere around $50,000. That's a lot for a 20-footer, but there's no other boat quite like Flicka.

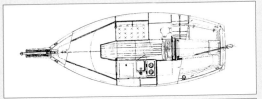

LOA	23'7"
LOD	20'0"
LWL	18'2"
BEAM	8'0"
DRAFT	3'3"
DISPLACEMENT	6,000 LB.
BALLAST	1,800 LB.
SAIL AREA	250 SQ. FT.
DESIGNER	BRUCE BINGHAM
PRICE NEW	NOT IN PRODUCTION
PRICE USED	$11,500–$13,100 (1980 MODEL) $21,900–$24,400 (1987 MODEL) $36,000–$40,000 (1992 MODEL) $62,600–$68,800 (1998 MODEL)
CONTACT	PACIFIC SEACRAFT CORP. 1301 E ORANGETHORPE AVE. FULLERTON CA 92831 714-879-1610 WWW.PACIFICSEACRAFT.COM POCKET YACHTS WWW.POCKETYACHTS.COM
SIMILAR BOATS	HURLEY 20 VIVACITY 21 WESTERLY PAGEANT 23 DANA 24 (ALSO BY PACIFIC SEA- CRAFT, AND IN PRODUCTION) BRISTOL CORSAIR 24

CRUISERS

QUICKSTEP 24

Designer Ted Brewer is best known for his cruising designs, many of them blue-water boats. He drew the lines of the Quickstep 24 in the late 1970s for aluminum construction. When that plan evaporated, the rights were sold to ocean racer Bill Stannard, who produced 23 hulls before turning the operation over to Gary Lannigan, marketing director for C. E. Ryder Corporation (builder of the Sea Sprite and Southern Cross cruisers) in the early 1980s. He and his wife Annie then started their own company to build the boat in fiberglass. The boat has an almost full keel, with cutaway forefoot and the so-called "Brewer Bite" just forward of the rudder. This is to reduce the wetted-surface area and enhance maneuverability. Although the boat is an adequate weekend cruiser for a couple or small family, the large cockpit also makes it a comfortable daysailer. As with the Alerion Express 28, this is a gentleman's boat, albeit smaller. Like the Alerion, many Quickstep owners are coming down from larger boats and appreciate the boat's high-quality construction, good looks, and easy handling under sail. It was sold with either inboard or outboard power.

LOA	23'11"
LWL	19'0"
BEAM	7'11"
DRAFT	3'4"
DISPLACEMENT	4,000 LB.
BALLAST	1,900 LB.
SAIL AREA	259 SQ. FT.
DESIGNER	TED BREWER
PRICE NEW	NOT IN PRODUCTION
PRICE USED	$8,050–$9,250 (1983 MODEL) $9,900–$11,300 (1986 MODEL)
SIMILAR BOATS	SEA SPRITE 23 COM-PAC 23 CAPE DORY 25

CRUISERS

CAPE DORY 25

The Cape Dory 25 was Cape Dory's first larger cruising boat; owner Andy Vavolotis obtained the molds for the Greenwich 24 from the Allied Boat Company and in 1973 transformed the full-keeler into a successful pocket cruiser. An outboard motor sits in a cockpit well. After the 25, the company retained Carl Alberg to design successively larger models. Narrow and with little freeboard, the Cape Dory 25 is a dated design, but traditionalists still adore the lines and underbody. The 25 was updated in 1981 with a beamier, heavier, deeper version called the Cape Dory 25D that sought to overcome the original boat's shortcomings. All specs below are for the 25, not the 25D.

LOA	24'10"
LWL	18'0"
BEAM	7'3"
DRAFT	3'0"
DISPLACEMENT	4,000 LB.
BALLAST	1,700 LB.
SAIL AREA	264 SQ. FT.
DESIGNER	GEORGE STADEL
PRICE NEW	NOT IN PRODUCTION
PRICE USED	$6,300–$7,200 (1974 MODEL)
	$8,900–$10,100 (1981 MODEL)
	$9,400–$10,700 (1982 MODEL)
CONTACT	CAPE DORY SAILBOAT OWNERS ASSOC.
	WWW.CAPEDORY.ORG
SIMILAR BOATS	SEA SPRITE 23
	COM-PAC 23
	QUICKSTEP 24

CRUISERS

CAPE DORY 300MS

Some say that motor sailers are neither fish nor fowl; others say that they are the best of both worlds, combining the aesthetic appeal of sail with the creature comforts of a powerboat. Although the Cape Dory 300MS, introduced in 1986 and built for just a few years, is admittedly not a great sailer—mostly because of the shallow keel and considerable windage of the pilothouse—it does OK, especially off the wind. For a 30-footer, it's beamy, with plenty of elbow room in the saloon. And the powerboat-style cockpit has space for a pair of captain's chairs. Best of all, the pilothouse has seats for three. It is enclosed on three sides; the aft side can be sealed by canvas curtains with acrylic windows for 360-degree visibility, even in nasty weather. Motor sailer styles vary considerably. Although the 300MS mimics powerboats in many ways, it retains the traditionally smaller cockpit and rounder hull form of the sailboat. Your choice depends on where you'll sail (the latter is better for offshore) and how quick you'll be to drop sail and motor (motoring a lot favors the powerboat style like the 300MS). Either way, motor sailers are not for high-performance sailors, but instead are for people who want a high degree of comfort and are realistic about their sailing interests.

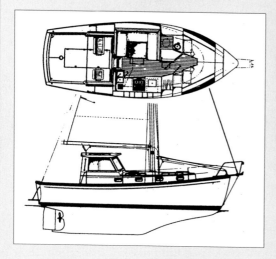

LOA	29'10"
LWL	26'6"
BEAM	11'5"
DRAFT	3'11"
DISPLACEMENT	11,500 LB.
BALLAST	4,500 LB.
SAIL AREA	442 SQ. FT.
DESIGNER	CLIVE DENT
PRICE NEW	NOT IN PRODUCTION
PRICE USED	$48,300–$53,100 (1986 MODEL) $77,000–$84,700 (1992 MODEL)
CONTACT	CAPE DORY SAILBOAT OWNERS ASSOC. WWW.CAPEDORY.ORG
SIMILAR BOATS	RAWSON 30 PH FALES 32 NAVIGATOR PEARSON 36 PH

ALBERG 30

More than 700 Alberg 30s were built during its record-breaking production run of 25 years between 1962 and 1987. All were built in Ontario by Whitby Boat Works. Carl Alberg worked for the U.S. Coast Guard much of his career, designing boats for commercial companies on the side. He drew the 28-foot 6-inch Triton for Pearson in 1958, and the Triton is credited with fueling the fiberglass auxiliary sailboat boom and helping the industry make the transition from wood to plastic. Later in his career, he designed nearly all the Cape Dorys for Andy Vavolotis. The Alberg 30 is a classic CCA (Cruising Club of America) type, with its relatively narrow beam, long overhangs and large mainsail. The full keel with attached rudder, though old-fashioned now, remains an excellent configuration for long-distance cruising, affording excellent directional stability, protection from submerged objects, and the capability to sit on its own keel against a seawall at low tide for performing repairs or maintenance. The interior is small by today's standards, but there are berths for four, an enclosed head, and a serviceable galley aft. Early boats had Atomic 4 gas engines; later models had Volvo diesels. The hulls are solid fiberglass, and overall construction is very good, though early models are getting quite old: check decks for oilcanning, tanks for corrosion, rudders for loose play, and chainplate attachments for leaks and rot.

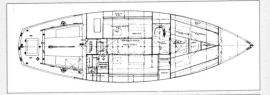

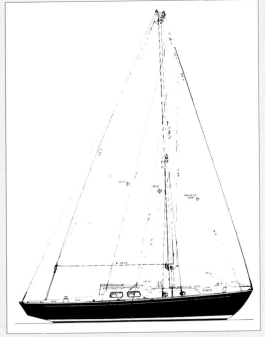

LOA	30'3"
LWL	21'8"
BEAM	8'9"
DRAFT	4'3"
DISPLACEMENT	9,000 LB.
BALLAST	3,300 LB.
SAIL AREA	410 SQ. FT.
DESIGNER	CARL ALBERG
PRICE NEW	NOT IN PRODUCTION
PRICE USED	$11,700–$13,200 (1965 MODEL)
	$17,300–$19,700 (1974 MODEL)
	$23,300–$25,900 (1981 MODEL)
	$31,600–$35,100 (1986 MODEL)
CONTACT	ALBERG 30 OWNERS ASSOC. WWW.ALBERG30.ORG
SIMILAR BOATS	BRISTOL 27
	PEARSON TRITON
	ALLIED SEAWIND 30
	ALBERG 35

CRUISERS

SOUTHERN CROSS 31

Tom Gilmer, a professor of naval architecture at the U.S. Naval Academy in Annapolis, drew the Allied Seawind 30, the first fiberglass boat to circumnavigate. Later, he updated the design as the Seawind II. He didn't design many production sailboats, and the next was this Southern Cross 31, with a hull very similar to the original Seawind (except that the Southern Cross is a double-ender). Clark Ryder, of Bristol, Rhode Island, built about 130 of them between 1976 and 1987. A number were sold as bare hulls for owner completion. The hull is cored with Airex foam in the topsides only. The deck and coachroof are cored with balsa. The hull-to-deck joint is an outward-turning flange that is more vulnerable to damage than inward-turning flanges. Ballast is internal. Bulkheads are tabbed to the hull. Overall construction quality is above average and suitable for offshore sailing. The Southern Cross 31 is fairly heavy, which affects light-air performance, but she has made good passages and will be comfortable at sea, which is more important. The cockpit is small, which is a desirable characteristic offshore. A 1981 boat had a base price of $62,500. If you're considering buying one, be sure you know whether it was factory- or owner-completed.

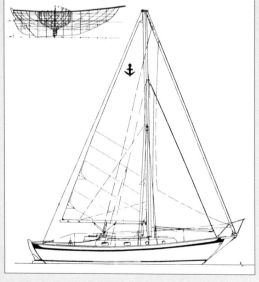

LOA	31'0"
LWL	25'0"
BEAM	9'6"
DRAFT	4'7"
DISPLACEMENT	13,600 LB.
BALLAST	4,400 LB.
SAIL AREA	447 SQ. FT.
DESIGNER	THOMAS S. GILMER
PRICE NEW	NOT IN PRODUCTION
PRICE USED	$40,400–$44,900 (1982 MODEL) $51,700–$56,800 (1986 MODEL)

CONTACT	SOUTHERN CROSS OWNERS ASSOC.
	C/O TREASURER/SECRETARY,
	   MICHAEL DESISTO
	P.O. BOX 142
	WEST BOOTHBAY ME 04575
	207-633-5838
	WWW.GEOCITIES.COM/
	   ~SOUTHERNCROSSOW/
	   INDEX.HTML

SIMILAR BOATS	ALLIED SEAWIND II MARINER 31 DOWNEASTER 32 WESTSAIL 32

PACIFIC SEACRAFT 34

Pacific Seacraft was founded in 1976, changed hands several times, and (as of 2004) is managed by Don Kohlmann, former owner of Ericson Yachts. This explains why Pacific Seacraft used to produce several Ericson models in addition to its line of traditional cruising boats. The 37 was launched in 1980, and the 34 was launched in 1984. The two are similar in appearance with canoe sterns (round) and double headsail sloop rigs. Hulls are solid fiberglass, with outer layers using vinylester resin to help prevent osmotic blisters. The deck is cored with end-grain balsa. An interior pan runs the full length of the boat. The finishwork below is well done and attractive. Headroom is 6 feet 4 inches. The galleys are large, for living aboard. Sailing performance is about what you'd expect for a moderately heavy cruising boat. The best point of sail is reaching. Motion is comfortable. The cockpit is small, which is good for offshore work because it minimizes the amount of water that could flood it; on the other hand, it can quickly get cramped with too many people aboard, and the absence of an afterdeck or side decks can make moving about the aft end of the boat a little tricky. All in all, an excellent couple's boat for blue-water cruising.

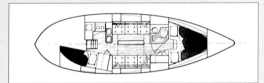

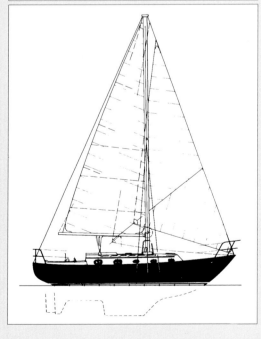

LOA	34'1"
LWL	26'2"
BEAM	10'0"
DRAFT	4'1" OR 4'11"
DISPLACEMENT	13,200 LB.
BALLAST	4,800 LB.
SAIL AREA	534 SQ. FT.
DESIGNER	WILLIAM CREALOCK
PRICE NEW	$190,000
PRICE USED	$59,900–$66,200 (1984 **MODEL**) $119,500–$131,000 (1992 **MODEL**) $232,000–$255,000 (2000 **MODEL**)
CONTACT	PACIFIC SEACRAFT CORP. 1301 E ORANGETHORPE AVE. FULLERTON CA 92831 714-879-1610 WWW.PACIFICSEACRAFT.COM
SIMILAR BOATS	MASON 33 CABO RICO 34/36 CALIBER 35 LRC PACIFIC SEACRAFT 37

CRUISERS

CALIBER 35 LRC

Caliber Yachts is run by brothers Michael (naval architect) and George (business manager) McCreary. After college, they built a boat in their garage and the following year (1980) started their own company. Their first offering was a 28-footer, followed by a 33. In 2004, the lineup is decidedly larger: the Caliber 35, 40, and 47, all with the suffix LRC (for long-range cruiser). That's the market that the McCrearys are going after, in a modern sort of way. All have long cruising fins, so the boats can sit on their own bottoms, careened against a wall if repairs are needed in faraway places. And the rudders are mounted on full-length skegs, which improves tracking and offers some protection. Inner forestays, especially if fitted with furling staysails, make reducing sail easier. Construction is above average, with a mostly wood interior; bulkheads are glassed to the hull and deck, making for a quiet sturdy boat. The 35 has eleven opening ports and five hatches, making for better ventilation than on most production boats. Michael McCreary's styling includes a lot of straight lines, which you either like or you don't.

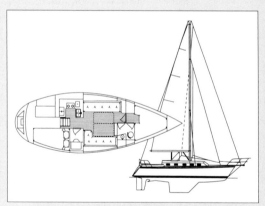

LOA	35'9"
LWL	29'10"
BEAM	11'4"
DRAFT	4'6"
DISPLACEMENT	13,100 LB.
BALLAST	6,100 LB.
SAIL AREA	563 SQ. FT.
DESIGNER	CALIBER YACHTS
PRICE NEW	$185,000
PRICE USED	$69,400–$76,300 (1991 MODEL) $80,300–$88,200 (1993 MODEL)
CONTACT	CALIBER YACHTS 4551 107TH CIRCLE N CLEARWATER FL 33762 727-573-0627 WWW.CALIBERYACHT.COM
SIMILAR BOATS	PACIFIC SEACRAFT 34 SAGA 35 TARTAN 3500

ALLIED PRINCESS 36

The Allied Boat Company of Catskill, New York, built sturdy cruising sailboats from 1962 to 1982. Its Seawind was the first fiberglass boat to circumnavigate. The Princess 36's springy sheer is distinctive. Standing on deck, you'll also notice that the bow is quite a bit higher than the deck amidships; going forward is like walking uphill, which is quite a contrast to the more common flattish sheers and horizontal decks. The hull is solid fiberglass, and the deck cored with balsa. The keel is long, with attached rudder. Ballast is internal; the keel cavity is part of the hull mold, and the cast ballast dropped in and glassed over. Such a keel doesn't provide the lift (necessary for better windward performance) that a fin keel does, but on the plus side, there are no bolts holding it on that can corrode or get bent in a grounding. The interior is all wood. There are three good sea berths. Headroom is 6 feet 4 inches. Speed under sail is just average (below average upwind), but the boat tracks well and when flying the mizzen, she can be trimmed to balance with minimal attention to the helm. That's what you want for offshore passages with a shorthanded crew. A great value for the dreamer on a small budget.

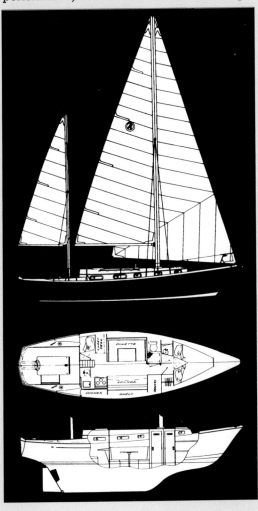

LOA	36'0"
LWL	27'6"
BEAM	11'0"
DRAFT	4'6"
DISPLACEMENT	14,400 LB.
BALLAST	5,000 LB.
SAIL AREA	595 SQ. FT. (SLOOP) 604 SQ. FT. (KETCH)
DESIGNER	ARTHUR EDMUNDS
PRICE NEW	NOT IN PRODUCTION
PRICE USED	$29,700–$33,000 (1973 MODEL) $49,100–$56,200 (1981 MODEL)
CONTACT	ALLIED PRINCESS 36 OWNER'S WEB WWW.GEOCITIES.COM/ THETROPICS/8005/ AP36PAGE.HTML
SIMILAR BOATS	ALLIED SEAWIND 32 HANS CHRISTIAN 34/36 PEARSON 365 ALLIED MISTRESS 39

CRUISERS

FREEDOM 36

Former advertising executive Garry Hoyt launched the Freedom 40 in 1977 and dazzled a lot of people—racers, cruisers, designers, and builders—with its unstayed cat ketch rig. Without an engine, it was also light and fast. The company he founded on the philosophy of making sailing simple, safe, and fun grew quickly and added smaller models—the Freedom 21, 25, and 33— that the public grabbed because they no longer had to grind winches trimming unwieldy genoas. Eventually, the ketches in the lineup gave way to sloops with large mainsails and vestigial jibs, or "blades." After Hoyt sold the company (to its builder, TPI, who in turn sold it to marketing director Paul Petronella), other designers were brought in. Gary Mull's first design for Freedom was this 36. Gone were Hoyt's curvy lines, replaced with sharper, crisper shapes. In most respects, the 36 looks like a lot of other racer/cruisers, with relatively flat sheer, fin keel, and elliptical rudder. The interior layout is spacious and straightforward, with a private stateroom aft, separate nav station, and U-shaped galley. Most 36s were sold with the sloop rig, though a few carried the ketch concept. Unlike the original 40, however, the mainmast is taller than the mizzen. Construction is above average. Speed under sail is a little less than average due to limited ways to increase sail area (no genoa, no spinnaker). But with a self-tending jib, she sure is easy to tack, and therein lies its appeal. Production was from 1986 to 1989.

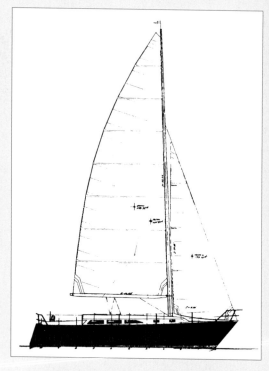

LOA	36'5"
LWL	30'7"
BEAM	12'6"
DRAFT	4'6" OR 6'0"
DISPLACEMENT	14,370 LB.
BALLAST	6,500 LB.
SAIL AREA	685 SQ. FT.
DESIGNER	GARY MULL
PRICE NEW	NO LONGER IN PRODUCTION
PRICE USED	$62,000–$68,000 (1986 MODEL) $72,700–$80,300 (1988 MODEL)
CONTACT	FREEDOM YACHTS 305 OLIPHANT LANE MIDDLETOWN RI 02842 401-848-2900 WWW.FREEDOMYACHTS.COM
SIMILAR BOATS	FREEDOM 35 FREEDOM 38 HERRESHOFF CAT KETCH 38 NONSUCH 30, 36

TAYANA 37

The popular Tayana 37 began life as the CT 37; it then had its name changed in 1979. The builder was Ta Yang of Kaosiung, Taiwan, which built 560 of these heavy displacement, double-enders. The Tayana 37 represents the better side of Taiwan boatbuilding during its heyday of the 1970s and 1980s. The interiors are all wood, with a great deal of solid teak and hand-carved detailing. It has a full keel with cutaway forefoot. Construction is strong, but the prospective buyer must be aware of certain areas, such as custom Taiwanese metalwork (which may be of low-quality alloys) and the inappropriate use of plywood (such as in cockpit seats). As with all boats, retain a competent surveyor before finalizing your purchase. Standard diesel engines have included Yanmar, Perkins, and Volvo. Spars may be wood or aluminum, with the latter much preferred. Perry himself recommends the cutter rig over the ketch. It has a reputation for being initially tender (it heels quickly and then stops, which some might object to, but this quality does take the snappiness out of the roll) and having some weather helm (which can be at least partly corrected with good sails and by raking the mast forward). This is a go-anywhere boat.

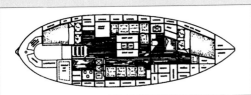

LOA	36'8"
LWL	31'10"
BEAM	11'6"
DRAFT	5'8"
DISPLACEMENT	24,000 LB.
BALLAST	7,340 LB.
SAIL AREA	864 SQ. FT. (SLOOP) 768 SQ. FT. (KETCH)
DESINGER	ROBERT PERRY
PRICE NEW	NOT IN PRODUCTION
PRICE USED	$59,300–$68,200 (1979 MODEL) $67,800–$74,500 (1982 MODEL) $123,000–$135,500 (1992 MODEL)
SIMILAR BOATS	HANS CHRISTIAN 34/36 MARINER 36 CT 37 AND 38 HANS CHRISTIAN 38

CRUISERS

CABO RICO 38

Cabo Rico sailboats are built in Costa Rica. The company's first facility was the corner of a British Leyland's Range Rover plant, a side interest of the manager, John Schofield. He produced his first boat in 1965; the first for the U.S. market was the Tiburon 36 ketch, designed by Bill Crealock. He's been Cabo Rico's primary designer ever since. The Cabo Rico 38 launched in 1979 and is still in production, along with an entire line of full keel cruisers ranging from 34 to 50 feet, as well as the Northeast line of motor sailers and Cambria sailing yachts. The 38 has moderately heavy displacement, an attractive sheer, cutter rig, and solid construction. The hull is cored with end-grain balsa, but not as in most boats; it is added to the inside of the solid glass outer skin, not for strength but for insulation, and then covered with a thin layer of glass. Threaded stainless steel plates are embedded in the deck laminate to which deck hardware is screwed. Ballast was originally encapsulated iron, but is now lead. The interior is beautifully made of exotic woods. The only fiberglass moldings are in the shower, engine bed, and icebox—perfect uses for them. As one would expect of a cruising boat like this, speed is only average, but she is comfortable to sail on and with a waterline of nearly 30 feet, she will make respectable passages.

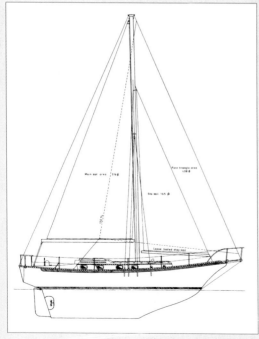

LOA	38'0"
LWL	29'3"
BEAM	11'6"
DRAFT	5'0"
DISPLACEMENT	21,000 LB.
BALLAST	7,800 LB.
SAIL AREA	778 SQ. FT.
DESIGNER	WILLIAM CREALOCK
PRICE NEW	$325,000
PRICE USED	$79,600–$87,500 (1982 MODEL)
	$154,500–$169,500 (1992 MODEL)
	$165,500–$181,000 (1993 MODEL)
CONTACT	CABO RICO CUSTOM YACHTS INC.
	2258 SE 17TH ST.
	FORT LAUDERDALE FL 33316
	954-462-6699
	WWW.CABORICO.COM
SIMILAR BOATS	ISLAND PACKET 37
	SHANNON 37
	ISLAND PACKET 38
	ISLAND PACKET 380
	CREALA 40
	ISLAND PACKET 40

ISLAND PACKET 38

Naval architect Bob Johnson and his wife started Island Packet Yachts in 1980 with the launch of a shoal-draft 26-footer. Their star rose as Cape Dory's set, so that today there is still really just one builder of full-keel cruising boats in the United States. But although Cape Dorys were deep and narrow in the traditional manner, Island Packets are shoal and wide—good for gunkholing in Florida Bay, but less desirable for crossing oceans. Still, many Island Packets do. The IP 38 was built between 1986 and 1993, with 188 being sold. Original base price in 1986 was $109,000; in 1993 it was $169,950, which is about what they sell for today. All Island Packets share certain features: cream-color gelcoat, molded bowsprit, cutter rig, full keel with attached rudder, and fiberglass pan interior. Headroom in the IP 38 is 6 feet 4 inches. Water capacity is 157 gallons, fuel capacity is 57 gallons. Auxiliary power is a Yanmar diesel. The IP 38 can sleep up to seven persons in three cabins.

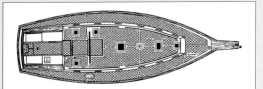

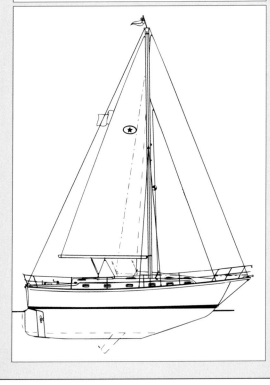

LOA	41'6"
LOD	38'0"
LWL	33'0"
BEAM	12'8"
DRAFT	5'0" (KEEL)
	4'0"–7'7" (KEEL/CB)
DISPLACEMENT	21,500 LB.
BALLAST	10,000 LB.
SAIL AREA	870 SQ. FT.
DESIGNER	BOB JOHNSON
PRICE NEW	NOT IN PRODUCTION
PRICE USED	$99,500–$109,500 (1986 MODEL)
	$146,000–$160,500 (1992 MODEL)
	$154,000–$169,500 (1993 MODEL)
CONTACT	ISLAND PACKET YACHTS
	1979 WILD ACRES RD.
	LARGO FL 33771
	888-SAIL-IPY (888-724-5479);
	727-535-6431
	WWW.IPY.COM
SIMILAR BOATS	ISLAND PACKET 37
	SHANNON 37
	CABO RICO 38
	ISLAND PACKET 380
	CREALA 40
	ISLAND PACKET 40

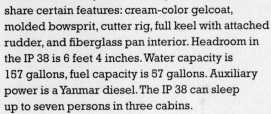

CRUISERS

PASSPORT 40

Passport Yachts was founded by Wendel Renken, who was essentially a U.S. developer/importer. The Passport 40, introduced in 1981, was first built at the King Dragon yard in Taiwan and later at Hi Yang. The boats are now imported by an Annapolis dealer. The Passport 40 illustrates how designer Robert Perry's thinking about cruising boats has evolved over the years (see the Valiant 40, opposite). Gone is the canoe stern in favor of a conventional transom, and the coachroof has considerable camber, which is stronger than the Valiant's flat coachroof. Perry describes the Passport 40 as having "asymmetrical waterlines, a wedge shape, and flat bottom. The Valiant 40 has symmetrical waterlines and higher deadrise." The keel is a long cruising fin, and the rudder is mounted on a skeg. The hull is solid fiberglass. Teak decks are ⅝ inch thick. There are ten bronze opening portlights with screens for ventilation. Joinerwork below is solid Burmese teak. Two layouts were offered, one with an offset double berth forward and another with the head forward. This is a high-quality, seaworthy passagemaker; although it is not capable of raceboat speeds, it will get you to your destination quickly. Production ceased around 1988.

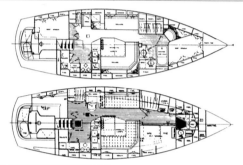

LOA	39'5"
LWL	33'5"
BEAM	12'8"
DRAFT	5'3" OR 5'9"
DISPLACEMENT	22,771 LB.
BALLAST	8,500 LB.
SAIL AREA	771 SQ. FT.
DESIGNER	ROBERT PERRY
PRICE NEW	NOT IN PRODUCTION
PRICE USED	$108,500–$119,500 (1984 MODEL) $139,000–$152,500 (1988 MODEL)
CONTACT	PASSPORT YACHTS 326 FIRST ST., SUITE 404 ANNAPOLIS MD 21403 410-263-0008 WWW.WAGNERSTEVENS.COM
SIMILAR BOATS	CALIBER 40 LRC VALIANT 40 TARTAN 40 PASSPORT 415

CRUISERS

VALIANT 40

When Seattle-based Robert Perry left his apprenticeship at Dick Carter's design office and hung out his own shingle, one of his first commissions was the Valiant 40. It was an immediate success and jump-started Perry's career. It also introduced the concept of the "performance cruiser" because many cruising boats before this time were more traditional, with heavier displacement and full keels. In 1973, the Valiant was considered quite light for offshore work; that's hardly the case today. The Valiant 40 has made numerous safe circumnavigations, including Dan Byrne's completion of the 1981–1982 BOC Challenge.

The boats were built by Uniflite and some had a fire-retardant resin called Hetron, which caused hull blisters and led to a class-action law suit. Uniflite declared bankruptcy in 1984, and the Valiant assets were sold to Rich Worstell, a Valiant dealer, who moved production to Texas. Despite these problems, the boat is very strong with a solid wood interior. There are good sea berths amidships and a double berth aft. The flat coachroof is distinctive. She sails very well. The 40 was eventually replaced by the Valiant 42.

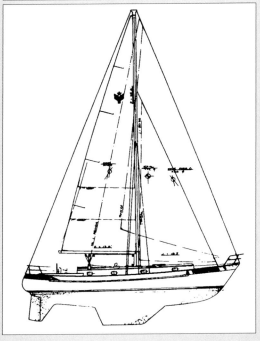

LOA	39'11"
LWL	34'0"
BEAM	12'4"
DRAFT	5'2" OR 6'0"
DISPLACEMENT	22,500 LB.
BALLAST	7,700 LB.
SAIL AREA	753 SQ. FT.
DESIGNER	ROBERT PERRY
PRICE NEW	NOT IN PRODUCTION
PRICE USED	$75,600–$83,100 (1975 MODEL)
	$98,400–$108,000 (1981 MODEL)
	$186,000–$204,500 (1991 MODEL)
CONTACT	VALIANT YACHTS
	500 HARBOUR VIEW RD.
	GORDONVILLE TX 76245
	903-523-4899
	WWW.VALIANTSAILBOATS.COM
	VALIANT YACHTS OWNERS ASSOC.
	WWW.OFFSHOREYACHTS.COM/
	ASSOCIATION.HTM
SIMILAR BOATS	CALIBER 40 LRC
	PASSPORT 40
	TARTAN 40
	PASSPORT 415
	VALIANT 42

CRUISERS

BLOCK ISLAND 40

The well-traveled Block Island 40 began as the Vitesse, a design commissioned by Dutch yacht importer Arie Van Breems, and built by American Boatbuilding in East Greenwich, Rhode Island. The first boat went down the ways in 1957. When the yard acquired ownership of the molds a few years later, the name was changed to Block Island 40, after the popular cruising destination off the Rhode Island coast. Connecticut sparmaker Metalmast produced a few BI 40s, with an ugly chopped-off stern, and the molds fell dormant until C. E. Ryder employee Eric Woods bought them in 1985 and started producing the original hull again. They were lovingly fitted out and finished, too. His aim was to build one boat for himself, but it took him 16 years and at least that many boats for others before he accomplished his goal. The yawl rig lets you to sail through rough weather "jib and jigger" (that is, without the mainsail), yet keep the sail plan balanced. This interior seems small by today's standards, although the beam is roughly the same as in many more modern boats; the difference is in lower freeboard and finer ends. The BI 40 is a classic, hall of fame cruising boat that is an absolute delight to sail. Eric went cruising in his and turned the company over to some folks in New Bedford, who apparently found old-fashioned boats a tough sell. Too bad.

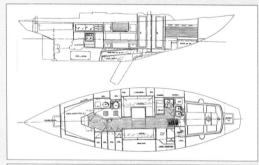

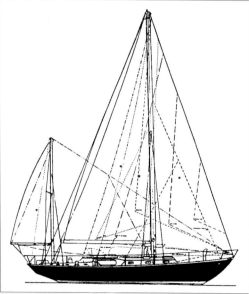

LOA	40'8"
LWL	29'2"
BEAM	11'10"
DRAFT	4'2"–8'10"
DISPLACEMENT	20,000 LB.
BALLAST	7,800 LB.
SAIL AREA	738 SQ. FT.
DESIGNER	BILL TRIPP
PRICE NEW	NOT IN PRODUCTION
PRICE USED	$38,200–$42,500 (1960 MODEL)
	$247,000–$271,000 (1997 MODEL)
	$334,000–$367,000 (2001 MODEL)
SIMILAR BOATS	HINCKLEY BERMUDA 40

BREWER 12.8/BREWER 44

These two similar boats evolved from the Whitby 42, a classic (1971) center-cockpit cruiser built for years by Whitby Boat Works in Ontario, Canada—the same company that built the Alberg 30 and 37. When the Whitby 42 was discontinued, consumer interest prompted Fort Myers Yacht and Ship-building to have Brewer update the design and continue production during the 1980s. The first revision was the 12.8, later replaced by the 44. Both are center cockpit cutters with a long keel–centerboard arrangement and a skeg-mounted rudder. The hull is cored with balsa only above the waterline, which provides stiffness and weight savings there, and keeps the core out of the water where it could conceivably get wet around poorly sealed through-hulls. The standard engine in the 12.8 was a 62 hp Ford Lehman diesel; in the 44, it was a 62 hp Perkins. The 135-gallon fuel tank gives a cruising range of about 700 miles. Interior finish quality is better in the 44 than the 12.8. The boat is well balanced and handles nicely. The boom on the 12.8 is quite high, which makes attaching the halyard and reefing difficult. The cockpit comfortably sits eight. A solid, well-built world cruiser that represents a good value compared with higher-priced Aldens and Hinckleys.

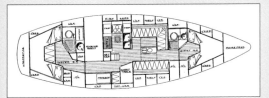

	BREWER 12.8	BREWER 44
LOA	42'0"	44'0"
LWL	33'9"	35'6"
BEAM	13'6"	
DRAFT	4'6" OR 5'2"	
DISPLACEMENT	23,850 LB.	27,500 LB.
BALLAST	9,000 LB.	12,000 LB.
SAIL AREA	867 SQ. FT.	867 SQ. FT.
DESIGNER	TED BREWER	
PRICE NEW	NOT IN PRODUCTION	
PRICE USED	$126,000–$138,500 (1986 12.8 MODEL)	
SIMILAR BOATS	BRISTOL 41.1, 42.2, 43.3, 45.5 WHITBY 42 HINCKLEY 43 CSY 44 LITTLE HARBOR 44 NORSEMAN 447 TARTAN TOCK	

CRUISERS

MASON 43/44

The Mason 43/44 and other Masons are built in the Orient and imported to the United States by Pacific Asian Enterprises (PAE), better known in recent years for the Nordhavn line of passagemaking motor yachts. In his long career, Al Mason worked with Carl Alberg, John Alden, and Sparkman & Stephens. The Mason 43 and 44 share the same hull but different decks. The 43 appeared in 1978 and was replaced by the 44 in 1985. About 200 were built. The Taiwanese builder is Ta Shing, probably the best in that country, and capable of very fine work. The 43/44 is a very traditional design with sweeping sheer, long overhangs, long cabin trunk, and moderately heavy displacement. The hull is solid fiberglass. There is a lot of solid teak on this and other Taiwan boats, which looks great as long as it is maintained, but keeping up with it can become a nuisance. The 43's companionway is offset to starboard, which means that on port tack, it is closer to the water. It was moved on centerline in the 44. Ketch and cutter rigs were offered. The aft cabin has both double and single berths. The double berth forward is offset to port, which is in some ways an improvement over the usual V-berth, although the person on the inside does have to crawl over his/her bedmate to get out. These are off-the-wind boats that have made circumnavigations. Top quality, but with complicated systems and oodles of teak; beware the maintenance.

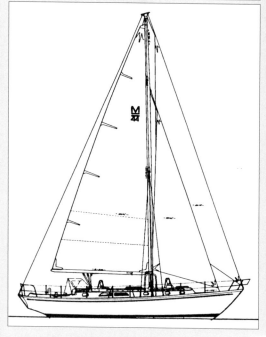

LOA	43'11"
LWL	31'3"
BEAM	12'4"
DRAFT	5'6" OR 6'3"
DISPLACEMENT	27,400 LB.
BALLAST	8,400 LB.
SAIL AREA	899 SQ. FT.
DESIGNER	AL MASON
PRICE NEW	NOT CURRENTLY IN PRODUCTION; SPECIAL ORDER ONLY
PRICE USED	$136,000–$160,500 (1980 MODEL) $150,000–$177,000 (1982 MODEL) $225,000–$247,000 (1989 MODEL)
CONTACT	PACIFIC ASIAN ENTERPRISES P.O. BOX 874 DANA POINT CA 92629 949-496-4848 WWW.NORDHAVN.COM
SIMILAR BOATS	BAYFIELD 40 HALLBERG RASSY 42 HANS CHRISTIAN 43 SHANNON 43 FUJI 45 KANTER ATLANTIC 45 MARINER 47 WESTWIND VAGABOND 47

J/24 (INTERNATIONAL)

J/Boats has been one of the most successful sailboat companies of the past 30 years, and it all began with the J/24. Rod Johnstone built the prototype in his Connecticut garage, and his brother Bob found a builder in TPI, and then sold the heck out of the boats. Today, this one-design keelboat numbers about 11,000, with licensed builders in South America and Europe. There are numerous large fleets around the country; national and world events are a big deal. Its incredible popularity belies some shortcomings, however, including difficulty learning to sail the boat competitively (although its many controls make for a good introduction to the world of big boat yacht racing) and a cluttered deck that has a reputation for bruising crew. Unlike the keelboats in the daysailer category, such as the Shields, the J/24 and other cabin boats have self-bailing cockpits that can't swamp.

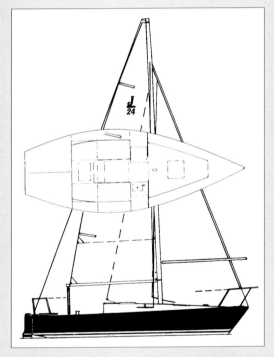

LOA	24'0"
LWL	19'5"
BEAM	8'11"
DRAFT	4'0"
DISPLACEMENT	3,100 LB.
BALLAST	950 LB.
SAIL AREA	261 SQ. FT.
DESIGNER	ROD JOHNSTONE
PRICE NEW	NOT IN PRODUCTION
PRICE USED	$6,850–$7,850 (1982 MODEL) $17,400–$19,700 (1993 MODEL) $33,200–$36,900 (2000 MODEL)
CONTACT	U.S. J/24 CLASS ASSOC. 7793 BURNET ROAD, #15 AUSTIN TX 78757 512-266-0033 WWW.J24CLASS.ORG/USA/ J/24 CLASS INTERNATIONAL WWW.J24CLASS.ORG
SIMILAR BOATS	MOORE 24 SAN JUAN 24 SHARK 24 TRIPP 26

MELGES 24 (INTERNATIONAL)

If the J/24 seems fast to you, wait until you get a ride on the Melges 24. Conceived as a semigenerational update of the J/24, it displaces almost half as much. Whereas the J/24 has a PHRF rating of around 170, the Melges 24 rates in the 90s. It was developed by Hans Melges, son of Harry "Buddy" Melges, the only skipper ever to win an America's Cup (1995) and an Olympic gold medal. The Melges family has been building scows and other boats in Zenda, Wisconsin, since 1943. The Melges 24 has many carbon fiber parts—mast, keel fin, and bowsprit—to reduce weight. The sprit is for flying an asymmetrical spinnaker. The bulb keel lifts straight up for trailering. This is a high-tech raceboat for experienced sailors (or wannabes) who groove on thrills!

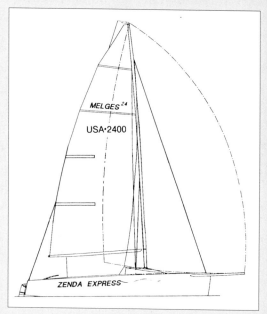

LOA	24'0"
LWL	22'0"
BEAM	8'2"
DRAFT	5'0"
DISPLACEMENT	1,750 LB.
BALLAST	620 LB.
SAIL AREA	380 SQ. FT.
DESIGNER	REICHEL/PUGH
PRICE NEW	$36,265
PRICE USED	$26,200–$29,000 (1998 MODEL)
CONTACT	MELGES BOAT WORKS N598 ZENDA RD. ZENDA WI 53195 262-275-1110 WWW.MELGES.COM U.S. MELGES 24 CLASS ASSOC. C/O JEFF JONES, PRESIDENT 53455 BELLAMINE SHELBY TWP. MI 48316 248-652-7244 INTERNATIONAL MELGES 24 CLASS ASSOC. WWW.MELGES24.COM
SIMILAR BOATS	J/80 TRIPP 26

EXPRESS 27

Designed in 1981, the Express 27 had a successful career in small keelboat racing, and helped to popularize lightweight, high-performance boats on the West Coast. Carl Schumacher, who died in 2002, apprenticed for Gary Mull for four years before opening his own practice in 1977. Besides the Alerion Express boats and the larger Express 37, Schumacher designed some 40 boats, ranging from One-Ton raceboats to world cruisers, and was involved in the San Francisco–based challenge for the 1987 America's Cup and its innovative front-rudder boat. Express 27s are still sought after and do not remain on the market for long. Molds for the boat surfaced in New Zealand in 2003, putting it back in production after a considerable hiatus. Hulls are laid up with vinylester resin and Klegecell cores. This is a great boat to race on San Francisco Bay, where there is a very active fleet.

SIMILAR BOATS

LOA	27'3"
LWL	23'9"
BEAM	8'2"
DRAFT	4'6"
DISPLACEMENT	2,450 LB.
BALLAST	1,100 LB.
SAIL AREA	276 SQ. FT.
DESIGNER	CARL SCHUMACHER
PRICE NEW	NZ$80,000
PRICE USED	$8,500–$9,800 (1984 MODEL)
CONTACT	DAVIE NORRIS BOAT BUILDERS INC. P.O. BOX 19702 11 NEWTOWN ST. CHRISTCHURCH NEW ZEALAND 64-3-3848454 WWW.NORRISBOATBUILDERS. CO.NZ EXPRESS 27 CLASS ASSOC. WWW.EXPRESS27.ORG
	ANTRIM 27

RACERS

J/30

The J/30 was the second boat designed by J/Boats, after the J/24. Between 1979 and 1986, 546 were built. They were built by Tillotson Pearson Industries (before the name was shortened to TPI) in Warren, Rhode Island. The hulls and decks are cored with end-grain balsa, a common stiffening material, though care must be taken not to get it wet (such as around through-hulls and deck hardware). Conceived as a racer/family cruiser, the J/30 is better as a racer. Although wide on deck, the beam is narrow at the waterline to make her fast in light air. The flip side is that it is initially tender. There are also some issues concerning control with the original rudder. When racing, it is expected that there will be four or five people sitting on the rail as human ballast. This, plus the "sit-on" rather than "sit-in" cockpit, makes the J/30 a less than ideal family boat. Nevertheless, for the performance-minded sailor who enjoys getting the last 1/10 knot of speed out of a boat, a used J/30 is an economical way to participate in offshore yacht racing.

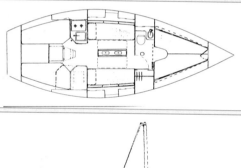

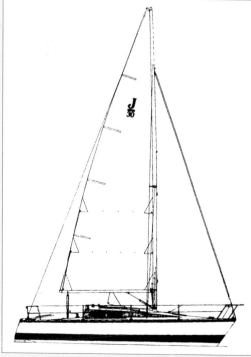

LOA	29'10"
LWL	26'0"
BEAM	11'2"
DRAFT	5'5"
DISPLACEMENT	7,000 LB.
BALLAST	2,100 LB.
SAIL AREA	461 SQ. FT.
DESIGNER	ROD JOHNSTONE
PRICE NEW	NOT IN PRODUCTION
PRICE USED	$23,700–$26,300 (1982 **MODEL**) $41,300–$45,900 (1990 **MODEL**)
CONTACT	J/BOATS INC. P.O. BOX 90 557 THAMES ST. NEWPORT RI 02840 401-846-8410 WWW.JBOATS.COM J/30 CLASS ASSOC. C/O CARL SHERTER 170 GRANDVIEW AVE. WATERBURY CT 06708 WWW.SAILINGSOURCE.COM/J30

SIMILAR BOATS	OLSON 30
	 TARTAN 30
	 OR MORE MODERN "SPRIT BOATS":
	    J/90, BRAVURA SPORTSTER 29,
	    MELGES 30, AND QUEST 30

J/105

For an idea of how raceboat design evolved between the late 1970s and early 1990s, compare the J/30 to the J/105. The two weigh about the same, though the latter is 5 feet longer! And sailing dead downwind with conventional spinnakers has given way to asymmetrical spinnakers set on short retractable bowsprits that make for faster and more comfortable legs when broad reaching. Like all J/Boats, the 105 is for people who like to go fast (and there are plenty of them); this model has been in production for more than 10 years with active fleets on all coasts. As a cruising boat, its main liability is the 5-foot 4-inch headroom below. The boats are built by TPI of balsa-cored fiberglass using the SCRIMP process.

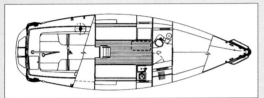

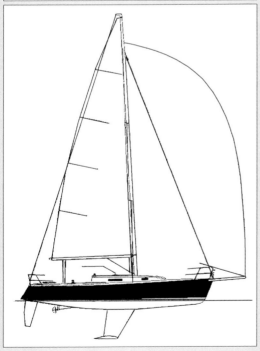

LOA	34'6"
LWL	29'6"
BEAM	11'0"
DRAFT	5'6" OR 6'6"
DISPLACEMENT	7,750 LB.
BALLAST	3,400 LB.
SAIL AREA	577 SQ. FT.
DESIGNER	ROD JOHNSTONE
PRICE NEW	$155,000
PRICE USED	$62,000–$68,000 (1993 MODEL) $114,000–$125,500 (2000 MODEL)
CONTACT	J/BOATS INC. P.O. BOX 90 557 THAMES ST. NEWPORT RI 02840 401-846-8410 WWW.JBOATS.COM J/105 CLASS ASSOC. C/O NELSON WEIDERMAN, TREASURER 127 SCHOONER DR. WAKEFIELD RI 02879 WWW.J105.ORG
SIMILAR BOATS	ANDREWS 35 J/106 J/110 MUMM 36

MUMM 36

Named after the champagne company that sponsors numerous yacht racing events, the Mumm 36 was designed in 1993 by Bruce Farr, the noted Kiwi designer now working in Annapolis, Maryland. The Mumm 36 is raced as a one-design keelboat. Competition is keen; to be competitive, you must spend tens of thousands of dollars per year on sails and equipment, crew expenses, and moving the boat to regattas around the country. It's for the hard core, but the rewards are commensurate with the involvement. Says Farr, "The world wanted it so we gave it to them—a strict one-design offshore racing keelboat capable of competing in ORC Category 3 events. The RORC was also looking for a one-design 36-footer for the small boat class of the Admiral's Cup, so the Mumm 36 was born. The Mumm 36 is an exciting one-design and IMS racer that provides extremely tight racing and high-performance, exhilarating sailing. A strong class continues on a national and international basis with over 100 boats launched to date."

LOA	35'8"
LWL	31'8"
BEAM	11'8"
DRAFT	7'4"
DISPLACEMENT	8,150 LB.
BALLAST	3,500 LB.
SAIL AREA	644 SQ. FT.
DESIGNER	BRUCE FARR & ASSOCIATES
PRICE NEW	NOT IN PRODUCTION
PRICE USED	$105,000–$115,000 (1995 MODEL) $126,500–$139,000 (1997 MODEL)
CONTACT	FARR YACHT DESIGN P.O. BOX 4964 613 THIRD ST., SUITE 20 ANNAPOLIS MD 21403 410-267-0780 WWW.FARRDESIGN.COM
SIMILAR BOATS	THOMAS 35 FARR 40

EXPRESS 37

Carl Schumacher, who designed the Alerion Express 28, was a West Coast designer who made a name for himself designing lightweight raceboats. The 1983 Express 37, which is a good example of his work, followed on the heels of the immensely popular Express 27 and was built by Terry Alsberg in Santa Cruz, California. The objective was to excel in ocean races, especially reaching and running. It met the minimum length requirements for the popular Transpac Race from California to Hawaii. The boats are well built, but the interiors are plain.

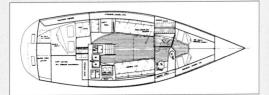

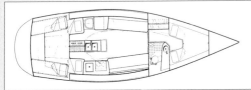

LOA	37'1"
LWL	30'10"
BEAM	11'6"
DRAFT	7'3"
DISPLACEMENT	11,000 LB.
BALLAST	4,500 LB.
SAIL AREA	638 SQ. FT.
DESIGNER	**CARL SCHUMACHER**
PRICE NEW	**NOT IN PRODUCTION**
PRICE USED	**$44,100–$49,200 (1984 MODEL)**
CONTACT	**EXPRESS 37 CLASS ASSOC.** **WWW.EXPRESS37.ORG**
SIMILAR BOATS	**J/35** **SCHOCK 35**

RACERS

FARR 40

The Farr 40 is raced as a one-design as well as under the IMS rule. Its builder, Carroll Marine, also built the Mumm 36, Mumm 30, and Corel 45 before going out of business in 2003. (A new builder is being sought.) Racing rules are managed by its designer, Farr International. The carbon fiber rig is simple by most standards: double swept-back spreaders, no running backstays (as would normally be required on fractional rigs), and small headsails (no overlapping genoas). The hull and deck are PVC and foam-cored fiberglass, vacuum-bagged, and oven-cured. Farr says that sailing the Farr 40 is "not beyond the capabilities of relatively inexperienced and mature crew members." The boat has had a very good record in both short course and offshore racing events.

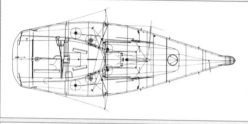

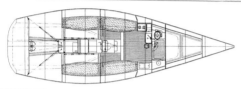

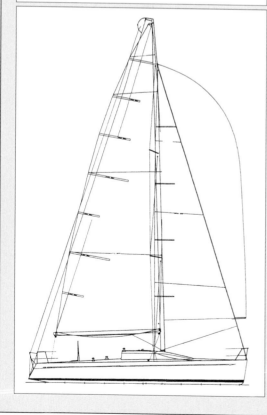

LOA	40'9"
LWL	35'3"
BEAM	13'3"
DRAFT	8'6"
DISPLACEMENT	10,917 LB.
BALLAST	5,039 LB.
SAIL AREA	1,050 SQ. FT.
DESIGNER	**BRUCE FARR**
PRICE NEW	**NOT IN PRODUCTION**
PRICE USED	**$185,000–$275,000 (VARIOUS YEARS FROM INTERNET)**
	$137,500–$151,000 (1997 MODEL)
	$375,000–$412,500 (2002 MODEL)
CONTACT	**FARR INTERNATIONAL INC.**
	613 THIRD ST.
	ANNAPOLIS MD 21403
	410-268-1001
	WWW.FARR-INT.COM
	FARR 40 ONE DESIGN CLASS ASSOC.
	FARR INTERNATIONAL INC.
	613 THIRD ST., SUITE 11
	ANNAPOLIS MD 21403
	410-268-1001
	WWW.FARR40.ORG
SIMILAR BOATS	**FARR 48**
	FRERS 41
	DEHLER 41 DS

SANTA CRUZ 52

Bill Lee, an engineering graduate of Cal Poly, has been both a yacht designer and builder. His portfolio of lightweight beamy racers began with the Santa Cruz 27, which helped popularize Lee's slogan: Fast is Fun! The Santa Cruz 52 was launched in 1993. A year later, Lee was forced to declare bankruptcy and lost control of the company. He maintains involvement as a consultant. Despite the flat-bottomed hull, the SC 52 is billed as a performance cruiser, but with emphasis certainly favoring speed. In recent years, even traditional cruisers are seeing the benefits of lighter-weight boats, in part because their speed may allow them to outrun a storm. But by definition, light displacement means a flatter bottom, and flatter bottoms have a tendency to pound when going to windward. The concept works best in a long waterline boat such as the SC 52.

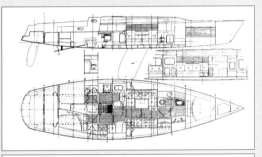

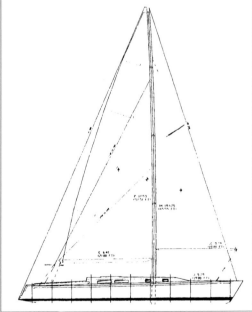

LOA	53'0"
LWL	46'6"
BEAM	14'0"
DRAFT	9'0"/6'0" (DEEP/SHOAL)
DISPLACEMENT	21,000 LB.
BALLAST	9,850 LB.
SAIL AREA	1,327 SQ. FT.
DESIGNER	BILL LEE
PRICE NEW	$654,000
PRICE USED	$432,000–$474,000 (1993 MODEL) $840,500–$923,000 (2002 MODEL)
CONTACT	SANTA CRUZ YACHTS 453 MCQUAIDE DR. LA SELVA BEACH CA 95076 831-786-1440 WWW.SANTACRUZYACHTS.COM TRANSPAC 52 CLASS ASSOC. WWW.FASTISFUN.COM/ TRANSPAC52RULES.HTML
SIMILAR BOATS	J/160

RACERS

HOBIE 16

During the 1950s, California surfer Hobie Alter began building lightweight surfboards with balsa and foam cores. In 1967, he turned his attention to sailboats, designing and producing the single-sail Hobie 14, a boat that could be easily towed to the beach and launched through the surf. Two years later, he introduced the Hobie 16 with main and jib. A strong international following assures big-time regattas, with more than 300 teams from more than 50 countries. Hobie has built more than 100,000 boats. Raced with two persons, the crew hikes out suspended by a trapeze. It doesn't get any more exciting than firing along at 15 to 20 knots with the windward hull airborne!

LOA	16'7"
BEAM	7'11"
DRAFT	4" BOARD UP
WEIGHT	320 LB.
SAIL AREA	218 SQ. FT.
DESIGNER	HOBIE ALTER
PRICE NEW	$7,995
PRICE USED	$900–$1,050 (1971 MODEL)
	$1,300–$1,550 (1981 MODEL)
	$2,800–$3,250 (1991 MODEL)
	$4,800–$5,500 (1998 MODEL)
CONTACT	HOBIE CAT CO.
	4925 OCEANSIDE BLVD.
	OCEANSIDE CA 92056
	800-HOBIE-49 (800-462-4349)
	WWW.HOBIECAT.COM
SIMILAR BOATS	NACRA 5.0
	PRINDLE 16

TORNADO

The Tornado was designed in 1967 specifically to compete in the Olympics. A selection committee chose the Tornado over numerous other boats. It first competed in the 1976 Olympics. The Tornado Class Association claims it is the fastest production catamaran in the world. "With the adoption of the New Rig in 2001," its Web site says, "the Tornado design includes an asymmetrical spinnaker, a double trapeze, a flat-top main sail, and a self-tacking jib." There are 1,200 class associations throughout the world, encompassing about 5,000 boats. The boat is capable of speeds of 15 to 18 knots upwind and down, and of 33+ knots reaching. Class rules allow the boats to progress with technology, especially the incorporation of new materials such as carbon fiber and Kevlar. Currently, there are no licensed builders in the United States.

LOA	20'0"
BEAM	9'11"
DRAFT	4" BOARD UP
WEIGHT	300 LB.
SAIL AREA	235 SQ. FT.
DESIGNER	RODNEY MARCH/TERRY PEARCE/ REG WHITE
PRICE NEW	NO U.S BUILDERS
PRICE USED	$2,100–$2,500 (1982 MODEL) $3,250–$3,800 (1986 MODEL) $10,500–$15,500 (RECENT MODELS)
CONTACT	U.S. TORNADO CLASS ASSOC. P.O. BOX 2598 DEARBORN MI 48124-2598 313-327-0897 INTERNATIONAL TORNADO ASSOC. WWW.TORNADO.ORG
SIMILAR BOATS	NACRA 6.0 NACRA F-18 PRINDLE 19 HOBIE 20 INTER 20

MULTIHULLS

CORSAIR F-27

The F-27 trimaran was designed by Ian Farrier around 1984. The patented folding mechanism collapses the two floats or amas in toward the main hull; beam then is a road-ready 8 feet 5 inches, making the boat legal for trailering. It is also possible now for this changeling to enter slips sized for monohulls. Construction is fiberglass cloth skins, Divinycell foam core, and vinylester resin, all vacuum-bagged. As one would expect, this is a very fast boat, with speeds in excess of 20 knots possible. Although it has made transoceanic passages across both the Atlantic and Pacific, a few have capsized, albeit while being raced and pushed hard. The interior is a bit tight, but serviceable. With the expansive trampolines and netting that constitute its "decks," this is a boat to enjoy topside. The boat was a success in southern California because it gave cruising sailors there (who have so few islands or coves, other than Catalina) some mobility. The favored destination is Baja, but because most people don't have time to sail their boats south, trailering the F-27 at 55 mph made the Mexican adventure very doable. This boat is for people who value performance over sumptuous interiors.

LOA	27'1"
BEAM	19'1"/8'5" FOLDED
DRAFT	1'2"–4'11" (CB UP, CB DOWN)
WEIGHT	2,600 LB.
SAIL AREA	446 SQ. FT.
DESIGNER	IAN FARRIER
PRICE NEW	NOT IN PRODUCTION
PRICE USED	$36,100–$40,100 (1990 MODEL) $63,900–$70,300 (1997 MODEL)
CONTACT	CORSAIR MARINE INC. 150 REED COURT CHULA VISTA CA 91911 877-FAST-TRI (877-327-8874) WWW.CORSAIRMARINE.COM
SIMILAR BOATS	F-28 TELSTAR 28

GEMINI 31/3000

When Tony Smith's Maryland boatyard burned in 1981, turning the molds of his Telstar 26 folding trimaran to ashes, he got back in business fast by resurrecting an old set of molds he had for the Aristocat 30 catamaran. He renamed it the Gemini and sold the dickens out of it, even back when many Americans were skeptical of multihulls. It didn't hurt that his price was considerably lower than other cruising multihulls available, which in the 1980s were mostly European imports such as Prout and Catalac. Continual refinements and upgrades have changed the appearance from a somewhat dowdy-looking cat to a much more modern vessel. The name has changed as well, from Gemini to Gemini 3000. Today it is the Gemini 105MC, with scoop transoms that lengthen the waterline, but basically it's the same hull. Smith doesn't tout the boat as an ocean passagemaker, but some have made major crossings. Unlike most cruising cats, the Gemini has centerboards, which definitely improve windward performance. Because weight destroys performance, most multihulls are necessarily built lighter than comparable monohulls, and the Gemini is no exception. It has lots of room, it's a good value, but it's not top quality.

LOA	30'6"
BEAM	14'0"
DRAFT	1'6"–6'9"
WEIGHT	7,000 LB.
SAIL AREA	425 SQ. FT.
DESIGNER	KEN SHAW/TONY SMITH
PRICE NEW	NOT IN PRODUCTION
PRICE USED	$11,400–12,900 (1982 GEMINI 31 MODEL) $48,400–$53,200 (1992 GEMINI 3200 MODEL) $78,100–$85,800 (1996 (GEMINI 105M MODEL) $143,500–$158,000 (2002 GEMINI 105MC MODEL)
CONTACT	PERFORMANCE CRUISING INC. 7364 EDGEWOOD RD. ANNAPOLIS MD 21403 410-626-2720 WWW.GEMINICATAMARANS.COM
SIMILAR BOATS	PDQ 32 SEAWIND 1000 GEMINI 105 ENDEAVOUR CAT 36

MULTIHULLS

PDQ 36

PDQ cruising catamarans, which (in addition to the 36) include the 32 Altair and 42 Antares, are built in Whitby, Ontario. The floats or amas have a waterline length-to-beam ratio of 12:1, considered ideal for cruising cats. It has a partial bridge deck forward, a nice compromise that saves some weight yet provides for some additional stowage. The hulls are solid fiberglass below the waterline and cored with Klegecell foam above. Vacuum bagging is used to achieve desirable glass-to-resin ratios. For easy maintenance there is no wood on deck (traditionalists may find this hard to accept, but hey, remember the bumper sticker that says, "I'd Rather Be Sailing!"). Below, there are two double berths forward; an aft stateroom can be configured as an office or guest cabin. The PDQ is offered in two configurations, Sports Cruiser and Long Range Cruiser (which weighs more). Adding a genset, air-conditioning, and electric windlass impairs performance. Speeds are normally in the 7- to 10-knot range, with speeds in the teens possible under the right conditions. This is a high-quality, high-price boat, but it has the right mix of performance and comfort.

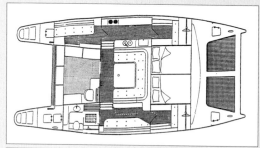

LOA	36'5"
LWL	34'4"
BEAM	18'3"
DRAFT	2'10"
WEIGHT	8,000 LB.
SAIL AREA	542 SQ. FT.
DESIGNER	ALAN SLATER
PRICE NEW	$204,900
PRICE USED	$118,000–$130,000 (1993 MODEL) $218,500–$240,000 (2000 MODEL)
CONTACT	PDQ YACHTS INC. 202 SOUTH BLAIR ST., #1-6 WHITBY ON L1N 8X9 CANADA 888-297-CATS (888-297-2287); 905-430-2582 WWW.PDQYACHTS.COM
SIMILAR BOATS	PDQ 32 SEAWIND 1000 GEMINI 105MC PROUT EVENT 34 PACKET CAT 35 TOBAGO 35 ENDEAVOUR CAT 36 LAGOON 37 SNOWGOOSE 37

LAGOON 380

The French builder Jeanneau was one of the companies that helped popularize cruising catamarans in the 1990s. The efforts of earlier builders, such as Catalac and Prout in the United Kingdom, to export boats to the United States were somewhat stymied by consumer fears of capsizing. The many virtues of multihulls, including unsinkability, have since been better appreciated. The Lagoon 380 replaces the Lagoon 37, built in the United States by TPI. The boats are now built in France, where Jeanneau is part of the Beneteau Group. Whereas the 37 had a sloped cabin trunk, the 380 has an abrupt vertical window to enhance visibility from the dinette/living area. There are two double berths, both aft, which are in direct contrast with the PDQ 36, in which they are forward. You have to decide where you want your views—in bed or at the table! Certainly, this is one of life's tougher decisions! The boats are well built, nicely finished, and correspondingly expensive. Before buying any multihull, take a test sail in choppy water to feel the quick, snappy motion. It's much different from a displacement monohull; some like it, some don't. The Lagoon line ranges from the 380 up to the 670.

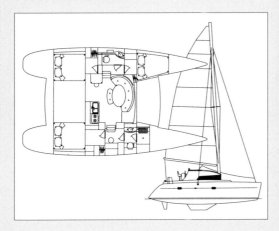

LOA	37'11"
LWL	36'1"
BEAM	21'4"
DRAFT	3'9"
WEIGHT	13,000 LB.
SAIL AREA	850 SQ. FT.
DESIGNER	MARC VAN PETEGHEM AND VINCENT LAURIOT PREVOST
PRICE NEW	$252,500
PRICE USED	$248,000–$272,500 (2002 MODEL)
CONTACT	LAGOON AMERICA 105 EASTERN AVE., # 202 ANNAPOLIS MD 21403 410-280-2368 WWW.CATA-LAGOON.COM
SIMILAR BOATS	TOBAGO 35 ENDEAVOUR CAT 36 PDQ 36 LAGOON 37 LIGHTWAVE 38 LAVEZZI 40 MAINE CAT 41 LEOPARD 42 MANTA 42

MULTIHULLS

Resources

Books

Badham, Michael, and Robby Robinson. *Sailor's Secrets: Advice from the Masters.* Camden, ME: International Marine, 1999. Over 1,000 tips, suggestions, evaluations, and nuggets of hard-won advice from more than 300 seasoned veterans.

Brogdon, Bill. *Boat Navigation for the Rest of Us: Finding Your Way by Eye and Electronics.* 2nd ed. Camden, ME: International Marine, 2001. Teaches small-boat navigation the way experienced skippers actually do it, by combining electronic aids like radar and GPS with visual observations, simple chartwork, common-sense piloting, and low-tech tricks that have worked for centuries.

Burgess, Robert F. *Handbook of Trailer Sailing.* 2nd ed. Camden, ME: International Marine, 1992. All you need to get started in the low-cost sport of trailer sailing.

Calder, Nigel. *Boatowner's Mechanical and Electrical Manual: How to Maintain, Repair, and Improve Your Boat's Essential Systems.* 2nd ed. Camden, ME: International Marine, 1996. Authoritative, hands-on instructions for diagnosing, repairing, and maintaining basic systems.

———. *How to Read a Nautical Chart: A Complete Guide to the Symbols, Abbreviations, and Data Displayed on Nautical Charts.* Camden, ME: International Marine, 2003. The best handbook on chart usage, from one of the most trusted names in boating.

Callahan, Steven. *Adrift: Seventy-Six Days Lost at Sea.* Boston: Houghton Mifflin, 2002. Amazing story of one man's survival in a life raft for 76 days.

Casey, Don. *Canvaswork and Sail Repair.* Camden, ME: International Marine, 1996. Tackle virtually any canvaswork project, including sails and sail covers.

———. *Inspecting the Aging Sailboat.* Camden, ME: International Marine, 1997. Expert advice on assessing a boat's quality, from structure to systems.

———. *Sailboat Electrics Simplified.* Camden, ME: International Marine, 1999. Handle electrical repairs and make improvements with ease.

———. *Sailboat Hull and Deck Repair.* Camden, ME: International Marine, 1996. Learn to seal joints, bed hardware, replace portlights, locate leaks, fix cracks and even holes, restore your hull's gloss, renew nonskid decks, and much more.

———. *Sailboat Refinishing*. Camden, ME: International Marine, 1996. Achieve a professional-looking finish on your boat's hull, deck, spars, wood trim, and in the cabin.

Colgate, Doris. *Sailing: A Ragged Mountain Press Woman's Guide*. Camden, ME: Ragged Mountain Press, 1999. A how-to sail book with a practical, down-to-earth, low-key approach perfectly suited to women's learning styles.

Compton, Peter. *Troubleshooting Marine Diesels*. Camden, ME: International Marine, 1998. Every step is illustrated, so users can work from illustrations alone.

Eldridge Tide and Pilot Book 2004. Boston: Robert White, 2003. Tables to aid in piloting for New England waters, including Long Island Sound.

Fletcher, Sue. *A Boater's Guide to VHF and GMDSS*. Camden, ME: International Marine, 2002. Straightforward and nontechnical, this book allows readers to quickly master and get the most out of their radios.

Gerr, Dave. *The Nature of Boats: Insights and Esoterica for the Nautically Obsessed*. Camden, ME: International Marine, 1992. A browser's reference to understanding how boats tick.

Gill, Paul G., Jr. *The Onboard Medical Handbook: First Aid and Emergency Medicine Afloat*. Camden, ME: International Marine, 1997. What to do when confronted with onboard emergencies.

Goodman, Di, and Ian Brodie. *Learning to Sail: The Annapolis Sailing School Guide for All Ages*. Camden, ME: International Marine, 1994. This book follows techniques perfected at the world-famous Annapolis Sailing School.

Henkel, Steve. *Boat Trailers and Tow Vehicles: A User's Guide*. Camden, ME: International Marine, 1991. How-to-do-it manual for worryfree trailering.

Hubbard, Richard K. *Boater's Bowditch: The Small-Craft American Practical Navigator*. Camden, ME: International Marine, 2000. A small-boat adaptation of the U.S. government's *American Practical Navigator*. An indispensable resource for beginning and advanced navigators.

Jarman, Colin. *The Essential Knot Book*. 3rd ed. Camden, ME: International Marine, 2004. Popular reference that covers the most practical knots, bends, hitches, whippings, and splices in everyday use by mariners.

Jones, Tristan. *Ice!* Dobbs Ferry, NY: Sheridan House, 1995. Tristan and Nelson, a one-eyed three-legged black Labrador, explore Arctic waters aboard *Cresswell*.

———. *The Incredible Voyage*. Dobbs Ferry, NY: Sheridan House, 1996. Spans six years of voyaging in *Barbara* and *Sea Dart*.

———. *Saga of a Wayward Sailor*. Dobbs Ferry, NY: Sheridan House, 2000. Tristan and Nelson go to the Mediterranean.

Kroenke, David. *Know Your Boat: The Guide to Everything that Makes Your Boat Work*. Camden, ME: International Marine, 2002. Easy-to-read introduction to the use and maintenance of the many systems found on power or sail boats.

Maloney, Elbert S. *Chapman Piloting and Seamanship: The Boating World's Most Respected Reference, Completely Updated and Revised*. 64th ed. New York: Hearst Books, 2003. Rules of the Road, USCG safety requirements, handling, navigation, weather, plus much other information.

Marino, Emiliano. *The Sailmaker's Apprentice: A Guide for the Self-Reliant Sailor*. Camden, ME: International Marine, 1994. A book as much about repairing, maintaining, and understanding sails as it is about making them.

Marshall, Roger. *The Complete Guide to Choosing a Cruising Sailboat.* Camden, ME: International Marine, 1999. Helps you understand your options and how to make the right boat selection.

Mustin, Henry C. *Surveying Fiberglass Sailboats: A Step-by-Step Guide for Buyers and Owners.* Camden, ME: International Marine, 1994. Expert advice on how to inspect a boat for problems, from structure to systems.

Pardey, Lin, and Larry Pardey. *Cruising in Seraffyn.* 25th anniv. ed. Arcata, CA: Paradise Cay Publications, 2001. The first book in the *Seraffyn* series. This edition has a new foreword, new appendixes, and color photos showing *Seraffyn* then and now (34 years later, with her new owners).

———. *Seraffyn's Oriental Adventure.* Arcata, CA: Paradise Cay Publications, 1996. The fourth book in the series finds the Pardeys halfway around the world, eight years into their meandering voyage.

Reed's Nautical Almanac 2004. Boston: Thomas Reed Publications, 2003. Tables to aid in piloting and navigation, published for various regions of the United States.

Rousmaniere, John. *The Annapolis Book of Seamanship.* 3rd rev. ed. New York: Simon & Schuster, 1999. Authoritative guide to handling a sailboat under sail and power.

Saltonstall, Jim, ed. *The Essential Sailor.* Camden, ME: International Marine, 1996. A complete course in the key techniques of basic sailing.

Seidman, David. *The Complete Sailor: Learning the Art of Sailing.* Camden, ME: International Marine, 1995. Straightforward text with instructive illustrations.

Smith, Hervey Garrett. *The Marlinspike Sailor.* Camden, ME: International Marine, 1993. How to splice line, tie the monkey's fist and Turk's head, plus other decorative ropework.

Snyder, Paul, and Arthur Snyder. *Nautical Knots Illustrated.* Rev. ed. Camden, ME: International Marine, 2002. With clear, simple explanations and 295 step-by-step photographs, you'll easily learn how to tie the 20 most useful knots and splices.

Spurr, Daniel. *Heart of Glass: Fiberglass Boats and the Men Who Made Them.* Camden, ME: International Marine, 2000, 2004. The story of how fiberglass boats transformed boating. Here are the legendary boats that built an industry; fascinating, especially if you enjoyed the brief reviews in *Your First Sailboat.*

———. *Upgrading the Cruising Sailboat.* 2nd ed. Camden, ME: International Marine, 1991, 1993. How to improve your boat for offshore passages and serious cruising.

———. *Yacht Style: Design and Decor Ideas from the World's Finest Yachts.* Camden, ME: International Marine, 1990. A full-color photographic collection of ideas to improve the look, comfort, and functionality of any cruising boat.

Sweet, Robert J. *GPS for Mariners.* Camden, ME: International Marine, 2003. Summarizes essential GPS concepts, explains the buttons, screens, and menus of a GPS receiver, and answers readers' questions.

Toss, Brion. *The Complete Rigger's Apprentice: Tools and Technique for Modern and Traditional Rigging.* Camden, ME: International Marine, 1998. The definitive reference on the art and science of rigging.

Vigor, John. *The Practical Encyclopedia of Boating: An A-Z Compendium of Seamanship, Boat Maintenance, Navigation, and Nautical Wisdom.* Camden, ME: International Marine, 2004. This handy reference gives sailors and powerboaters quick access to just the right amount of information needed to answer most questions and solve most problems.

———. *Boatowner's Handbook.* Camden, ME: International Marine, 2000. A handbook with timesaving tips and golden rules on everything from buying paint and adhesives to drilling pilot holes, showing navigation lights, and rigging your boat.

Wing, Charlie. *One Minute Guide to the Nautical Rules of the Road.* Camden, ME: International Marine, 1998. A quick-reference situation guide.

———. *How Boat Things Work: An Illustrated Guide.* Camden, ME: International Marine, 2004. Eighty principal devices and systems are covered with simple explanations of parts, tips for disassembly and assembly, and instructions for troubleshooting, maintenance, and repair.

Wittman, Rebecca J. *Brightwork: The Art of Finishing Wood.* Camden, ME: International Marine, 1990. All the information you need to avoid frustrations and costly mistakes and derive the greatest possible satisfaction from a process that can be its own reward.

———. *The Brightwork Companion: Tried-and-True Methods and Strongly Held Opinions in Thirteen and One-Half Chapters.* Camden, ME: International Marine, 2004. Guides you through every step of refinishing your boat's wood trim with a stripped-to-the-essentials presentation designed for quick reference.

Magazines

Blue Water Sailing, P.O. Box 268, Newport, RI 02840; 401-847-7612; www.bwsailing.com. The authority on offshore sailing, voyaging, and world cruising.

Cruising World, P.O. Box 420235, Palm Coast, FL 32142-0235; 866-436-2461; www.cruisingworld.com. Articles range from easy sailing destinations to fairly complex technical subjects.

Good Old Boat, 7340 Niagara Lane North, Maple Grove, MN 55311-2655; 763-420-8923; www.goodoldboat.com. Emphasis on creating a community of sailors, keeping boats afloat, and pride of ownership.

Ocean Navigator, P.O. Box 569, Portland, ME 04112; 207-772-2466; www.oceannavigator.com. For the offshore sailor.

Practical Sailor, P.O. Box 420235, Palm Coast, FL 32142-0235; 800-829-9087; www.practical-sailor.com. Unbiased boat reviews both in the twice-monthly newsletter and in the two-volume *Practical Boat Buying* anthology.

SAIL, 98 North Washington St., Boston, MA 02114; 800-745-7245; www.sailmag.com. Regular articles on new boats and gear, ask the experts, and cruise notes.

Sailing, P.O. Box 249, Port Washington, WI 53074; 800-895-2596; www.sailingonline.com. Full of beautiful pictures and instructive material on all aspects of sailing.

Small Craft Advisor, P.O. Box 676, Morro Bay, CA 93442; 805-771-9393; www.smallcraftadvisor.com. Offers boat reviews, interviews, where to sail, and how-to articles.

Soundings, 10 Bokum Rd., Essex, CT 06426; 800-244-8845; www.soundingsonline.com. The nation's boating newspaper.

Web Sites

The Boating News, http://theboatingnews.com. Selects 25 news stories twice a day from the world's best publications and Web sites to provide a wide range of unabridged articles about yachts and yacht racing, marinas, waterways, fishing, sailing, powerboats, shoreline regulations, and other subjects of importance to recreational boaters.

Boat Owner's World, www.boatowners.com. The world's most complete boating portal.

Boats Yachts Marinas, www.boatsyachtsmarinas.com. An online magazine for boaters and the boating industry.

Boat Trader Online, www.boattraderonline.com. Thousands of boats listed for sale.

DIY boat owner, www.diy-boat.com. Online marine maintenance magazine.

Equipped to Survive, www.equipped.org. The definitive source for independent reviews and information on outdoor gear, survival equipment, and techniques.

Marinersguide.com, www.marinersguide.com. Detailed information on almost every port in the United States.

SailNet, www.sailnet.com. BoatCheck reviews written by owners. Also has a learning to sail section.

U.S. Coast Guard, www.uscgboating.org. The official Web site of the U.S. Coast Guard Office of Boating Safety.

Marinas

BoatingOnTheWeb.com, http://boatingonthe web.com. Boating and marina information.

Boatowners.com, www.boatowners.com/marinasindex.htm. Provides a master list of U.S. marinas.

BoatUS, 880 South Pickett St., Alexandria, VA 22304-4695; 703-823-9550; www.boat america.org/marinas. Directory of marinas and membership discounts.

Marina Info, www.marina-info.com. The largest online marina directory from super yacht marinas to the smallest marina.

MARINAMATE.com, 800-SERVE-91 (800-737-8391); www.marinamate.com. Has thousands of marinas listed online.

Marinas.com, www.marinas.com. View marina facilities throughout the United States and abroad.

Organizations

American Boat & Yacht Council (ABYC), 3069 Solomons Island Rd., Edgewater, MD 21037; 410-956-1050; www.abyc.com. ABYC has been developing and updating the safety standards for boatbuilding and repair for 50 years.

American Sailing Association, P.O. Box 12079,

Marina del Rey, CA 90295; 310-822-7171; www.american-sailing.com. America's sail education authority.

Boat Owners Association of the United States (BoatUS), 880 South Pickett St., Alexandria, VA 22304-4695; 703-823-9550; www.boat us.com. Directory of marinas and membership discounts. Also provides marine insurance quotes and services.

National Association of Marine Surveyors, P.O. Box 9306, Chesapeake, VA 23321-9306; 800-822-6267, 757-638-9638; www.nam surveyors.org. NAMS members survey new and used vessels to determine condition and value.

National Safe Boating Council, P.O. Box 509, Bristow, VA 20136; 703-361-4294; www.safe boatingcouncil.org. Its mission is to enhance the safety of the recreational boating experience through education and outreach.

Society of Accredited Marine Surveyors (SAMS), 4605 Cardinal Blvd., Jacksonville, FL 32210; 800-344-9077; www.marine survey.org. SAMS is an organization of professional marine surveyors who have come together to promote the good image and general well-being of their profession.

US Sailing, 15 Maritime Dr., Portsmouth, RI 02871; 401-683-0800; www.ussailing.org. Their mission is to encourage participation and promote excellence in sailing and racing in the United States.

Boat Loans

BoatUS Finance, 880 South Pickett St., Alexandria, VA 22304-4695; 800-365-5636; www.boat us.com/boatloans.

Essex Credit Corporation, 2200 Powell St., Suite 1200, Emeryville, CA 94608; 866-ESSEX-4-U (866-377-3948); www.essex credit.com.

First Commercial Corporation of America, P.O. Box 439, Allenwood, NJ 08720; 800-55-FIRST

(800-553-4778); www.boatfinance.com.

Ganis Credit Corporation, 7985 113th St., Seminole, FL 33772; 866-240-4112; www.ganis credit.com.

Scott Financial Services, 914 South Wolfe St., Baltimore, MD 21231; 800-556-0666, 410-675-6700; www.marineloan.com.

Insurance

American Marine Underwriters, P.O. Box 439, Allenwood, NJ 08720; 877-AMU-INS-1 (877-268-4671); www.boatinginsurance.com.

BoatUS Marine Insurance, 880 South Pickett St., Alexandria, VA 22304-4695; 800-283-2883; www.boatus.com/insurance.

Gowrie, Barden & Brett, 70 Essex Rd., Westbrook, CT 06498; 800-BOAT-911 (800-262-8911); www.boatinsure.com.

John G. Alden Insurance Agency, 89 Commercial Wharf, Boston, MA 02110; 800-J G Alden (800-542-5336), 617-227-7670; www.john galden.com.

Premier Marine Insurance Managers Group, 800 Fifth Ave., Suite 4100, Bank of America Building, Seattle, WA 98104; 800-589-4208; www.boatinsurance.com.

Discount Retailers

Aurora Boat Care Products, 7015 Ordan Dr., Suite 11, Mississauga, ON L5T 1Y2, Canada; 866-214-3444, 905-564-4995; www.aurora marine.com.

BoatUS, 880 South Pickett St., Alexandria, VA 22304-4695; 703-823-9550; www.boatus.com.

Defender Industries, 42 Great Neck Rd., Waterford, CT 06385; 800-628-8225; www. defender.com.

West Marine, P.O. Box 50070, Watsonville, CA 95077; 800-BOATING (800-262-8464); www.westmarine.com.

Index

Illustration Credits

Thanks to Justin Thompson for sharing images from his incredible collection of boat brochures.

All drawings by Christopher Hoyt unless otherwise noted. All photos supplied by author unless otherwise noted.

Page	Credit
ii	Alison Langley photo
xii–1	Photo courtesy Doris Colgate, from Colgate and Colgate: *Fast Track to Cruising*
5–7	Daniel Forster photos
9	Ensign plans courtesy Ensign Spars Inc.
10	Photo courtesy International Marine
11	O'Day 22 plans courtesy Cape Cod Shipbuilding Co.
12	O'Day 23 plans courtesy Cape Cod Shipbuilding Co.
13	Catalina 270 plans courtesy Catalina Yachts
14	Pearson 30 plans courtesy Pearson Yachts
15	Ted Brewer, from *Ted Brewer Explains Sailboat Design* (top); Bruce Bingham, from Spurr: *Upgrading the Cruising Sailboat* (bottom)
17	Shannon Shoalsailer plans courtesy Shannon Yachts; rig drawings by Bruce Bingham, from Spurr: *Upgrading the Cruising Sailboat*
18	Valiant 50 plans courtesy Valiant Yachts
20	Photo courtesy U.S. J/24 Class Association
21	Express 37 plan courtesy Express 37 Class Association
22	Photo courtesy Corsair Marine Inc.
28	Courtesy the manufacturers
39	Henry C. Mustin (concept), Jim Sollers (illustration), from Mustin: *Surveying Fiberglass Sailboats*
40–41	Rob Groves illustrations from Casey: *Inspecting the Aging Sailboat*; captions by Don Casey
42–43	Jim Sollers (upper left); other illustrations by Rob Groves, from Casey, *Inspecting the Aging Sailboat*; captions by Don Casey
45–50	Steve D'Antonio photos
51	Jim Sollers from Casey: *Inspecting the Aging Sailboat*; labels by Don Casey
57	Courtesy the manufacturers

58–59   David Seidman (concept), Kelly Mulford (illustration), from Seidman: *The Complete Sailor*

60   David Seidman (concept), Kelly Mulford (illustration), from Seidman: *The Complete Sailor* (top and right); Bill Seifert (concept), Jim Sollers (illustration), from Seifert: *Offshore Sailing* (bottom left)

61   Nigel Calder, from *Nigel Calder's Cruising Handbook* (left); David Seidman (concept), Kelly Mulford (illustration), from Seidman: *The Complete Sailor* (right)

62   Catalina 22, courtesy Catalina Yachts; Gemini 105, courtesy Performance Cruising; Cabo Rico 38, courtesy Cabo Rico Custom Yachts, Inc.; IMI Crosby/Frigoboat, from Calder: *Refrigeration for Pleasureboats* (bottom right)

63   Photo courtesy Doris Colgate, from Colgate and Colgate: *Fast Track to Cruising*

71   Jonathan Klopman

77   Photo courtesy Paul and Arthur Snyder, from Snyder and Snyder: *Nautical Knots Illustrated*

84   David J. Schuler photo (left); right photo courtesy Paul and Arthur Snyder, from Snyder and Snyder: *Nautical Knots Illustrated*

85   Courtesy Charlie Wing, from Wing: *How Boat Things Work*

94   Photos courtesy Paul and Arthur Snyder, from Snyder and Snyder: *Nautical Knots Illustrated*

96–98   David Seidman (concept), Kelly Mulford (illustration), from Seidman: *The Complete Sailor*

105   David Seidman (concept), Kelly Mulford (illustration), from Seidman: *The Complete Sailor*

110   Steve D'Antonio photo

112   Island Packet photo, courtesy Island Packet Yachts; photos top right and bottom left [2] courtesy Bill Seifert, from Seifert: *Offshore Sailing*; bottom right photos [2] courtesy David Westphal, from Hinckley: *The Hinckley Guide to Yacht Care*

113   Cabo Rico photo, courtesy Cabo Rico Custom Yachts, Inc.; middle right photo courtesy Bill Seifert, from Seifert: *Offshore Sailing*; bottom right photos [2] courtesy David Westphal, from Hinckley: *The Hinckley Guide to Yacht Care*

121   Photo courtesy Doris Colgate, from Colgate and Colgate: *Fast Track to Cruising*

124–25   Richard K. Hubbard (concept), Kim Downing (illustration), from Hubbard: *Boater's Bowditch*

126   Ship's compass photo courtesy Ritchie Navigation; hand-bearing compass photo courtesy Celestaire, from Hubbard: *Boater's Bowditch*

141   Courtesy Bruce Bingham, from Spurr: *Upgrading the Cruising Sailboat*

146–47   Nigel Calder (concept), Jim Sollers (illustration), from Calder: *Nigel Calder's Cruising Handbook*

150   Charlie Wing, from Wing: *Rules of the Road: A Captain's Quick Guide*

151   Photo courtesy Doris Colgate, from Colgate and Colgate: *Fast Track to Cruising*

160–61   David Kroenke (concept), Jim Sollers (illustration), from Kroenke: *Know Your Boat*

162   David Kroenke (concept), Jim Sollers (illustration), from Kroenke: *Know Your Boat* (top)

163   David Kroenke (concept), Jim Sollers (illustration), from Kroenke: *Know Your Boat*